THE CIVIL SERVICE IN LIBERAL DEMOCRACIES

The
Civil Service
in
Liberal
Democracies

An Introductory Survey

EDITED BY J.E. KINGDOM

R

ROUTLEDGE
London and New York

First published 1990
by Routledge
2 Park Square, Milton Park, Abingdon, Oxon, OX14 4RN

Simultaneously published in the USA and Canada
by Routledge
a division of Routledge, Chapman and Hall, Inc.
29 West 35th Street, New York, NY 10001

Transferred to Digital Printing 2004

British Library Cataloguing in Publication Data

The civil service in liberal democracies: an
   introductory survey.
   1. Western world. Civil service
   I. Kingdom, J.E. (John E. *1939–*)
   351'.000981'2

   ISBN 0-415-00493-4
       0-415-04456-1 (pbk)

Library of Congress Cataloging in Publication Data

The Civil service in liberal democracies: an introductory survey /
   edited by J.E. Kingdom.
      p. cm.
   Includes index.
   ISBN 0-415-00493-4. – ISBN 0-415-04456-1 (pbk.)
   1. Civil service – Europe – Case studies. I. Kingdom, J.E., 1939–
JN94.A67C58 1989
351.6'094–dc20   89-10338
                                             CIP

CONTENTS

PREFACE   vii

1.   INTRODUCTION   1
     J. E. Kingdom

2.   BRITAIN   11
     J. E. Kingdom

3.   CANADA   35
     J. E. Kingdom

4.   FRANCE   64
     B. G. Owen

5.   IRELAND   90
     M. McManus

6.   ITALY   119
     R. E. Spence

7.   SWEDEN   143
     B. M. Jones

8.   THE UNITED STATES   163
     J. A. Chandler

9.   WEST GERMANY   182
     A. R. Peters

     INDEX   208

PREFACE

One problem encountered by students of public administration
and politics is that their introduction to the subject area
is based entirely on the case of a single country. This
ethnocentric approach has a severe drawback in that it tends
to limit students' perspectives, leaving them unaware of
alternative institutional frameworks, practices, and ethical
norms, and thereby reducing their capacity to understand any
particular country. Ideally students should be made aware
that each case represents but one, culture-bound example
belonging to a much wider empirical domain.

While it is possible for students studying at an introductory level to turn to books devoted to particular countries,
or to books of comparative study per se, they will experience
problems of access posed by the quantity of the material and
of complexity in methodology. For this reason there is a
tendency for the comparative dimension to be ignored in
courses at the level of GCSE, A-level, BTEC Ordinary and
Higher Certificates and Diplomas. This book is intended to
provide an opportunity for such students to gain some rudimentary knowledge of other systems of government. Although it
does not aim to apply comparative methodology in the strict
sense (that is, it does not postulate generalised hypotheses
to be tested across a wide empirical domain), an attempt is
made to isolate for examination a number of foci which together can constitute a framework for some simple comparison
by students.

In the country-based chapters which follow each author
has endeavoured to follow a common basic pattern, though each
had complete freedom to diverge following his own individual
perceptions and judgements concerning the salient features of
the particular country.

The authors are grateful to Brenda Christmas for undertaking the exacting task of preparing the camera-ready copy.

Chapter 1

INTRODUCTION

J. E. Kingdom

CIVIL SERVICES AS A SUBJECT FOR COMPARISON

Comparison must proceed upon the identification of a framework of similarity in the objects being compared. In the
area of government and public administration it is common to
seek such similarities in structures and/or functions. Prima
facie, the study of civil services is unambiguously structural rather than functional. However, the notion of function
remains present since the underlying rationale of the structures is essentially functional.

Civil services provide an obvious focus for comparative
study for reasons such as the following. As well-established
structures they are highly visible, and their formal function
is very clearly defined. In addition, their role and organisation lie at the centre of a number of important debates
which transcend national boundaries, relating for example, to
efficiency, the distribution of power within the state, the
role of the state in society, and the operation of democracy.

In principle, civil services are agents of governments;
they are established to fulfil the function of rule implementation, the 'rules' being, for the most part, the policies of
the state. However, in reality it is not possible to discern
a perfect identification of structure with function; civil
services are not mono-functional, they do not merely implement policies; neither is the function of implementation their
sole preserve. In most modern states the latter function is
dispersed among a range of agencies, including institutions
of local government, various ad hoc bodies, and nationalised
industries. The greater the amount of public administration
carried out by such semi-autonomous agencies of the state,
the more important it becomes to focus attention, not on the
function of implementation, but on the role of the civil
service in policy-making, control and regulation.

Introduction

The Concept of Bureaucracy

Civil services are characteristically organised as bureaucracies; indeed, the terms are almost synonymous. The strict meaning of 'bureaucracy' is government by officials, or members of bureaux, and as such it carries decidedly pejorative connotations. However, following the extensive organisation studies of the sociologist Max Weber, it is common for social scientists to employ the term to denote a certain kind of organisation. Weber outlined his view of the ethical purpose of bureaucracy through his depiction of an ideal type of organisation form. This was a prescriptive model, the adoption of which would afford a protection against the dangers of arbitrary rule by officials in an increasingly complex modern state. It was characterised by rationality, impersonality, formal rules of procedure, and a centralisaton of authority.

The Concept of the Civil Service

The term 'civil service' has a British ring, and derives from that part of the East India Company through which sovereignty in colonial India was exercised, the Indian Civil Service. This was seen as a particularly effective form of organisation for public administration. Many of its admired practices were used as an example for the nineteenth-century reform of the central administration of the mother country, and the term 'Home Civil Service' gained acceptance. Civil servants of the Crown could be distinguished from other servants of the Crown such as politicians, the military, and the judiciary (Hughes 1954: 17)

In 1854 the Northcotte-Trevelyan report carried an official seal of approval for the term in its very title: <u>Report on the Organisation of the Permanent Civil Service</u>. From here it was given statutory endorsement in America when, in 1883, as part of the reform movement, the government established the United States Civil Service Commission. Various other countries have adopted this nomenclature to designate that part of the bureaucracy where recruitment lies outside the political process.

The term received a definitive enunciation in 1931 by a British Royal Commission, the Tomlin Commission:

> Those servants of the Crown, other than holders of political or judicial offices, who are employed in a civil capacity and whose remuneration is paid, wholly and directly, out of monies voted by Parliament (Tomlin 1931: para. 9).

It is this body of public administrators which is the focus

of attention in the present study, even in countries where the term 'civil service' is not commonly employed. Nevertheless, the extent to which the behaviour of other actors, including politicians and their political appointees, has a considerable bearing on that of the civil servants cannot be excluded from the analysis.

The Underlying Questions

Public servants in developed polities are expected to operate within a framework constrained by both political and ethical parameters, arising from public expectations as well as from the constitution. These constraints can be understood in terms of two well-known dichotomies articulating respectively the distinctions between politics and administration, and between public and private administration (Kingdom 1986).

The Politics-Administration Dichotomy

An important watershed in the quest to understand the nature of public administration occurred in 1887, when Woodrow Wilson published a paper outlining prescriptively his view of its nature (Wilson 1887). Wilson drew a distinction between the activities of politics and administration, and argued that administrators were outside the political process, concerned only with the impartial implementation of the policies created by the politicians. This stood as a classic statement, which identified an area of professional activity, distinct from the hurly burly of politics, which could be seen as a respectable and permanent career.

Today one finds this proposition widely employed (overtly or covertly) by the mass media, politicians, and practising administrators for their own purposes. It may be used as a depiction of the way things actually are (a descriptive statement), or as an ethical guide to the way things should be (a prescriptive statement). Indeed such a prescription was particularly appropriate for the time it was advanced, as a basis for attacking widespread public corruption in America. However, whichever way the statement is used it is highly misleading, and it is (usually) discredited by academics.

In behavioural terms it has been demonstrated as entirely untenable. Countless studies, as well as the commonsense observation of practitioners, testify to the fact that ethical judgements made by administrators intrude into the policy-making process at all levels. Civil servants cannot be portrayed as apolitical eunuchs.

The proposition is equally untenable, though more dangerous, when taken as an ethical prescription of an ideal. In this context the distinction parallels that which can be made between fact and value; the implication being that the administrator is concerned with one and not the other; that is, that he is relieved of moral responsibility for the <u>means</u> he employs in pursuit of given (politically determined) <u>ends</u>. At all levels above the most menial, public administration requires the exercise of judgement and choice. If the administrator believes himself to operate in a value-neutral manner with no framework of moral constraint, administration becomes little more than a pattern of 'uncontrolled, opportunistic adaption' (Waldo 1955: 64).

The Public-Private Administration Dichotomy

This second dichotomy is logically connected with the first, and relates to the extent to which public administration may be distinguished from administration in the private sector. If one rejects the distinction between politics and administration it becomes logically necessary to accept this second distinction, because policy-making in the public sector clearly differs profoundly in terms of process, content, and ethical purpose, from that in the private sector.

Of course the act of distinguishing between public and private administration is not the same as suggesting that the two sectors are themselves physically separate or self-contained. Indeed the contrary is the case. The role of government in the modern, advanced societies examined in this volume brings it into intimate contact with the private industrial, commercial and business institutions at numerous points. It is this very interpenetration which sometimes leads to a failure to appreciate fully the essential, and significant, difference between the two forms of administration.

THE FRAMEWORK FOR ANALYSIS

In seeking an understanding of the political and ethical parameters in which civil services operate one generates a series of crucial perspectives for study, and indeed, comparison; these are outlined below as a framework for analysis. Subsequent chapters will apply this framework to various countries.

Political Setting

A civil service, perhaps more than any other institution, reflects the values and norms of the society it serves. It is not only an expression of the nature of the polity, it is

a provider of many services, and for most citizens is far
more a practical part of daily life than the political
institutions. The role and nature of the civil service is in
large measure shaped by the texture of the political culture,
which defines the expectations and demands made of it. For
this reason we sketch the principal features of the political
systems and political cultures of the states studied as a
prelude to the examination of their respective civil services.

A political culture is essentially the sum of the attitudes and psychological orientations which citizens hold towards the political practices and institutions of the state.
Although these vary at the fine-tuning level, members of the
western-style liberal democracies examined here share certain
fundamental attitudes with respect to the notion of the civil
service. Generally there is a higher level of acceptance of
the bureaucratic form of organisation than is found in non-
liberal democratic systems, as is evidenced in the abortive
attempts to install British Whitehall-style bureaucracies in
undeveloped polities. There is a confidence in rationality
in policy-making, members of society are prepared to accept
the application of generalised rules in solving particular
problems, and expect them to be applied impersonally and uni-
versally. There is a high level of trust in bureaucracy,
with people willing to countenance a high degree of official
intervention in their private lives.

Historical Background

In addition to contemporary social and cultural factors,
civil services, like all institutions, are also the products
of their past. Although they have sometimes been subject to
periods of radical reform, their practices and structures
have generally evolved through a test of experience and the
acceptance of precedent. In day-to-day administration civil
services must themselves take cognizance of their pasts
because the rigorous ethical codes which characterise public
administration in liberal democracies demand that rules be
applied uniformly over time. Most countries recognise
important watersheds in their bureaucratic history in which
basic principles were laid down as a guide to future gener-
ations, and the documents associated with these are often
venerated and dignified with an almost constitutional status.
The pattern of historical development can furnish a useful
focus for comparison. Indeed, there are several cases where
the bureaucratic history of one country has directly influenced that of another through emulation. Accordingly this
topic forms an early part of the analysis of each chapter.

The Political Executive

We use the term political executive to designate the effective political leadership of the state; that is, the
Cabinet, Prime Minister, or President. We have noted that
civil services can be functionally defined as agencies of
rule implementation. This view sees the administrative
machine as a body without any internal source of motivation;
it is like a car without a driver. If the bureaucracy were to
be entirely self-motivating it would represent a manifestation
of the administrative state feared by Weber, Kafka, Orwell
and others. However, in a liberal democracy the prime motivation is expected to emanate from within the political
system, finding its resolution in the institution of the
executive. For this reason a study of the nature of the
political executive becomes important in a study of the civil
service.

A variety of questions can be examined, such as whether
the executive is singular or plural, stable or unstable,
dignified or effective, and legitimate in its authority. It
is also important to examine how it gains information and
advice, how it reaches decisions, and to ascertain the nature
of its relationship with the other political and state
institutions. One particularly important issue concerns the
civil service-executive interface; in some systems it is
argued that the seniormost civil servants are virtually
members of the executive. Certainly no modern executive
could work without extensive civil service penetration and
support.

Structure

The factors considered in the preceding sections underpin the
study because they are instrumental in shaping the civil
service in any country. A further necessary preliminary to
study is the establishment of a concrete picture of the
structure in real-world organisational terms. One needs to
examine the overall departmental pattern, the size and nature
of the individual departments, their functional responsibilities, their expenditure levels and so on. It can also be
important to study physical location, and the extent to which
the agencies are centred upon the capital or dispersed
throughout the state in a pattern of field administration.
Some countries have a variety of alternative forms of
administrative agency enjoying varying relationships with the
executive and political institutions. The presence of such
bodies influences the role of the civil service, sometimes
undermining, and sometimes elevating, its importance.

Introduction

The Bureaucrats

Civil services are social organisations, a fact which provides
an elaborate set of dimensions for analysis. One can examine
issues such as behaviour within the organisation, the social
and educational backgrounds of the senior administrators, and
the provision made for the education of bureaucrats both
prior to their employment, and on an in-service basis. In
some societies it is appropriate to note the ethnic composition of the bureaucracy, as well as the extent to which the
career opportunities are equally distributed between the
sexes. The criteria for recruitment, and subsequent promotion, can furnish another important basis for analysis and
comparison. Characteristically, liberal democracies formally
espouse the merit principle as a dominant selection criterion,
but even so 'spoils' systems operate in some countries,
enabling politicians to dispense rewards for services
rendered; and in others a more vaguely defined exercise of
patronage enables those in positions of authority to gain
additional leverage by placing loyal sycophants in key positions. In reality one finds elements of all three practices
in most developed polities.

The relationships between the different types of bureaucrats is another important area for comparative analysis. The
broad distinction between specialists and generalists has
been the subject of particular interest to scholars in the
post-war era. The reason for this is, in large measure, the
increased complexity in the subject matter of modern government, resulting in an influx of technocrats, who have demanded
a greater share of influence within the organisation.

Another dominant theme in a study of the sociological
aspects of public bureaucracy is the class composition of the
upper echelons of the hierarchy. At these senior levels the
ability to influence the content of public policy is considerable, and it becomes of interest to democratic theorists to
consider the question of whether such influential roles
should be entrusted to what is often a social elite. The
traditions of different countries lead to contrasting values
and practices with respect to this issue.

Control and Accountability

It is a central tenet of liberal democratic government that
the civil service should be subject to popular control. The
public administrators are custodians of the national interest,
and while the processes of education and socialisation are
usually intended to inculcate a proper degree of sensitivity
to this goal, it is also considered proper that the constitution, the political institutions, and the structure of the
bureaucracies impose a variety of additional controls.

7

Introduction

One of the principal means of securing popular control is through some mechanism of accountability. In a representative democracy this lies in the political institutions, most notably the elected assemblies. However, a pluralist political system provides other, less formal, kinds of control including the mass media, and interest groups. The extent to which the bureaucracies make information available to the public through both formal and informal channels represents a crucial issue of accountability today, and affords a further point of comparison.

The judiciary can also play an important part in the control of public bureaucracy, particularly where the principle of the rule of law is fundamental to the constitution. Certain countries have special systems of administrative law prescribing codes of behaviour for adminstrators per se which do not apply to ordinary citizens.

In addition to the external controls imposed through the mechanisms securing public accountability there are the internal controls which the bureaucracy imposes upon itself. These include the controls politicians enjoy in the nature of their constitutional relationship. The effectiveness of this, as well as other aspects of this relationship, has formed the basis for much analysis which can be utilised when adopting a comparative perspective. In the first place there are internal controls implied in the very nature of the bureaucratic form of organisation, resulting from the well-codified sets of rules and procedures, and the characteristically hierarchical patterns of authority.

There are also the ubiquitous financial controls which lie at the heart of almost all governmental behaviour. The basis of financial control often derives from constitutional rights held by popular assemblies in matters of taxation. In addition there is increasing recognition of the political reality that the resources available to government are limited and must be allocated between competing objectives. This latter requirement tends to elevate the position of the financial agencies within bureaucracies to the extent that they become supremely powerful, a fact which in itself raises another set of issues for consideration.

Management

As organisations, civil services require management in much the same way as any other organisation, and recent years have seen the emergence of a managerial debate in the civil services of many developed countries. This can centre on various areas such as personnel management, financial management, and the application of techniques designed to promote efficiency and effectiveness. Countries reveal differences in the extent to which they are prepared to utilise such techniques.

Introduction

For some the danger of creating a technological elite represents an inhibiting factor, in others the techniques, often
developed in the private sector, are viewed as fundamentally
inappropriate given the special nature of public administration. Management debates are of particular importance because
they involve a consideration of the nature and goals of public
administration in a society. For some political forces of the
right, the notions of managerialism and efficiency are
bugaboos with which to intimidate public bureaucracies and
reduce the role of the state in society through cuts and
privatisation.

Policy-Making

We have already observed the artificiality of the distinction
between politics and administration in practice. At all
levels, the process of implementation itself calls for the
exercise of judgement on the part of the bureaucrats, and the
effect of this can often influence the nature of the policy.
Furthermore, at the senior levels the public servants formally enter into the policy-making process through their relationships with the political members of the executive. To
this relationship the bureaucrats bring a considerable
expertise born of long experience, advanced education,
intellectual sophistication, and sometimes a high degree of
self-confidence engendered by membership of the upper strata
of society. Politicians do not always share these qualifications, which means that the relationship between the two can
be contentious, and perhaps a threat to democracy itself. The
manner in which the dangers are perceived and contained
represents a significant focus for comparison.

CONCLUSION

The following chapters will address some of these areas and
questions. In certain countries a particular debate may be
considered to be of greater salience than it is in others,
but for the most part you should be able to find in this
framework a basis for:

1. acquiring basic information about an important aspect of
   the political systems of a number of countries;
2. gaining an increased understanding of some of the
   important concepts associated with the study of public
   bureaucracy;
3. developing, through (albeit limited) comparison, a
   greater insight into the nature and role of public bureaucracy in any particular country;
4. generating further questions relating to public

administration which may be profitably explored through comparative study;
5. acquiring a rudimentary appreciation of the benefit of using a comparative approach.

REFERENCES

Hughes, E. (1954) 'Civil Service Reform 1853-1855', Public Administration, 32, 17-51.

Kingdom, J. E. (1986) 'Public administration: defining the discipline - Part I', Teaching Public Administration, VI, 1-13.

Tomlin (1931) (Chairman) Report of the Royal Commission on the Civil Service, 1929-31, Cmd 3909, London, HMSO.

Wilson, W. (1887) 'The study of administration', Political Science Quarterly, 2, 192-222.

Waldo, D. (1955) The Study of Public Administration, New York, Random House.

Chapter 2

BRITAIN

J. E. Kingdom

POLITICAL SETTING

It is usual to find the British constitution described as
unwritten, but this is only true in the sense that there
exists no single legal document which is formally termed the
Constitution. There are in fact various laws of constitutional
significance, and there is a great corpus of authoritative
constitutional writing in which scholars and lawyers discuss
the constitution as it is, and as they think it ought to be.
It remains true, however, that a number of important constitutional practices are followed with rigidity although they are
nothing more than conventions. The fact that Britain does not
have a formally written constitution is thus not of great
significance for the practice of government and politics. A
binding authoritative constitution does exist and politicians
and public administrators are no less constitutional in their
behaviour than their counterparts in those countries which do
have a formally designated document.

The absence of a written constitution is convenient for
students of the subject as a means of understanding how the
practices of modern government and politics have evolved. The
essential feature is continuity: the present constitution
retains many of the institutions and practices of earlier
centuries, including of course a highly visible monarchy. Many
of the ceremonial aspects of Parliament recall different
epochs in its development; indeed, one of the chambers in this
bicameral assembly, the House of Lords, remains entirely
undemocratic, drawing most of its members from the aristocracy
on a hereditary principle. Of course, the effective power of
the House of Lords is small, the real authority having passed
to the elected chamber, the House of Commons. The monarchy
and the House of Lords are but two examples from a substantial
number of constitutional relics whose functions have
dramatically changed but which serve to illustrate the link
with the past. Britain has moved from being a monarchy to a
liberal democracy with little overt social revolution or

11

constitutional engineering.

Not all scholars, or British citizens, approve of this kind of constitutional development. Some argue that the absence of a Bill of Rights, for example, leaves the people in a vulnerable position before the authority of the state. Others see the preserved vestiges of the country's aristocratic past as repugnant reminders of the cruelty and suffering inflicted by past rulers upon ordinary citizens.

Political Culture

Walter Bagehot, in a seminal nineteenth-century study of British politics, opined that there existed within British popular feeling a certain deference towards authority manifesting itself in various ways, including a demonstrable affection for the symbols of the state, particularly the monarchy, and a liking for strong government. Bagehot's methods were by no means scientific, and he wrote before the Labour Party had become a left-wing force in British politics, yet his observations that 'no feeling could seem more childish than the enthusiasm of the English at the marriage of the Prince of Wales', written during the reign of Queen Victoria, could well have been evoked to describe the popular response to the same parallel event taking place over one hundred years later in 1981.

In 1963 the political scientists Almond and Verba also detected signs of popular deference, declaring that 'strong subject orientations have persisted despite the development of more active participant orientations'. The study also confirmed Bagehot's view concerning the predilection for firm government.

The deference within society is manifested in other ways. The education system, for example, contains a duality permitting private, fee-charging establishments which cater for those able and willing to purchase education (the public schools), to exist alongside a state system which provides the education for the great majority. The established professions, particularly law and medicine, are similarly able to extract and preserve a high degree of deference from ordinary people. A classic study of the medical profession in Britain by Eckstein notes as characteristic the 'self-effacing attitudes laymen generally assume when confronted by the professions' and a belief that 'doctors always know best what is good for the organisation of medicine'. Elsewhere Eckstein has argued that there is a congruence in the social attitudes shown towards the various institutions in any state, so the political deference is constantly reinforced through a general habit of deference learned and consolidated throughout life in the process of socialisation.

A corollary of deference is an acceptance of secrecy: and

secrecy - the preservation of a mystique - is certainly a
characteristic of British institutions. Thus it is no surprise
to find that it is also a characteristic of British public
administration. Indeed, as recently as 1982, one commentator
was by no means alone in expressing the view that 'Britain is
about as secret as a state can be and still qualify as a
democracy'.

In electoral terms the tradition of deference manifests
itself in a marked preference for right-wing governments in
the form of the Conservative Party. The Labour Party was
formed as the left-wing alternative early in the century, but
did not gain power until 1929, and has never succeeded
in becoming the 'natural' party of government. Even amidst
alarming levels of unemployment and social unrest, following
a period of eight years' Conservative rule under Prime
Minister Margaret Thatcher, the result of the 1987 general
election was to give the government a substantial majority in
Parliament. Although it is true that the nature of the
British electoral system (which is not proportional representation, and is very hard on minority parties) contributed
to this result, it remains true that a vast number of working-
class people support the Conservative Party in spite of its
aristocratic antecedents, and its further shift to the
political right.

HISTORICAL BACKGROUND

Like the other institutions of the constitution the British
civil service has evolved, rather than been created on the
basis of some rationally conceived blueprint. The origins of
a number of the important departments of state lie in the
divisions of the royal household. However, the modern civil
service in Britain may be distinguished from its antecedent
organisations by a number of characteristics, including a
system of appointment and promotion based upon merit,
sometimes involving competitive examination; avowed political
impartiality; permanence; and a unified organisational
structure embracing a variety of departments under a single
identity. Of course there is debate as to the extent to
which these characteristics represent actual reality rather
than an ideal.

The modern civil service is largely a creation of the
nineteenth century, and may be seen as a product of the
industrial revolution which spawned the machines, factories,
and commercial institutions serving to place the country in a
position of international pre-eminence. The new class of
businessmen which emerged, and ascended to power and wealth
as a result of industrialisation, was irked by what seemed
the ineptitude, corruption, and inefficiency of the traditional institutions of state administration, and would have

little truck with evolutionary explanations of constitutional
development. Inspired by the utilitarian ideas of Jeremy
Bentham, and the philosophical radical movement, they
reformed local government, the police force, the legal system,
the electoral system, and indeed the apparatus of central
administration which was to become a unified 'civil service'.
    Gladstone, himself a member of the new order, commis-
sioned an official enquiry into the question of the machinery
for central administration which, in 1854, produced the blueprint for reform. This is well known as the Northcote-
Trevelyan report. Prior to this, there was no single unified
organisation which could be termed a civil service; the
separate departments of state pursued their respective
affairs autonomously. By contemporary standards the organisations were very small, the Treasury for example contained
fewer then a hundred employees. Recruitment was largely on
the basis of patronage and nepotism, with no serious attempts
made to test aptitude or ability; some entrants could neither
read nor write. There were no clear lines of authority, no
uniform basis for the payment of salaries, and at the senior
level, no clear distinction between administrative and
political office, so that administrators were not expected
to be politically impartial, or to see themselves in any
philosophic sense as guardians of the national interest.
    The driving force in framing the report was Sir Charles
Trevelyan who, as a one-time member of the Indian Civil
Service, a highly efficient form of colonial administration,
was a zealot in the cause of administrative reform at home.
The separate departments were to be amalgamated into a single
whole which would be termed the Home Civil Service (a title
which distinguished it from colonial organisations while
recognising the debt to them), members of which would be
expected to move between departments in the course of their
careers. The report was premised upon the assumption that
the work of the state administration fell into distinct
categories of intellectual quality. This it was believed,
should be reflected in the structure of the administration
and its patterns of recruitment and promotion. In order to
improve the quality of entrants the report advocated examinations for recruitment, which were to be set and assessed by
an external body. Subsequent promotion was to be in accordance with a career pattern and based on merit, objectively
assessed by superiors.
    The stress upon examinations, particularly for the upper
echelons, placed a premium on university education, though
the report did not specify which disciplines were to be
regarded as relevant; the emphasis being on intellectual
excellence as such. Consequently the university curriculum,
as it was, became the principal determinant of the educational
qualifications of candidates. The nineteenth century had seen,
under the influence of prominent educationalists such as

Thomas Arnold, something of a renaissance in classical
education, which was regarded as a training in moral virtue
as well as an intellectual pursuit demanding the greatest
rigour. The universities of Oxford and Cambridge were the
prime repositories of such knowledge; the more technical
subjects being largely neglected and left to other
institutions of inferior status.

Thus the Northcote-Trevelyan Report wrought a major
reform of the central administration. However, as we shall
see later in this chapter, it also left a legacy which was to
prove problematic: new twentieth-century conditions replaced
those of the nineteenth century for which it was designed.

THE EXECUTIVE

The British executive consists of the Prime Minister and the
Cabinet, all of whom are politicians with seats in Parliament,
the majority being from the House of Commons. On the rare
occasions when a person is chosen as a Cabinet member who is
not in Parliament it is usual for him to contest a by-
election at the first opportunity, or to be awarded a life-
peerage enabling him to become a member of the House of
Lords. Membership of Parliament is crucial in order to
secure executive responsibility to the assembly. Civil
servants themselves are not formally part of the executive
though they may work very closely with the Cabinet and Prime
Minister.

The Cabinet usually consists of about 15 to 22 members
who are chosen by the Prime Minister from his or her own
party, the one with a majority of seats in the House of
Commons. It has not been the practice in Britain to form
coalition governments, in a political system which tends to
follow the two-party model. However, the growth of the new
Social Democratic Party, and its 1988 merger with the hitherto
moribund Liberal Party, led some to believe that the two-
party system was under threat. In a multi-party system the
British executive might be formed from more than one party
with the choice lying largely with the leader of the largest
party in the coalition, but subject, no doubt, to a process of
bargaining. An alternative prediction concerning the rise of
the new party might be that it would merely replace one of the
existing parties, so that the two-party system would reassert
itself, as was the case when, at the beginning of the century,
the Labour Party supplanted the Liberals. The principal reason
for this is found in the effects of the electoral system,
which is not designed to ensure proportional representation,
and which causes third parties to be grossly under-represented
in Parliament. The general election of 1987 saw the opposition
parties damaging each other's chances by splitting the anti-
Conservative vote in the various single-member constituencies,

and talk of a coalition government was made to look ridiculous
when the Conservatives were returned to office with 42.3 per
cent of the votes cast (only 0.1 per cent down on the 1983
result), and an overall majority of 100 seats. The Liberal-
Social Democratic Alliance, which had threatened to force
coalition government into British politics, acquired only 22
seats.

In the nineteenth century Walter Bagehot saw in the
Cabinet the 'efficient secret' of the constitution. It was
the 'buckle' which joined the executive to the legislature in
a fusion of powers which ensured the successful legitimation
of its policies. In the 1960s a debate emerged concerning
the role and authority of the Prime Minister within the
Cabinet, and Richard Crossman, an academic and practising
politician, popularised the view that British government had
become presidential in character, with successive Prime
Ministers having arrogated to their position the powers which
Bagehot believed lay with the Cabinet. General elections had
become gladiatorial contests between the two party leaders,
with success conferring a personal mandate on the victor and
affording greater legitimacy and authority than that available
to ordinary Cabinet members.

Asquith, a Liberal Prime Minister at the beginning of
the century, had expressed the view that the office was what
any individual might choose to make of it; a view given
support by Harold Wilson, who held office for some nine years,
though he cast doubt on the idea that the office could ever
bequeath unbridled power. The tenure in office of Margaret
Thatcher has probably seen more extensive recourse to the
prime ministerial armoury than has been the case with any of
her predecessors in peacetime. Whether her dominant style of
leadership will leave a lasting impression on the nature of
the British executive remains to be seen. For a number of
critics of the presidential trend, the dominant prime minister
model represents a threat to the deliberative, consensus-
building style of executive leadership which is held to be a
particular strength of British government.

The ministers who form the Cabinet tend to have responsibilities for leading the various departments of state, but a
minority may be ministers 'without portfolio', with more
vaguely defined duties. There is a hierarchy within the
Cabinet, those holding certain posts of traditional importance
such as Home Secretary, Chancellor of the Exchequer, and
Foreign Secretary, being of generally superior status to
others. The senior ministers are said by some observers to
form an 'inner cabinet' around the Prime Minister and to take
certain important decisions without the participation of the
other Cabinet members. There is further differentiation
within the ministerial hierarchy with Secretaries of State
responsible for whole departments and other ministers responsible for what might be termed sub-departments.

The Cabinet and its committees are serviced by a secretariat; a body of considerable prestige and importance, which is itself part of the civil service. The head of this is the Cabinet Secretary, who is probably one of the most influential public figures in the country, being, as he is, at the centre of all state deliberations. The minutes taken by the secretariat become the directives for action by the departments, so that the accuracy of the interpretation placed on Cabinet discussion is of crucial importance. This is by no means an uncontentious role; indeed, Richard Crossman, in his diaries, expressed some grave doubts on the ability of the Cabinet secretariat to reflect accurately the spirit of Cabinet policy. Under Mrs Thatcher the role of the Cabinet Secretary, in the case of Sir Robert Armstrong, became rather akin to that of a permanent secretary to the Prime Minister, and contributed to the presidential trend.

The departmental responsibilities of ministers is another debated aspect of the working of the executive. It is argued that these responsibilities are onerous and compel ministers to immerse themselves in detail to the exclusion of their collective role of taking the wider view of government policy. Various suggestions for reform have been made. One such is the creation of a small 'super-cabinet' of non-departmental ministers. Though there have been some experiments this suggestion does not seem attractive to politicians. One reform which has been implemented has been the creation of 'giant' departments, through a process of amalgamation, the heads of which are able to take a broad view over a larger section of the government's total remit.

A development around the executive which has been taking place over a long period, but which has accelerated and gained more attention during the Thatcher governments, has been the introduction of prime ministerial and ministerial advisers from outside government, including the academic world (not necessarily British) and the private sector. The Prime Minister herself developed what some saw as a veritable prime ministerial department containing experts on most areas of policy, as well as those concerned with public relations, the media, and the presentation of government policies.

Prior to the Thatcher premiership, there were some commentators who saw in the development of pluralism (or its narrower variant, corporatism), in which various pressure groups within society played a critical part in policy-making, a diminution in the power of the executive. Others saw an increase in the power of the senior civil servants. However, whether singular, or plural, the British executive has, by the late 1980s, reasserted itself as the decision-making centre of the political system. This has had important implications for the civil service.

Britain

STRUCTURE AND FUNCTIONS

Though regarded as a single entity, the British civil service
is organised on a departmental basis. This structure is not
laid down constitutionally and can be freely changed by the
Prime Minister of the day. Nevertheless there is a degree of
stability, and some departments, such as the Treasury and the
Home Office, have long histories, with origins in parts of
the royal household. There are various small departments but
the main ones at the time of writing are as follows:

Ministry of Agriculture, Fisheries and Food
Ministry of Defence
Department of Education and Science
Department of Energy
Department of the Environment
Department of Health
Department of Social Security
Department of Trade and Industry
Department of Transport
Foreign and Commonwealth Office
HM Treasury
Home Office
Law Officers' Department
Lord Chancellor's Department
Northern Ireland Office
Scottish Office
Welsh Office

The functions undertaken by the British civil service
have developed in nature, scope, and scale. Before the nineteenth century central public administration had been mainly
regulatory. The industrial revolution offered no serious
challenge to this role, resting as it did on the basis of
minimal government and maximum private enterprise. The
thrust of the argument of the reforming philosophical
radicals was that government should seek only to remove any
fetters which might inhibit the free play of market forces.
Legislation was intended to bring the pursuit of private
interest into harmony with the public interest, so that
individuals seeking the maximisation of their own utility
would ipso facto be conducing the wider public good.
However, paradoxically, the industrial revolution did
call for a more interventionist state, and the scope of
government activity increased with large-scale reform of the
poor law, the development of a public health movement, a
growth in the role of the state in the provision of education,
and a strengthening of the agencies of law and order.
Although the reforms brought about by these movements mainly
involved local government, they also increased the role of
the central administration as a regulator. A prime mover in

18

all these reforms was Edwin Chadwick, a man whose allegiance
to Benthamite centralist principles was abundantly evident.
In the early years of the twentieth century the role of
central government was further extended and became increasingly positive through an education act (1902), an old-age
pensions act (1908), a labour exchanges act (1909) and a
national insurance act (1911). The positive role of the
state was further advanced during two world wars, and the
powers acquired during these times of emergency were never to
be fully relinquished. In addition, the post-war period saw
an acceptance of Keynesian principles of economics, entailing
a crucial role for the central government in the regulation
of the economy.

A development concomitant with the increase in the
functions of the central government has been the enlargement
in the scale of the undertaking. This was occasioned by a
continuing population growth caused by an increased birth
rate, an increased average life expectancy, and some immigration. This enlargement led to a substantial increase in the
practice of delegated legislation, whereby the civil service
itself actually makes certain laws. In 1929 Lord Hewart made
a detailed critique of the effects of this practice, and
warned of the rise of a 'new despotism'. Notwithstanding the
dangers the trend has proved irresistible and Parliament has
been obliged to content itself with regulation of, rather
than any reduction in, the volume of such official-made
legislation.

More recent civil service growth has taken place at the
periphery. A network of field agencies has extended the
tentacles of the centre into the regions to stand alongside
the range of non-departmental agencies which configure the
administrative landscape of the state, including the public
corporations which run the nationalised industries, the
National Health Service which is administered regionally by
ad hoc bodies, local government, and a diverse array of ad hoc
quasi-autonomous public agencies.

In responding to the increase in civil service functions
it has been necessary to consider whether to entrust new
responsibilities to existing departments, or to create further
departments on an ad hoc basis. This problem was officially
addressed in 1918 in the report of the Haldane Committee on
the machinery of government. The committee recommended the
adoption of the 'functional principle'; that is, the second
of these solutions. This principle has largely dominated the
allocation of responsibilities to departments within the
British civil service, although one can also find evidence of
other rationales including the clientele (e.g. Education),
area (e.g. the Welsh, Scottish, and Northern Ireland
Offices), and process (e.g. the Treasury). In 1970 a white
paper on the machinery of government reaffirmed the adherence
to the functional principle.

Indeed, the functional principle for the allocation of
responsibilities can be found throughout the public sector in
Britain, a fact which may be a reflection of the evolutionary
pattern of development, where ad hocery rather than planning
predominates. This is seen in the nineteenth-century local
boards (responsible in their localities for particular
functions such as public health, schools, hospitals, burial
of the dead, roads and so on), the post-war structure of some
nationalised industries, the National Health Service, and a
host of quasi-autonomous bodies. Even the all-purpose local
government authorities are organised internally on the basis
of functionally specific departments.

In 1968 the Fulton Report on the civil service recommended some subdivision within departments on a functional
basis, through the establishment of agencies concerned with
defined areas of work and with greater autonomy from the
normal pattern of ministerial responsibility. These agencies
would be held accountable only for the extent to which they
were able to achieve their broad objectives. This model of
structure has found little favour within departments, though
there are some examples, one being the Property Services
Agency, which is responsible for the physical fabric, such as
the buildings of the civil service. Though remaining part of
the Department of the Environment this body enjoys
considerable autonomy in terms of personnel and financial
policy.

The size of departments is another factor which has been
seen as important. Since the 1950s there has been a trend
towards the creation of larger entities through a process of
amalgamation of functionally related departments. Departments formed by the process of amalgamation include the
Ministry of Defence, the Foreign and Commonwealth Office, the
Department of Health and Social Security, the Department of
Trade and Industry, and the Department of the Environment.

One of the most important of the advantages which this
reform was intended to offer was increased co-ordination
between the related areas of administration, though there is
substantial doubt as to the extent to which this has been the
case. By the 1970s the misgivings began to lead to some
retreat from the policy: in 1974 Energy (under pressure from
the fuel crisis) was removed from the Department of Trade and
Industry, in 1976 Transport was re-established outside the
Department of the Environment and in 1989 Health and Social
Security parted company. Nevertheless, the general picture
remains one of larger departments, with Environment, Social
Security, and Defence well established and employing over
half of all civil servants.

Although there is considerable concentration upon
London, the civil service structure is widely dispersed
throughout the country by means of field agencies; some 75
per cent of all civil servants work outside the capital. The

regional offices remain formally within the hierarchical
framework of authority and responsibility, but in practice
the pressures of day-to-day administration result in a
substantial degree of discretion devolving upon the local
officials.

Another area of debate relating to the structure of the
civil service concerns its total size. Critics have
portrayed the public sector in general, and the civil service
in particular, as fat, lazy, and inefficient, and the Thatcher
years have seen a general slimming down in a quest for greater
efficiency.

The Fulton Committee advocated the hiving-off of certain
functions to specially created, quasi-autonomous agencies
which would cease to be part of the civil service. In 1968
the postal and telecommunications service was hived off in
this way and made a public corporation. In 1973 and 1974,
the responsibilities of the Department of Employment for the
administration of employment exchanges, industrial training
and health and safety at work, and industrial arbitration
were hived off to newly created agencies named respectively
the Manpower Services Commission, the Health and Safety Commission, and the Advisory Conciliation and Arbitration
Service. The removal of functions from the ambit of the
civil service is held to have important implications for the
manner in which they are administered. Because the quasi-
autonomous bodies are granted greater freedom from ministerial control it is hoped that they will exercise more
imagination and flair in the conduct of their business, and
in some cases it is appropriate for them to operate according
to private-sector-style commercial critiera.

However, by 1987 parts of the Manpower Services
Commission were being reclaimed into the Whitehall embrace,
demonstrating the great flexibility of the civil service.
Structural change is visible and can have symbolic significance. A new government, anxious to give the impression of
dynamism, may well find it easier to change structure than it
is to alter substantive policies, attitudes, and processes.
It is certainly true that governments have tended to begin
their terms of office with some widely publicised form of
structural reform.

THE BUREAUCRATS

Though it has never been formally defined, the term 'civil
servant' is usually reserved for those working in the civil
service itself and does not include employees in the large
range of other public agencies. The politicians heading the
ministries are not, of course, themselves civil servants.
Today the civil service in Britain employs some 600,000
individuals, though about 100,000 of these are classified as

industrial civil servants and not, for the most part, engaged in public administration as such.

There is wide agreement that the Northcote-Trevelyan Report of the nineteenth century left a considerable legacy in the reforms it inspired with respect to recruitment practices. The stress on the value of university education represented a marked improvement on earlier recruitment patterns, but the acceptance of the existing university syllabus resulted in the recruitment of generalists, the products of the classical education greatly valued by Victorians for its character-building effects, rather than specialists, the products of a more scientific education. This tradition endured into the twentieth century, notwithstanding the fact that considerable advances took place in the newer intellectual disciplines, including the natural and social sciences.

Other traditions also endured. In the nineteenth century the universities of Oxford and Cambridge stood alone as centres of intellectual activity, and not unnaturally it was from these institutions that the entrants to the higher ranks of the service came. Even though the twentieth century saw the emergence of a network of provincial universities, this propensity to recruit from Oxford and Cambridge persisted, with examinations favouring such candidates, and consequently discouraging applications by graduates from the newer centres of higher education. A further effect of this recruitment pattern was a social composition in the upper echelons of the service which could only be described as elitist. For historical reasons the ancient universities recruit disproportionately from the public schools, which belong to the private education sector where attendance is effectively reserved for the children of the wealthy.

Since the second world war there has been mounting criticism of the recruitment pattern perpetuated by the civil service in Britain, much of which comes from academics and politicians of the left. Two principal allegations constitute the gravamen of their case. In the first place there is the tendency of the 'Oxbridge' candidates to have studied subjects of little relevance to the problems of modern society: this has led to ineffectual public policy in a number of crucial areas. Secondly, the elitist social background of the civil servants casts doubt on their ability to understand the problems of ordinary people, and makes them unresponsive to the leadership of socialist-inspired governments.

The Fulton Report echoed these criticisms and offered a large number of recommendations aimed at reducing social elitism, including the establishment of a civil service college, improving in-service training practices, and increasing the role of specialists. However, in spite of much public discussion and enthusiasm, little real change

occurred. A decade later the House of Commons Select
Committee on Expenditure conducted an inquiry into the
post-Fulton civil service and found little change in
practices, structures, or in the criticisms made by those
questioned.

A major barrier to reforms of the kind advocated has
been the fact that those charged with implementation, i.e. the
senior civil servants, are themselves products of, and for
the most part apologists for, the very system under attack.
Of course it may well be that the elitism manifest within the
civil service is symptomatic of a greater elitism which is
fundamental to British culture, which is in turn linked with
the deferential nature of society. Marxists would allege
that no remedy can come from direct action towards civil
service reform, rather it must focus on the fundamentals of
society. The response to the Fulton Report was decidedly
feeble and could be seen as supportive of such a view.

Thus there is in Britain no systematic education system
for senior civil servants such as exists in France. There
are courses with a substantial public administration component
offered at undergraduate level in British institutions of
higher education, but these are usually at provincial
universities or polytechnics, and graduates have modest
career aspirations, tending to enter local government, the
National Health Service, or the intermediate ranks of the
civil service.

Today, if we ignore the criticisms of social elitism, the
formal basis for the recruitment and promotion of civil
servants is merit. Civil servants are not appointed for their
political views. They are supposed to be politically neutral,
and able to serve governments of any complexion. However,
during her term of office, Mrs Thatcher has exercised certain
hitherto-unsuspected prime ministerial powers in order to
influence appointments at the very senior levels of the
service. This was possible because, rather fortuitously, a
number of permanent secretaries reached retirement during the
period. In addition, she has accelerated a post-war trend
towards the appointment of political sympathisers to advisory
positions within the civil service. It is possible that
these tendencies will be continued by her successors, in
which case the character of the British civil service may
become, in some respects, a little more like that of public
bureaucracy in the United States, and the French civil
service with its ministerial cabinets. Mrs Thatcher has
expressed the view that civil servants should be committed to
the success of the government's policies; and this sentiment
has also been expressed by politicians of the left who have
felt themselves impeded by official intransigence or
lethargy.

ACCOUNTABILITY

The principal avenue for the public accountability of the
civil service in Britain is Parliament. A doctrine of
individual responsibility dictates that each minister is
answerable to the House for anything which takes place within
his department (or sub-department). This means that any
Member of Parliament can, on his own initiative, or on that
of one of his constituents, ask a parliamentary question on
any aspect of the work of the civil service. In this the
civil service differs from other public agencies such as the
public corporation, local government, the National Health
Service, and the variety of smaller quasi-autonomous bodies
where the extent of ministerial responsibility is limited.
     Various corollaries flow from this doctrine of the
individual responsibility of ministers for the work of their
departments: the civil servants are not themselves expected
to address Parliament or the public on questions of policy;
when praise or blame is apportioned civil servants are not
mentioned by name; and ministers are held vicariously culp-
able for any errors emerging in the work of their departments
and can be called upon to resign in serious cases. However,
in practice all these principles are breaking down. Leading
civil servants are increasingly addressing themselves to the
public, civil servants have even been named and blamed in
cases where mistakes have been uncovered, and for a number of
years the actual resignation of ministers has reflected
political expediency on the part of the government rather
than any sense of constitutional imperative. Even the answerability of ministers to Parliament is subject to political
expediency, with Prime Ministers and ministers taking pains
to evade questions which might cause embarrassment.
     In addition to individual responsibility there is a
doctrine of collective responsibility, which means that the
ministers forming a government are considered to share responsibility for all policies, and should resign en bloc if
defeated in Parliament. This doctrine has little significance
today other than to bind members of the government to the
expression of a single view, which again is entirely a matter
of political expediency, offering no improvement in accountability. Failure to support the 'official' party line may
result in resignation, voluntary or otherwise. The reason
that responsibility through the operation of these doctrines
can be so easily evaded is that they are conventions rather
than legal prescriptions. They evolved in an earlier era,
before the advent of the modern mass political parties, with
their strict internal discipline, which now dominate most
parliamentary procedures.
     Another form of accountability is secured through the
financial process. The historical basis of all parliamentary
control over the executive derives from its role as the

provider of finance through taxation. The financial accounts
of all civil service departments are examined by means of a
specialist body of members, the Public Accounts Committee.
The deliberations of the committee are assisted by a constitutionally independent figure, the Comptroller and Auditor
General, working through his own department, whose role is to
audit accounts and report any irregularities. From time to
time causes célèbres emerge through this process, generating
much media coverage and public discussion. The permanent
secretary of each department is the chief accounting officer
and as such he can be called before the Public Accounts
Committee to answer its questions. On these occasions the
committee is able to utilise the advice of experts from
outside Parliament. Nevertheless, the effectiveness of the
process is subject to some debate and certain commentators,
who have been closely involved, have expressed doubts that the
powers of the committee are as great as the textbooks usually
suggest.

The Public Accounts Committee has provided a model for
further experimentation in accountability through select
committee scrutiny, which has taken place since 1964. The
civil service has put up a stout resistance to the use of
such committees by Parliament, and has shown some reluctance
to assist their deliberations. The principal justification
for such truculence has been, rather ironically, the argument
that it would interfere with the doctrine of individual
responsibility. At present there are twelve committees of
this kind. Their remits are closely linked with the areas of
policy covered by particular departments, including agriculture, defence, education, employment, environment, foreign
affairs, home affairs, industry and trade, social services,
transport, and the Treasury. Two further committees examine
the activities of the Welsh and Scottish Offices.

Some observers see in the committees the key to a revit-
alisation of accountability through Parliament. For many of
the advocates of reform, the congressional committees in the
United States have represented something of an ideal to which
the British system might aspire. However, at present, the
British variants can be regarded as no more than a pale
shadow of their influential US counterparts. The British
executive and civil service display considerable powers to
evade scrutiny, as a number of recent events have
demonstrated.

The avenues of accountability described above are somewhat removed from the lives of ordinary people. It is a
cause of concern to some that there is in Britain no special
system of administrative law, operating through a separate
system of courts such as the Droit Administratif in France.
However, recourse may be made to the ordinary courts in a
number of ways. Actions by public bodies which are outside
their statutory powers may be declared ultra vires, and

application may be made for the issue of High Court writs which compel public authorites to act in a proper manner, or cease acting improperly. In addition, the courts are supplemented by a system of administrative tribunals which can consider disputes arising between the citizen and a public body. This system has grown up ad hoc, and there exist doubts both on the extent of the independence of the tribunals from the administrative bodies themselves, and on the efficiency with which they are able to dispense justice.

The machinery for accountability was extended in 1967 by the creation of the office of a Scandanavian-style ombudsman to investigate complaints of maladministration made by the public. At this time Parliament was fearful of a further erosion of its own power, and in order to appease these misgivings the new system was tied to the old, so that all complaints intended for the ombudsman had, in the first instance, to be addressed to a Member of Parliament, who would act as a 'filter', taking up some of the complaints himself, and passing others on to the new official; appropriately termed the Parliamentary Commissioner for Administration. The absence of a direct channel of public access is seen by many as a weakness of the system, and it is something of an anomaly that complaints against the National Health Service, which is not part of the civil service, may be made directly to a Health Service Commissioner, who is in practice the same person as the Parliamentary Commissioner. There are other criticisms made of the system which centre on features such as the lack of 'teeth' of the commissioner (he can only recommend remedial action not enforce it), limitations on his jurisdiction, lack of initiative on the part of successive incumbents in the office, and an absence of public awareness. Nevertherless, the system continues to evolve and there are a number of achievements recorded.

We have seen that the constitutional means of ensuring public accountability of the civil service can all be subject to criticism. It is argued that defects are mitigated by the pluralistic nature of the British political system, which involves opposition parties, pressure groups of various kinds, and the mass media. The interaction of these with the executive can effectively heighten the level of accountability by demanding information from the civil service, and educating, involving, and affecting the aspirations of the public with respect to government. Of course this form of accountability can also be subject to criticism. Pressure groups and parties are always motivated by partisan considerations, with some considerably more powerful than others, and the mass media can be accused of bias, or the trivialisation of political information.

CONTROL

The concept of accountability is closely allied with that of
control. The very rationale of individual responsibility is
that the minister is considered to be in control of the
activities of his department. In theory, this political
control exceeds that which the executive can have over any of
the other forms of public agency. In practice, however, the
great size of many of the departments, the vast amount of
delegated legislation, the Herculean workload of ministers
(which extends beyond their departmental roles, since they
remain ordinary Members of Parliament while they are
ministers), and certain of the management structures in use,
mean that ministerial control is far from total, with considerable autonomy and discretion lying with officials. Indeed,
one of the principal arguments for the dominance of the
generalist-type civil servant is based on the acceptance that
he will frequently be acting on behalf of the politician (who
is essentially a laymen), and must therefore be able to think
in a similar way.
     The machinery by which control over the civil service in
Britain is exercised reflects the bureaucratic form of
organisation, incorporating a pyramidal hierarchy with each
level receiving direction from the one above, and with the
minister, or secretary of state, at the apex. The hierarchy
is partly political in composition, with ministers and junior
ministers set below the secretary of state.
     The interface between the politicians and the civil
servants is a particularly sensitive point in the hierarchical
chain. There has been considerable debate on the extent to
which the politicians can gain the committed loyalty of the
bureaucrats, of whom critics have alleged political
insensitivity and even obstructionism. Civil servants at the
senior levels in Britain have a number of advantages over
their political masters. They are highly educated, they have
long experience and understanding of the working of the
bureaucratic machine in minute detail, they have great
security of tenure, they are cloaked in anonymity, the views
they express are regarded as secret, they are charged with
the implementation of policy, and they have unique access to
official information, which they are able to filter before it
reaches the minister. The suspicion that the officials play
an over-dominant role in the policy-making process is
strengthened by an increasing post-war tendency of governments
of left and right to have recourse to the appointment of
advisers from outside the service whose political allegiance
is overtly sympathetic to their policy objectives. However,
the underlying principle of appointment on the basis of
merit, rather than by political patronage, means that an
incoming government should not face overtly ideological
opposition from the bureaucracy.

Control over the civil service also comes through
finance. In a formal sense the House of Commons controls the
manner in which the executive raises and spends money. This
control is exercised through various processes which centre
on a scrutiny of the annual estimates of future expenditure,
the longer-term spending plans of the departments, the
government budget which makes proposals for taxation, and the
annual financial accounts of the departments. In practice
the party system means that these processes give very little
real control to Parliament itself, but they do lead to other
forms of control.

The Treasury, which is itself under the control of the
Prime Minister and the Chancellor, has come to inherit the
formal controls of Parliament through its responsibility to
oversee all government expenditure in order to prepare the
estimates, the economic forecasts, and the Budget etc. The
role of the Treasury is ubiquitous and overbearing, with
officials entering into lengthy bilateral negotiations with
all departments in the determination of their expenditure
levels, and hence influencing their substantive policies.
Thus it becomes possible to speak of a system of Treasury
control within the civil service. This control has been the
subject of considerable criticism, and the Treasury is blamed
for a number of Britain's economic failings, including low
capital investment, an over-emphasis on short-term objectives
such as securing a balance of payments, the size of the
public sector borrowing requirement, and inflation. The
general tendency of the Treasury has been to reduce
expenditure by departments; a goal which characterised the
Victorian governments under which this system was created.

The hold of the Treasury was reduced in the 1960s,
following the introduction of the Public Expenditure Survey
Committee (PESC) process which was designed to modify the
narrow, short-term approach to public expenditure control.
However, subsequent 'crises' in PESC, and a determinedly
monetarist stance of the Thatcher governments since 1979,
have served to re-establish this central dominance. This in
turn has made it easier for the politicians to control the
policies and resultant expenditure levels of the departments.

MANAGEMENT

Problems over the manner in which the civil service is
managed is another focus of topical debate in Britain.
Ministers can be said to have managerial as well as policy-
making roles, though the skills of the former are not
necessarily those of the latter. Furthermore, the senior
civil servants tend to see themselves, not as managers, but
as policy-makers. Thus it is not surprising that, when
diagnosing civil service ills, critics place considerable

emphasis upon what is perceived as an absence of managerial skills; particularly in the higher reaches. A major thrust in the Fulton Report was for greater attention to the acquisition and use of managerial skills, with in-service courses, the establishment of the civil service college referred to earlier, and the creation of a new department charged with responsibility for the implementation of new management techniques throughout the service. These recommendations, and a number of others (including the identification of units of work suitable for transference to sub-departmental agencies with limited accountability) were implemented, but with little lasting impression. We have noted that the civil service college was not a success, and the Civil Service Department, established to promote management techniques throughout the service, was wound up in the 1980s.

In 1970 the new Conservative government announced a firm intention to introduce a more managerial style into the civil service. Certain reforms were implemented, and businessmen from the private sector were brought into government, but once again there was little lasting impact. Efforts to import private-sector managerial skills have been renewed since 1979 by the Thatcher governments. Influential figures from commerce and industry have been brought in to scrutinise the management practices of the civil service, and to promote change. The durability of reforms wrought under this regime remain in some doubt however; some commentators believe that a change of Prime Minister will see the civil service revert to its earlier practices.

It is argued that the culture of public administration in the British civil service is antithetical to private-sector-style management. Public adminstration is seen as unique in character, with particular ethical and practical contingencies which render lessons from the profit-orientated world of private business fundamentally unsound. Other factors which inhibit the use of private-sector-style management techniques in the British civil service include the fact that all ministers are politicians, who retain their parliamentary seats as well as the full range of duties associated with membership of the House, the dominance of the generalist administrator, the doctrine of individual ministerial reponsibility, the dominance of the Treasury, and a career structure based on length of service which is essentially non-competitive. Opponents of this view argue that the civil service resists managerial reforms through institutional inertia, and the pursuit of self-interest at high cost to the national interest. The ethos of the upper echelons has been characterised as more like that of the senior common room in one of the older universities than of the board rooms of the twentieth-century industry which shapes the environment of modern government.

However, at the lower levels of the civil service, where there is a greater proportion of work of a routine nature, a managerial style is in greater evidence, and there has even been some pioneering work in the use of various techniques. Nevertheless, the impact of politics and the ethical demands of public administration continue to create problems, so that the quest for efficiency remains something of a perennial occupation.

POLICY-MAKING

The underlying theory of the British variant of representative democracy is that ministers, as the representatives of the people, to whom they are responsible through Parliament, are the makers of all public policy. They receive any praise or blame for the manner in which they exercise this function, and they may be removed from office en bloc by the popular vote expressed at a general election if the policies have not met with widespread satisfaction.

However, in practice the policy-formation process is not as simple as this. We have seen that a number of factors, such as the expertise of civil servants, the heavy work-load of ministers, the sheer size of the scope of government involvement in social and economic life, and the increasing complexity of the subject matter and technology associated with policy in modern times, make it inevitable that civil servants themselves play a considerable part in the process. The conventions of the constitution, and of political life, recognise this fact, and much work in Whitehall is avowedly policy orientated, with a complex network of official inter-departmental committees formed, and reformed, to reflect changing policy concerns.

However, policy influence extends beyond the civil service. There exists within British society a range of organised interests, some with considerable power, which intrude directly (through bargaining and negotiation), and indirectly (through the desire of the formal policy-makers to appease them and gain their support). These organisations are often placed in strong positions with respect to the shaping of public policy by virtue of expertise which they uniquely possess. Policy towards the National Health Service, for example, could not be made without the assistance of the British Medical Association, and agricultural policy similarly requires the involvement of the National Farmers Union. If policy is disliked by the powerful pressure groups they can often render the legislation unworkable, as was the case in the 1970s when the trades unions objected to industrial relations legislation.

This pluralism in policy-making has been an accepted part of British political culture, and it can be defended by

the usual arguments concerning the defects in the formal
system of representative democracy. What is not so clearly
understood is the role of the civil service in this
pluralism; in fact the system serves to increase the policy-
making power of officials. Although pressure groups may
attempt to influence policy in a number of ways, including
efforts to change public opinion, access to the mass media,
and contact with Members of Parliament and ministers, a
number of prominent case studies testify that the most
effective avenue of access is via the civil service.
Relationships between bureaucrats and leaders of certain
groups are conducted quietly, even covertly, through a series
of informal relationships. Representatives of the groups
also sit, along with the civil servants, on various official
government advisory and consultative bodies which exist in
their hundreds in Britian.

The pluralism which operates in Britain does not form a
single monolithic system; it is fragmentary, with a number
of relatively autonomous 'sub-governments' or policy communi-
ties. These bring together, in an intimate relationship, the
leading interests and civil service departments associated
with a particular area of policy. If these representatives
and the civil servants are in close accord on some matter of
policy, the scope for ministerial influence is severely
restricted.

We have already noted that since 1979 governments under
Mrs Thatcher have sought to curb or harness the policy-making
power of the civil service in various ways. One method has
been through prime ministerial influence in the appointment
of permanent secretaries in order to conduce bureaucratic
compliance with government objectives. Another has been the
introduction into the civil service of businessmen and
techniques from the private sector, the use of outside
advisers, and attempts to reduce the size of the service
which have tended to undermine morale.

In addition, government style has moved away from the
consultative, consensus-seeking mode of policy-making implied
in the pluralist model. The post-war consensus has been
severely criticised by the Thatcher government; one member
spoke of the 'post-war funk'. A number of strong interest
groups have been humbled, particularly the miners, who paid
heavily for their defeat of the Heath government in 1974.
The British trades union movement has been weakened by
legislation and exclusion from negotiation; even the medical
and legal professions have had their wings clipped, and the
Confederation of British Industries has found itself in
opposition to the government on a number of occasions.

Nevertheless, the policy-making role of the civil
service in a modern, highly developed state such as Britain
cannot be underestimated. It is difficult to believe that
governments can ever change in the long term the fundamental

relationships which are brought about by the environment in which policy-making takes place. It is for this reason that features such as the composition and ideology of the civil service remain of perennial interest to observers.

CONCLUSION

The British civil service in the twentieth century remains largely a product of the previous century, retaining many vestiges from its past. Apologists for the system would point to characteristics such as a dominant ethic of public service, and a political neutrality betokened in a total subordination to the political will of the government of the day. Furthermore, the permanence of the officials can give a continuity to policy which would otherwise be lacking in a political system which knows little of coalition governments, and sees a complete changeover of the party of government following electoral defeat of an incumbent. Similarly, the civil service can be said to impose a moderating influence on policy and steer forces of left or right towards a via media which is said to be a virtue to be found throughout British political history.

The service offers to employees a permanent career structure, free from the vagaries and vicissitudes of private industry, and guarantees salaries which are substantial, though not comparable with those available in the private sector for similar levels of responsibility and qualifications. Promotion is largely on the basis of merit, not characterised by enervating cut-and-thrust competition.

Critics of the British civil service are by no means mute. One body of thought portrays the service as a bastion of elitism, an arm of an 'establishment' which embraces the upper strata of the traditional professions: the armed forces, the Church of England, the City (i.e. the financial institutions), and an aristocracy headed by a royal family. In the nineteenth century such a coincidence of interests may have been functional in the development of economic and social life, but today it can be portrayed as anachronistic and dysfunctional for the majority of the population.

Other criticisms draw attention to the overbearing role of the Treasury, which damages the economy, an excessive preoccupation with secrecy (i.e. secrecy from the British people), the absence of experts in policy-influencing positions, and the lack of managerial skill within the service, particularly amongst the upper echelons. The relatively cushioned existence offered to employees, who are prepared to forego the salary levels available in the private sector (though they receive various other prestigious honours such as knighthoods and life-peerages), may be seen to attract a rather dull kind of administrator without

innovatory ability, flair, or personal drive. Politicians of
right and left have commented on the bureaucratic inertia
which greeted their would-be policy innovations. There is
also the allegation that the civil service in Britain is too
big. This can mean either that it is overstaffed and
inefficient or that the role of the state itself is too
large. We have seen that the Conservative government, which
took office in 1979, would appear to agree with a number of
these latter criticisms, and has introduced various experts
in management, and the substance of policy. In addition it
has reduced the size of the civil service and has begun a
programme of privatisation of nationalised industries.
    For these and other reasons, explored in earlier
sections, it may be that the British civil service is in a
state of change. However, the evolutionary nature of British
constitutional history, and the capacity of the service to
resist outside influence, demonstrated in the fate of the
recommendations of the Fulton Report, counsel caution in any
predictions. Almond and Verba believed that the deferential
and secretive nature of society, together with the preference
for strong government, provided a basis for 'the maintenance
of an efficient and independent administrative culture'.
This suggests a highly stable organisation, well able to
defend its norms and practices against external forces.

REFERENCES AND FURTHER READING

Almond, G. and Verba, S. (1963) The Civic Culture, Princeton,
    Princeton University Press. (A classic, but much criticised
    study. See also the more recent evaluation in the same
    authors' 1980 book, The Civic Culture Revisited, Boston,
    Little, Brown.)

Bagehot, W. (1963) The English Constitution, London, Fontana.
    (A reprint of the nineteenth-century classic.)

Birch, A. H. (1964) Representative and Responsible Government,
    London, Allen and Unwin. (A classic treatment of its topic.)

Brown, R. G. S. and Steel, D. (1979) The Administrative
    Process in Britain, London, Methuen. (Provides a helpful
    insight into the place of the civil service within the
    machinery of government, and offers a good theoretical
    basis for further study.)

Eckstein, H. (1960) Pressure Group Politics, London, Allen
    and Unwin. (Dated, but still a useful account of pressure
    group relations with the civil service.)

Garret, J. (1980) Managing the Civil Service, London,
Heinemann. (Garret, associated with the Fulton Report, has
long been an advocate of civil service reform, and an acute
critic of developments.)

Greenwood, J. R. and Wilson, D. J. (1984) Public
Administration in Britain, London, Allen and Unwin. (A
well-constructed basic text.)

Kellner, P. and Crowther-Hunt, Lord (1980) The Civil Servants:
An Enquiry into Britain's Ruling Class, London, Macdonald.
(As plain Norman Hunt, one of these authors played a
central role in the Fulton enquiry and has vigilantly
chronicled civil service shortcomings ever since.)

Pitt, D. and Smith, B. (1981) Government Departments,
London, Routledge & Kegan Paul. (An authoritative account.)

Riddell, P. (1985) The Thatcher Government, Oxford, Basil
Blackwell. (Examines the considerable impact of the
eponymous Prime Minister.)

Chapter 3

CANADA

J. E. Kingdom

THE POLITICAL SETTING

The Constitution

Canada is regarded as a liberal democracy with a constitution
containing written and unwritten elements, owing much to the
influence of Britain, the ex-colonial power. The written
part of the constitution is the British North America Act of
1867, which formally granted independence. However, Canada is
unlike Britain in that it is a federation and the constitution
must apportion authority between the federal and provincial
levels of government. Although the nature of the federal-
provincial relationship has changed since the nineteenth
century, Canada has continued to recognise the British monarchy as the sovereign authority in its system of government.
The Crown is represented by a Governor General, who is advised
by the Canadian Privy Council, the efficient part of which is
the Cabinet headed by the Prime Minister.
    Canada has a Parliament in the form of a bicameral
assembly, consisting of an appointed Senate, and an elected
House of Commons. The formal role of Parliament is that of
legislation, but most legislation is framed by the Cabinet,
which is able to rely on the support of its party majority in
the House of Commons, so that the effective role of the House
is one of scrutinising the executive, and providing a forum
for political debate. It is the concern of reformers to
strengthen the ability of the House to perform its role.
    The members of the Senate are appointed by the Prime
Minister, and its function is not unlike that of the British
House of Lords, which represents traditional aristocratic
authority against popular forces. The Senate tends to represent the wealthy classes, though there is also an element of
geographic representation, in that Senators are drawn from
the regions. However, this House has little effective power,
and rarely disagrees with the House of Commons. The Cabinet
is not drawn from its members, and is not responsible to it.

Like the British House of Lords, its continued existence is a
source of debate.

As the popularly elected chamber, the House of Commons
is the effective part of the legislature. All money spent by
government must be sanctioned, and bills containing proposed
legislation must pass through a series of deliberative stages
during which they will be publicly examined and perhaps
amended.

The fundamental rights of citizens are derived from the
British constitution and have their roots far back in the
Magna Carta. The practical enforcement of such rights rests
with the judiciary. The courts in Canada form a single
hierarchy at the top of which is the Supreme Court of Canada.
Below this are the courts of appeal of each of the ten
provinces. All senior judicial appointments are made by the
federal government. The federal nature of the constitution
tends to elevate the role of the judiciary in the constitution, when it is called upon to adjudicate on the relative
jurisdictions of the federal and provincial governments.
However, much of the practical determination of this relationship has rested with politicians, whose ad hoc compromising
has been necessary to render the confederation viable under
changing circumstances.

Political Culture

The political culture of Canada is, perhaps to a greater
extent than in other countries, considerably influenced by
geographical factors. In the first place the country is
extremely large, a fact which can create communication
problems. These are exacerbated by physical barriers of some
enormity, including the Rockies, the prairies, the Great
Lakes, and even some territory of the United States. The
separate provinces exhibit considerable differences in
natural conditions, and their respective economies reflect
this. Further fragmenting tendencies arise from the distinctive historical developments of the individual provinces, the
effects of which remain today. Though a young country,
Canada has an extended lineage in the histories of the colonising powers, from which the present population is descended.
There is also a more modern form of 'colonising' influence
arising from the close proximity to the greatest power in the
western world: the United States exerts a ubiquitous social,
economic, and cultural influence through penetration at
numerous points.

There is some doubt as to whether one can meaningfully
speak of a distinctive Canadian political culture at all, but
it has certainly been the intention of political leaders at
the time of federation, and ever since, to forge a political
identity through a process of 'state building'. In spite of

all such efforts there remains one fundamental dualism in
Canadian political culture, arising from the successive
colonisation by the French and the English, so that today
French Canadians and English Canadians exist as distinctive
social groups. This broad dichotomy has its manifestation in
ethnic, religious, philosophical, economic, and political
terms which cannot be ignored, though, having considered
them, we may look for more homogenising aspects of Canadian
political culture.

The French Canadians are mainly concentrated in Quebec,
where the sense of ethnic separation is reinforced by a
powerful Roman Catholic Church. This has actively promoted
the persistence of a distinctive subculture. The church has
tended to deprecate materialism, and worldly achievement. It
has supported a veneration of ascriptive status such as that
of the family, the aristocracy, and indeed the church itself.
The result was a reputation for lack of enterprise on the
part of the Quebecois, a small-town parochialism, and an
unwillingness to be impressed by those professions, usually
pursued by the ambitious, which tend to be held in popular
respect in other western societies. Recent decades have seen
a breaking down of these traditions amongst younger members
of the society, who have been unwilling to accept the
economic leadership of English Canadians and the United
States which had become the norm.

In contrast, the English Canadians who dominate all the
other provinces, espouse values more similar to those of the
United States. Such religious influence as there is would
support the protestant ethic of hard work, and the spirit of
individualism leading to respect for achievement and material
gain. The economic success of Canada, even in Quebec, is
largely to be attributed to the endeavours of the English
Canadians, who have seen in the abundant natural riches of
the country an opportunity to create a standard of living far
superior to that which might have been considered their birth-
right in the mother country. However, the English Canadians
do not hold the values of egalitarianism and materialism in
the same measure as do Americans. The early settlers combined
elements of Lockian philosophy respecting life, liberty, and
property, with traditional Tory notions of an organic society
with functional divisions, including a paternalistic ruling
class, maintaining social stability.

The social pluralism resulting from the basic dualism
discussed above does have fragmentary manifestation, including
politically inspired separatist movements in Quebec. Nevertheless, it is possible to identify a homogeneous political
culture in Canada which actually draws on these traditions.
The act of federation is itself an acknowledgement that the
individual provinces can gain more than they will lose in
merging to form a larger entity under a single leadership.
The acceptance of federal leadership was demonstrated in 1970

in the acceptance by a substantial majority of a highly
centralist War Measures Act.

Generally speaking, Canadians display deference towards
institutions and authority. This is a more positive characteristic in the case of the English Canadians following the
old English Tory traditions, who willingly delegate authority
to political leaders. In the case of the French Canadians,
deference is accepted as a proper response to institutions
such as the church and family, but is granted rather more
grudgingly to the political institutions. In both cases,
class status of elites within society tends to confer legitimacy. There has been something of a tradition of aristocratic rule inherited from the colonial era, which saw the
monopolisation of the highest public offices by an elite
group, termed the family compact. This has bequeathed to the
Canadian political culture an underlying conservatism. Conservatism, of a kind, has also been fostered by the French
Canadian respect for traditional values and patterns of
authority.

However, Canadians are probably less deferential than
the British. The respect for the Governor General does not
match that displayed in England towards the Queen; and there
are rumbling republican movements. Canadian deference is
more a product of a materialistic pragmatism, which is content to permit freedom to political leaders to attend to state
business, while allowing individuals to pursue their own interests in a comfortably affluent society. Thus the Canadians
have tended to look for pragmatic, rather than charismatic
leaders. Britain in the nineteenth century, and the United
States in the twentieth, have provided sufficient political
glamour, so that the Canadians have been able to seek more
prosaic virtues at home. They place less emphasis on symbol-
ism and ceremony than most nations, and look to politics for
practical policies which will maximise their satisfactions.
Certainly, Diefenbaker and Trudeau have been seen as charismatic, but the longest-serving Prime Minister has been
Mackenzie King, a colourless leader of the Liberal Party whose
skill lay in a practical approach to balancing the conflicting
demands from such a diverse society. The flamboyant life-
style of Brian Mulroney has not earned popular approval. In
spite of the unprecedented economic boom achieved by 1987,
Canadians were sceptical about the lavish interior decorations
to the Prime Minister's official residence inspired by his
wife Mila.

Participation by ordinary citizens in political life is
by no means high. Local government is seen as largely apolitical, with political parties playing very little part. Man-
hood suffrage did not come until the late nineteenth century,
and the vote was withheld from the female population of Quebec
until 1940. The effect of successive waves of immigration,
temporarily creating sections of the population without full

political rights, has served to reduce participatory levels
and aspirations. Research reveals that Canadians generally
lack knowledge on political matters, and show little interest
in gaining information. There is some justification in
regarding the political culture as only quasi-participative.
    The lack of popular interest in politics may be explained
in terms of a high degree of satisfaction with, and confidence
in, the institutions and working of government and public
administration. It certainly cannot be explained logically,
in terms of laissez faire, and the rugged individualism embedded in the spirit of the frontiersman, since the Canadian government permeates, in a positive way, most aspects of social
and economic life. Even before the first world war government
could be described as collectivist. Subsequently war, and
the depression of the 1930s, led to the emergence of a complex
welfare state, and to the acceptance of Keynesian economic
principles. Various important parts of the economy are
nationalised, and most private sectors can expect subsidies
and support in times of crisis. The French Canadians have
been traditionally more opposed to the extended economic role
for the state, which could be seen as conducive to industrialisation and an erosion of certain human values, but since the
1960s the provincial government in Quebec has promoted
economic growth in line with the pragmatic materialism of
English Canada.

Political Parties and Interest Groups

The most formal manifestation of the political process is in
the political parties. Since confederation there have been
two major parties in Canada - the Liberals and the
Progressive Conservatives. These have fought each other for
office, while sharing a broad conservative consensus on much
policy. Other parties have formed with more committed ideological stances, often in opposition to the dominant capitalist values. For example, the Progressive Party gained 65
seats in the 1921 election though it disappeared within a
decade. In 1961 The New Democratic Party was formed with the
intention of espousing a more socialistic position, while
making a wide electoral appeal, in order to rival the established parties. Other parties flourish in particular provinces.
In 1935 the Social Credit Party formed in Alberta but later
became dominant in Quebec. Smaller parties have been able to
exert some influence over policy when their support has been
required during periods of minority government, though their
members have not been able to enter the Cabinet.
    The non-ideological nature of the stances of the two
major parties reflects the broad consensus amongst Canadians
in general, and a rejection of class-based politics. Indeed,
with an exceedingly high general standard of living, the

majority of Canadians see themselves as belonging to a single
(middle) class. Federal politics have been relatively low
key, with the rumbustious style more apparent at the provincial level. It is also within the very nature of federalism
to demand a broad tolerance of diversity within parties in
order to forge an election-winning alliance. The Liberal
Party has proved the best able to reflect the political
desires of Canadians and has held office for over 50 years
this century.

The major parties are supported by teams of voluntary
workers, organised at all levels throughout the country,
though power within parties tends to remain at the centre,
and the general level of participation is not high.

What are the implications of the Canadian political
culture for its federal civil service? The deferential
attitudes mean that bureaucracies can enjoy a high degree of
legitimacy and control, with the possibility of secrecy where
desired. It also means that bureaucracy can be largely
dominated by the middle class, who are able to weld together,
in a mutually reinforcing manner, social prestige and professional status. The dualism resulting from the French ethnic
subculture sees little representation of the Quebecois in the
federal bureaucracy, where the dominant elite class consists
of English Canadians.

The low levels of interest taken by the population in
politics is another factor conducing the power of the bureaucrats, in that it reduces calls for scrutiny. The freedom of
interest groups to enter the decision-making process can also
contribute to bureaucratic authority, when civil servants can
be the principal negotiators with the groups' representatives.
The superior social status of senior civil servants can serve
to reduce the levels of expertise at the top by introducing
non-technical criteria into the recruitment process.

The aspects of the political culture of Canada discussed
above have wide implications. The deference, and willingness
of individuals to delegate freely to political leaders, opens
the door to other, less formal forms of political activity in
which those who are well organised can pursue their own
objectives through negotiation with government. Thus the
Canadian political culture is highly pluralist, with many
interest groups involving themselves in the process of policy
formation. The tendency is reinforced by the nature of the
major political parties. These remain ideologically vague in
order to maximise their appeal to voters, with the result
that, when in office, they are obliged to seek a sense of
policy direction from the interest groups, which of course are
not ideologically vague. The involvement of such groups is
seen as legitimate, and their freedoms to meet and articulate
their views unhampered derive from constitutional guarantees.

However, the largely materialist ethos has resulted in a
dominance of the pluralist decision-making process by a

complex of commercial and industrial interests in a pattern of
interaction which may be better described as some variant of
corporatism. This is institutionalised in the existence of
the upper house of Parliament, the Senate, where a body of
some 100 individuals, not elected but chosen by the Prime
Minister, provide functional representation for the major
economic interests.

HISTORICAL BACKGROUND

Considerable changes have taken place in the federal bureaucracy in Canada since confederation in 1867. The role of the
state at this time was minimal, mainly concerned with the
provision of defence, postal services, justice, law and order,
and certain public works. Accordingly, the skills of the public servants were also limited, amounting to little more than
basic literacy and numeracy, and many appointments were made
on the basis of patronage exercised by politicians in power.
As the confederation grew, the economy became more complex,
and the advantages of a greater degree of collectivism became
apparent, so that the state could assist the process of developing capitalism while at the same time acting to mitigate
some of its harsher social consequences.
    The depression of the 1930s was instrumental in hastening
the acceptance of a changed attitude towards the responsibility of the state for its citizens. At first the greater state
involvement was achieved through regulation, but this gave way
to a more positive role in the embryonic development of what
was to become a fully fledged 'welfare state'. The post-war
period saw an acceptance of Keynesian principles of economic
management, placing the state in a pre-eminent position in
the economy. It became necessary to act to control the level
of economic activity, to intervene further in the lives of
citizens, and to increase state revenue through an enlarged
tax base and public borrowing. It was during this period
that the federal civil service grew considerably in size, and
assumed what may be termed its modern form.

THE EXECUTIVE

Constitutionally speaking, the head of state, or chief executive, in Canada is the British monarch acting through her
representative, the Governor General. Like the monarch, the
Governor General plays a ceremonial rather than effective
role in the system of government.
    The efficient executive head is the Cabinet led by the
Prime Minister, though neither of these are actually mentioned in the BNA Act. The origins of the Canadian Cabinet
lie in the Privy Council, a body formally charged with the

function of advising the Governor General. Once chosen, Cabinet members formally gain their authority by being sworn in
as members of this Council. Though remaining privy councillors for life, they lose executive authority once they cease
to be members of the Cabinet. The Prime Minister and Cabinet,
as such, are not directly elected by the people, though they
are of course popularly elected as members of the House of
Commons.

As in the case of Britian, the Prime Minister is the
party leader able to command the support of the House of Commons. He has the right to choose the other members of the
Cabinet, and he restricts his choice to members from his own
party, even if his government requires the support of another
party. The act of forming the Cabinet represents a considerable power of patronage for the Prime Minister, giving him
great influence over the political careers of his colleagues.
However, there are a number of important constraints on his
freedom in this respect. For example, it is conventional to
secure equitable representation of the regions in the country,
and to secure a voice for the major interests. However, in
the final analysis, the right to choose the Cabinet is an
important political resource of the Prime Minister, and one
which he can be expected to operate to his own advantage.

The Prime Minister's power of patronage extends beyond
the appointment of his Cabinet to a number of state positions
including the Lieutenant Governors, members of the judiciary
and of the Senate. In addition, and in spite of the official
commitment to the merit principle of recruitment, it is possible for the Prime Minister to make senior appointments to the
civil service. Brian Mulroney, coming to office in September
1984 following a long period of Liberal rule, secured a
considerable number of changes in the federal bureaucracy in
this way.

As in Britain, there are those who fear that the power
of the Prime Minister is too great vis-a-vis the other members
of the cabinet, and see in the organisation of the executive
threatening presidential features. The power has been increased over recent decades, with the development of personal
staffs consisting of parliamentary secretaries and special
advisers. Pierre Trudeau strengthened the office considerably
in this way, creating a team of advisers covering a wide
range of government policy areas, including some normally
under the control of the provinces.

The Cabinet works through a number of committees covering
the main policy areas such as the economy, foreign affairs and
welfare. These are co-ordinated by other, overarching committees, concerned with matters like federal-provincial
relations, the economy, finance, and planning.

The size of the Cabinet is not fixed, but a number of
factors such as the size of the federal bureaucracy itself,
and the competing demands of interests from society, tend to

create pressures for a relatively large team, usually of over
25 members. This tendency is countered by the existence of
an inner cabinet - consisting of ministers from the departments of central importance such as Justice, Defence, and
External Affairs - which considers policy in terms of broad
outlines.

The cabinet system is serviced by a secretariat known as
the Privy Council Office. This serves to link the executive
head with the bureaucracy through a two-way transmission of
information, and the communication to the appropriate department of Cabinet decisions requiring bureaucratic action. To
some extent the Privy Council Office can be seen as an instrument of the Prime Minister, in that it shares his overarching,
co-ordinating function. Through the office he is also able to
manage the Cabinet's business and decide the order and
content of the agenda.

Initially there was suspicion at the idea of civil servants being so close to the political decision-making process,
and the development of a cabinet secretariat owes much to the
British experience. In 1927, Prime Minister Mackenzie King
commissioned a study of the British cabinet secretariat which
had developed under Lloyd George to meet the demands of the
first world war. However, it was not until a quarter of a
century later that a Canadian version of the institution
emerged, also under the pressure of war. In both cases the
success of the innovation owed much to the commitment of a
dedicated civil servant, Hankey in the case of Britain, and
Heeney in Canada.

The executive head in Canada has a great deal of power
within the system. The formal constraints inherent in the
principle of the separation of powers which can limit the
actions of the American President are absent, since the Prime
Minister remains a member of the House of Commons, wherein
his party remains in control of the majority. Within the
Cabinet he enjoys the unrivalled supremacy of the British
Prime Minister. Furthermore, the ability to make top civil
service appointments represents a power akin to that of the
President. The main constraints are probably political rather
than constitutional, deriving from the balance of support
within his party, from public opinion, and from the activities
of interest groups. As in many liberal democracies, the
office can be what is made of it, permitting considerable
scope for variation in reflection of the personality of the
incumbent.

STRUCTURE

In 1901 the Canadian federal government had some 12,000
employees; today this figure stands at over 400,000, with
about 268,000 of these in the civil service as such. Approx-

imately one in twelve working people in Canada is employed by the government. However, the proportion of public servants employed by the federal government has declined relative to those in provincial and local bureaucracies since the second world war; a fact which reflects, not any lessening in the authority of the federal government, but a growth in the concept of partnership between the centre and the provinces.

The federal civil service is by no means a monolithic body, being organised into a large and fluctuating number of departments which together share the totality of bureaucratic responsibility. In contrast to Britain, where the major departments have evolved historically over hundreds of years from the sections of the royal household, all departments are created by statute. Responsibilities are allocated largely in accordance with the functional principle; though even a cursory examination reveals evidence of other principles, including process, clientele, and, not surprisingly in a country as large and diverse as Canada, area. The complex basis upon which departments now appear to be established testifies to an evolutionary factor much like that of older constitutions. The structure reflects the following areas.

Agriculture	Communications
Consumer and Corporate Affairs	Employment and Immigration
	Environment
Energy, Mines and Resources	Finance
External Affairs	Indian Affairs and Northern Development
Fisheries and Oceans	
Industry, Trade and Commerce	Economic Development
Science and Technology	Social Development
Justice	Labour
National Defence	Health and Welfare
National Revenue	Post Office
Public Works	Regional Economic Expansion
Supply and Services	Veterans' Affairs
Transport	

There is a hierarchical pattern within the departmental structure, the most prestigious being the traditional ones such as Finance, Justice and External Affairs. The large geographical size of the country, and the federal nature of the constitution, mean that a number of departments operate through field agency structures, with locations throughout the country. Examples of these include Agriculture, Veterans' Affairs, Transport, and Defence. A number of the departments reflect particularly Canadian characteristics, such as Indian Affairs and Northern Development, Fisheries and Forestry, and Mines and Resources. In spite of the enormous growth in the role of government, and the size of the civil service, the number of major departments has grown only slowly: from 14 at the time of confederation, to around 27 at the present.

The essential feature of the government departments is
the extent to which they are answerable to Parliament through
the minister. The internal organisation of each department
may be depicted as a pyramid composed of sub-units, progressively subdividing from the top in order to allocate aspects
of the total portfolio. Each unit is considered responsible
to the one above, in a chain of command and responsibility
which culminates in the minister's relationship with
Parliament.

The strict pattern of control and accountability implied
in the responsibility of the minister to Parliament has,
particularly since the second world war, been viewed with
misgivings for its allegedly negative effects on efficiency,
and the system has been subject to some modification. Departmental corporations, such as the Agricultural Stabilisation
Boards, have been created to fulfil certain supervisory and
regulatory functions. While remaining part of the departmental structure, these agencies are not subject to the full
rigours of the formal chain of ministerial responsibility.

There has also been a growth of agencies outside the
formal civil service structure altogether, which are collectively termed Crown Corporations, and together employ some
207,000 public servants. These bodies have varying degrees
of freedom from the detailed control of ministers, and
responsibility to Parliament is restricted. These fall into
a number of categories.

Firstly there are agency corporations such as Atomic
Energy of Canada Limited, and the Royal Canadian Mint, employing some 8,000 people. These are concerned with the management of trading or service activities on a quasi-commercial
basis, and the management of procurement, construction, or
disposal operations. Secondly there are proprietory corporations which, rather like the public corporations in Britain,
manage industries providing goods and services for public
consumption in a commercially viable manner. Examples in
this category include Air Canada, the Canadian Broadcasting
Corporation, and the Canadian National Railways. These are
normally self-financing, and beyond the system of parliamentary appropriations. However, they are required to submit
reports and accounts to Parliament through an appropriate
minister, and must gain parliamentary approval in order to
secure certain kinds of financing, including parliamentary
grants or loans, the issue of capital stock to the government,
and by borrowing from the capital market with government
guarantee.

There is also a group of unclassified corporations
ranging extremely widely to include for example, the Bank of
Canada, the Canadian Wheat Board, and the Company of Young
Canadians. Each body in this category is established and
governed by special act, letters patent, or article of incor-
poration, which defines its particular relationship with

government, but in all cases there is a high degree of freedom. The main control is through the appointment of auditors,
although, of course, the government always has the option of
bringing any one within the other categories mentioned, thereby subjecting them to the more rigorous provisions of the
general legislation in the Financial Administration Act.

Finally, there are corporations which, although established in the same way as the unclassified corporation, are
only partly owned by the state, through the purchase of
capital stock. These are termed mixed, or joint enterprises
and the remaining shares are held by private investors or
provincial governments. Well-known examples of such bodies
are the Canadian Development Corporation, and Panarctic Oils
Limited. They remain outside the provisions of the Financial
Administration Act.

Thus it can be seen that the Canadian political culture
permits a high degree of autonomy to the agencies of public
administration, resulting in a complex and varied structure.
However, the civil service, with its tight level of control
and accountability, remains central to the whole system,
playing a dominant role in key policy areas, and remaining
close to the processes of central resource allocation and
policy-making. Clearly the high degree of political control
afforded by the government department remains valued, though
the presence of a large quasi-autonomous sector helps to
create an environment in which such control is constantly
questioned.

Federal-Provincial Relations

The Canadian civil service has one set of structural problems
which is not necessarily shared with other central government
bureaucracies; these arise from the federal nature of the
state. The relationship between the two levels of government,
each sovereign in its own legally defined area, results in a
continuing debate over the real extent of their respective
powers. This balance of power has shifted in a see-saw manner
since confederation in 1867.

Initially the consensus was for a high degree of centralisation under the impetus of the spirit of nation-building.
After some 20 years this gave way to a movement towards a
more genuine form of federalism, with the provinces enjoying
a greater level of autonomy. The first world war resulted in
a return to centralism for reasons of national emergency.
After this, increasing urbanisation and industrialisation led
to further growth in the activity of the provincial governments, with a greater demand for the services assigned to
this level, including education, health, and welfare. The
second world war again heralded a period of centralism, but
this was not so easily relaxed at the conclusion of the war

owing to the acceptance of the Keynesian principles of macro-
economics, which required the federal government to assume a
management role in the state economy. This trend was
strengthened by a range of factors including the demands for
equity in the provision of services throughout society, and a
growing enthusiasm for the concept of a Canadian identity.

However, since the 1960s, the movement has been towards
provincial autonomy. This has been partly occasioned by some
of the failures of federal policies, and has received added
impetus from the ambiguous loyalties of the French Canadians.
In the 1960s Quebec provincial government became more aggres-
sive in its assertion of the rights of French Canadians to
share in the country's prosperity. In promoting this goal
they demanded various freedoms from central government intervention, resulting in a compromise relationship which has
been termed 'co-operative' federalism.

Today it is probably true to say that virtually all
civil servants, at whatever level, spend some of their time
dealing with matters which have an intergovernmental dimension. The federal civil servants have counterparts in the
provinces, with whom they negotiate and plan across a wide
range of policy areas where there are shared interests or
responsibilities. In addition, there are some members of the
civil service who specialise in understanding and operating
intergovernmental machinery, which has grown up and become a
crucially important permanent feature within the Canadian
structure of public administration. This has evolved mainly
since the second world war, and involves elected politicians
at the formal decision-making level, in the Federal-Provincial
Relations Office, and a range of public servants representing
all levels of the bureaucratic hierarchies, functioning in a
network of official agencies.

There are certain dangers in the existence of this intergovernmental bureaucracy. Some fear that it will heighten
conflict within the system, others charge that it will enhance
the power of the bureaucrats vis-à-vis the elected politicians. Many provincially administered programmes are financed
by the federal government, and this can lead to difficulties
in securing accountability. Ultimately there is the question
of public access. The layered nature of the system can prove
puzzling to the citizen, and render it more susceptible to
administrative obscurantism and secrecy. Furthermore, a
number of the goals sought through the federal-provincial
relationship are mutually contradictory: for example, decentralisation of the federal bureaucracy (involving the
appointment of local candidates to field agencies) conflicts
with the merit system; provincial autonomy inhibits a nation-
ally equitable provision of services; and a stronger local
tax base defeats centrally sponsored equalisation of richer
and poorer provinces.

It is possible that federal-provincial relations will

prove one of the most important public issues of Canada in
the immediate future. The duality in the political culture
adds to the sensitivity of the problem. The federal system
requires a unique form of management if it is to be successful; interests must be balanced and values must be
reconciled in a system of political and social pluralism.

THE BUREAUCRATS

The politically significant upper echelons of the Canadian
civil service consist of some 4,500 officials, including the
deputy ministers, who are the administrative heads of the
departments (comparable with the British permanent secretaries), and senior executives (comparable with British under-
secretaries).

Merit and Patronage

Today the bureaucrats are full-time, permanent officials
recruited and promoted on the basis of merit. It was in 1908
that the first steps were taken to establish the merit system,
with the abolition of the exercise of political patronage in
making appointments to the civil service. The Civil Service
Commission was created in 1917 to act as an independent body
in the furtherance of the merit principle. In subsequent
decades the system was developed and entrenched throughout the
public sector and the federal service has led the provinces
in this respect. Indeed, patronage has remained widespread
in Quebec, and in New Brunswick it was not until the 1970s
that the practice of the wholesale hiring and firing of civil
servants associated with changes in government was discon-
tinued.
     For the most part, it is the merit system, based on the
British ideal of political impartiality, which commentators
and academics advocate for all levels in the Canadian civil
service. However, the country is physically adjacent to the
United States, where the spoils system remains predominant at
the senior levels of public bureaucracy. This generates certain tension in Canada, with politicians showing some unease
in their attitude to the question of the career patterns of
those bureaucrats with whom they must work most closely in
the implementation of their policies.
     Certain non-British characteristics remain within the
Canadian system. One of these is a tradition that a substantial proportion of the upper echelons of the service is recruited from outside the service; from industry, commerce,
and the academic establishment. Though this pattern of recruitment has a number of advantages in terms of forging links
with the outside world, it is criticised for its effect on the

morale of the career civil servants who are, as a consequence,
afforded restricted access to the uppermost positions. This
also reduces the capability of the service to produce its own
leaders.

More importantly, the practice opens the door to the
exercise of political patronage. The appointment of individuals whose careers have been well developed elsewhere means
that they may well have clearly formed political ideas. It
is unlikely that a government will appoint anyone lacking
sympathy with its own ideology and objectives. The question
arises whether an incoming government will feel able to wait
for the natural pattern of retirement to take effect before
making such appointments. In addition, there is the threat
to impartiality posed in the possibility of creating new
posts in order to enhance the degree of partisan support
within the bureaucracy.

Civil servants are forbidden by law to take part in
political activity. The principle was challenged in the
courts in 1984 prior to the general election when Michael
Cassidy, one of the candidates, applied for an injunction
suspending the law in order to permit civil servants to take
part in the campaign. The injunction was refused on the
grounds that civil servants might campaign for a particular
candidate, or party, in the expectation of subsequent career
advantage.

An important test of the political impartiality implied
in the merit system occurred in 1957, when the Progressive
Conservatives acceded to power after a lengthy period of
Liberal rule. The administrative establishment which had
been built up under the Liberals was believed to be sceptical,
and out of sympathy with the policy objectives of the new
government and its leader John Diefenbaker. The suspicion
was reciprocated, and the incoming Prime Minister established
a number of independent sources of advice in the early years
of his administration. Nevertheless, the civil service remained substantially intact and the bureaucrats were adjudged
to have served the new government loyally.

The situation was repeated in 1984, when the Conservatives won a massive election victory enabling them again to
replace a Liberal government of long standing. The new Prime
Minister, Brian Mulroney, appeared extremely suspicious of the
bureaucracy, and made immediate moves to strengthen the
government's hand by means of enlarged personal advisory
staffs for ministers. In January of the following year the
Prime Minister confirmed that he intended to bring about the
'largest single change in senior personnel in the history of
the Canadian civil service'. The following May he announced
a wide-ranging early retirement plan aimed at removing some
750 senior public servants, including deputy ministers.
Critics saw this as a purge of Liberal sympathisers, and
argued that the vast majority of those eligible for retirement

under the scheme had actually been appointed by the independent Commission.

The Prime Minister also made some significant appointments at the top of the civil service. Within the first year he appointed Paul Tellier as Clerk to the Privy Council, the equivalent of the British Cabinet Secretary, and the most powerful position in the federal bureaucracy. Amongst a number of other changes he placed Stanley Hartt, a Montreal lawyer who was known to be a personal friend, in the vital position of deputy minister of finance. The principle of making these and other appointments roused criticism from opponents, who were particularly vocal when two sons of John Crosby, the justice minister, were appointed legal agents of the federal government in Newfoundland. In response, the Prime Minister announced measures to prevent nepotism in recruitment, calling upon five of the senior civil servants he had recently appointed to subject themselves to a screening process by parliamentary committee. However, the gesture was largely symbolic because the committee would have no actual power of veto.

By the end of 1987 Prime Minister Mulroney, in spite of an unprecedented economic boom, was languishing at the bottom of the public opinion polls as a result of his failure to live up to the anti-nepotism rhetoric of his earlier promises. His business-orientated Cabinet appeared to many commentators to be rife with corruption. His former assistant, Bill Fox, commented publicly that the charges of patronage 'hang like a storm cloud over his government'. It is clear that the operation of the merit system at the upper levels of the Canadian civil service is by no means as evident as in Britain. Indeed, roughly speaking one could argue that the Canadian position is somewhere between those of Britain and the United States.

Unionism

Finally, it should be noted that, increasingly, bureaucrats at various levels have a developing sense of political will in pursuit of their self-interest. They have shown themselves ready to challenge the government on issues of various kinds. For example, they called for a parliamentary enquiry into official contracting policies, where they alleged the government to be wasting money, in an extension of the patronage system through the hiring of outsiders to do work which the existing public agencies could do themselves. In 1985 the Conservative moves to make manpower cuts were hotly opposed in an overtly political manner. The various unions combined to form a Public Service Alliance and mounted press, radio, and television campaigns to voice their opposition, and gain public support. They also organised huge picketing operations outside the office of the Treasury Board.

Canada

Social Background

The high educational qualification required of members of the
federal civil service in Canada, together with a pattern of
recruitment which included much importation of expertise from
academic, industrial and commercial life, results in the
dominance of those with elitist family backgrounds. In
addition, there is traditionally a preponderance of Anglo-
Canadians, the racial group identified with the wealthy
establishment in Canada, a substantial proportion of whom
have been educated in private schools.
   The result of this is a homogeneous service with a consensus of ideological and intellectual values. This effect
is reinforced by the wider life-style of the bureaucrats. In
contrast to their counterparts from Britain and the United
States, senior Canadian federal civil servants live in a
small, closely knit city, with a small-village atmosphere,
tending to socialise together in an exclusive manner outside
working hours. Thus there are strong pressures on those who
might enter the service without the accepted values to
conform. This is true even to the extent that French-speakers
have traditionally tended to eschew their first language in
favour of English, though this tendency is opposed by a movement towards bilingualism. The federal bureaucracy may thus
be regarded as an elite group within society.

Ethnic Representation

The cultural pluralism within Canadian society means that the
federal civil service has to consider a particular issue of
bureaucratic composition not shared by all liberal democracies. This is particularly manifest in the issue of the language spoken within the organisation and with the public. It
is argued by some that the bicultural nature of society should
be reflected in its institutions of public administration
through the recruitment of both French and English Canadians
in proportions which reflect those existing in the population
at large. The goal of a policy of this kind is national
unity, rather than bureaucratic rationality; which would of
course dictate the application of the pure merit principle.
   Following confederation, a tradition of recruitment
emerged which favoured English-speakers, in which French
Canadians were obliged to adopt the English language as the
basis for all communication. Thus they became Anglicised and
ceased to reflect their ethnic group effectively. It is this
tradition which has been the stimulus for the call for
bilingualism as an official policy.
   The federal civil service has probably moved further in
the direction of bilingualism than the majority of the
provinces. Until 1962, the requirement, laid down in an act

51

of 1918, was that administrators should speak the language of
the majority of the community they were to serve. In 1961
Parliament decreed that the language qualification should be
such that no section of society was linguistically disadvantaged in their dealings with the public service. Various
measures have followed this, including the requirement of a
second language facility in new entrants, and recruitment
programmes aimed specifically at French-speaking universities.
In 1964 a Public Service Language School was opened in order
to increase the second-language skills of those already in
post.

Measures of this kind were officially endorsed by the
Prime Minister in 1966, as constituting a basis for an equitable participatory democracy, and the further implementation
of the bilingual policy was entrusted to a specially created
Secretariat on Bilingualism located within the Privy Council
Office, and directly responsible to the Prime Minister. By
1984 some 330,000 public servants were Francophones. This
figure represented 27.2 per cent of all public servants, a
percentage roughly equal to their occurrence in the
population at large.

However, the policy of increasing the employment of
Francophones remains controversial, with Conservatives arguing
that it is not in the interests of efficient administration.
In 1973 a Progressive Conservative MP complained to the
Canadian Human Rights Commission that three federal departments had practised ethnic discrimination by taking special
measures to increase the number of Francophone employees. The
case was dismissed on the grounds that language abilities were
not the same as ethnic origins. There are also allegations
that the Francophones are not politically impartial; that
they support a particular kind of socialism. In 1984 'hate
literature' was widely circulated within the civil service by
an 'Anglo Resistance Movement' attacking an influx of 'French
carpet-baggers' with political motives.

The question of ethnic representation in the composition
of the civil service has latterly been seen in even wider
terms. In 1982 it was reported that of 4,700 senior management positions in the civil service, only 22 were held by
Canadians of aboriginal, Indian descent. In 1985 the federal
government acknowledged that minority groups in general were
unrepresented in the civil service; they formed 1.7 per cent
of all federal public servants, but 4.0 per cent of the population generally. Since this time Parliament and successive
governments have sought to increase the recruitment of
Francophones.

ACCOUNTABILITY

The pattern of accountability of the Canadian federal civil service derives from the British model of individual and collective responsibility. Ministers are almost all drawn from the House of Commons and retain their positions as MPs. They are thus able to answer directly to the assembly for all actions carried out by their departments. Collective responsibility decrees that the Cabinet will all stand by the same policy, and would resign en bloc if the House withdrew its support: an unlikely eventuality in an era of strong party discipline. Individual responsibility means that particular ministers accept responsibility for the activities of their departments, and ensures that the House will always have some named member of the government to question and, if necessary, blame for any failings. In the case of serious departmental error it is possible to call for a ministerial resignation.

A corollary of individual responsibility is that civil servants remain anonymous in the face of public scrutiny. However, there has been some decline in this tradition resulting from a number of developments. Reforms in the estimates procedure and in the standing committee system of the House of Commons mean that civil servants regularly testify before members in order to explain and defend policies. An increase in federal-provincial dealings again places civil servants in representative, and visible, positions on various joint boards, and consultative and negotiating committees. The wide acceptance of pluralistic methods of decision-making means that civil servants frequently have to negotiate with representatives of interests and appear at public forums to explain departmental policies. The general feeling amongst the public and the media that civil servants should share their knowledge, and not seek to shroud their activities in a cloak of secrecy, has further led to considerable relaxation in the requirement of anonymity.

Accountability, if it is to be effectively enforced, requires an adequately informed public. There have been some problems in this respect. The sheer size of the organisation can make it remote, impersonal and difficult to penetrate. There has also been a preoccupation with official secrecy, with documents being rather hastily placed beyond the public's eyes through formal classification as secret, and thus officially entombed for 30 years. In 1969 a task force reported with some alarm on the level of public ignorance, particularly amongst the young, the poor, the under-educated and the unemployed, and various measures were taken to make government more accessible and to disseminate information. An agency was established called Information Canada, to work through regional and local agencies.

There is, in addition, a particular accountability problem in the Canadian system of public administration arising

from the deliberate purpose in the machinery of government to
reduce accountability in order to secure other administrative
goals. This is demonstrated in the post-war growth in the
various forms of non-civil-service public bodies described
above. The essential feature, which all these share to some
degree, is the ability to operate outside ministerial control,
and hence outside the scrutinising eye of Parliament. In
this way they are enabled to operate differently from the
civil service departments in a number of significant respects:
they can make decisions on a commerical basis of the profit-
maximising kind; they can secure the service of a range of
professional and other experts who would not normally be, or
wish to see themselves as, civil servants; they are enabled
to enter functional areas new to the state; they can make
judgements which might seem unsuitable for politicians to be
linked with in, say, aesthetic or moral matters; and they
can often operate in a more flexible and speedy manner than
is traditional in the civil service.

This deliberately attenuated system of accountability has
its critics. It is argued that, in addition to evading democratic control, the quasi-autonomous agencies are more easily
prey to the attentions of the interest groups. An alternative
criticism alleges that the existence of this sector conceals
the full extent of the involvement and influence of the state
in society. Reformist writers advocate the strengthening of
the ability of Parliament to examine the activities of the
boards and commissions, or the reduction in their number in
favour of an enlarged civil service. However, it is probably
quite commensurate with the acquiescent nature of Canadian
political culture to tolerate a high level of public administration outside the control and scrutiny of elected
representatives.

The idea of a Scandanavian-style ombudsman, as an aid to
public accountabiltiy, has been discussed in Canada since the
early 1960s. The first provincial move in this direction was
made in Alberta in 1967, with the appointment to such a position of the retiring head of the Royal Canadian Mounted Police
Force. By 1982 nine provinces had adopted versions of the
system, but in spite of the fact that a number of bills have
been introduced into Parliament, an ombudsman system has not
yet been introduced at the federal level.

This development may also be explained in terms of the
Canadian political culture, which tends to accept bureaucracy
and government in a passive manner. However, it is likely
that the office will be established before long, since government has been sensitive to citizens' rights in a number of
ways, through the creation of a number of institutions such
as a Correctional Investigator for Penitentiary Services, a
Human Rights Commission and a Commission for Official
Languages, all of whom fulfil investigatory services on the
behalf of citizens.

CONTROL

Control may be considered under two heads: political and
financial.

Political Control

Political control over the civil service is exercised formally by the Prime Minister and his ministerial team. This
control seeks two broad objectives: the direction of a particular department by its minister, and the direction of the
departments collectively in pursuit of a coherent, integrated
government policy. The internal organisation of each department may be depicted as a typically bureaucratic pyramid, progressively subdividing the portfolio of the department into
its detailed units of responsibility. Each tier on the pyramid is considered responsible to the one above, in a chain of
command and control which culminates in the minister's
relationship with Parliament.

The role of the deputy minister (the senior civil servant
within the department) is crucial in the control relationship,
though there can be an uncomfortable sense of ambivalence.
The constitutional duty of the deputy, as derived from the
British model, is to serve his political master loyally, but
the fact that the Canadian Prime Minister plays a greater role
in the appointment (and dismissal) of the senior administrators than does his British counterpart leaves the deputy with
two masters to serve. The political nature of appointments
creates a further problem for political control, in that
deputy ministers appointed during one regime may be felt to
be out of sympathy with an incoming government of a different
political complexion.

Another element of the debate on political control of
the civil service concerns the conflict between the long-term
aims of the individual departments and the political goals of
the ministers. Senior administrators can be skilled in
reducing the range of choice available to their political
masters. One minister expressed a fairly typical view when
she explained how she was expected 'to accept the unanimous
recommendation of the Department ..... Seldom if ever was I
given the luxury of multiple choice options on matters of
major import' (quoted in Winn 1985).

Financial Control

The regulation of public expenditure levels lies at the heart
of the control over the civil service in Canada. The underlying principles are derived from the British model, where
all proposals for expenditure and taxation must receive prior

approval from Parliament, and all accounts must be examined
post hoc. However, the reality of party politics in
Parliament has meant that control by these means is largely
mythical and symbolic; in practice the power to control
through finance was inherited by the Treasury Board and its
secretariat. The Board was originally created in 1867 as a
statutory committee of the Privy Council, possessing strong
powers of centralised financial co-ordination and control
over the departments. The powers of the Board are of course
available as tools of government control.

It was the traditional responsibility of the Board to
determine the budgets of the departments, and prepare the
estimates for presentation to Parliament. Broadly speaking
this has involved two functions: the determination of the
total level of government spending, and the allocation of
funds between programmes. The traditional approach of the
Board to its responsibility has been to practise containment,
to keep public expenditure down through a detailed scrutiny
of individual expenditure items, with little regard for the
policy objectives behind the proposals.

The effect of this was criticised in the early 1960s by
the Glassco Commission, which wished to see greater financial
autonomy for the departments. The report argued that financial control should be concerned only with broad categories of
expenditure, leaving departments to manage the detailed allocation of their resources within programmes. Following these
recommendations a number of reforms were implemented. The
pre-audit responsibilities of the Comptroller of the Treasury
were delegated to the departments so that they could, in
effect, authorise their own expenditures; and the Treasury
Board was reconstituted to take a less restrictive view of
its financial control function.

Under the reformed system the main agent of central
control became the Auditor General, operating in a post hoc
manner as the watchdog over the departmental accounts. This
represented a considerable weakening of central financial
control because he could only draw attention to expenditure
issues after the event, and was a servant of Parliament
rather than the administration.

Subsequently the Auditor General himself was to criticise
this loss of central control, which he argued was the result
of a misreading of the Glassco recommendations. His comments
were underlined in an alarming rise in public expenditure
during the 1960s and early 1970s. The area of financial management and accountability was examined again by another royal
commission in 1976. This recommended a reinstatement of the
central agencies of control, and led to the creation in 1978
of the office of Comptroller General, located within the
Treasury Board Secretariat, to monitor financial control
systems and related administrative practices, a mandate conferring wide powers.

In 1979 the government inaugurated a Policy Expenditure and Management System (PEMS) designed to make financial decision-making more rational. This had elements in common with the PESC system introduced in Britain in the 1960s. It represented a logical extension in the process of centralising financial control in that it was concerned with the allocation of funds between departments on the basis of rational centrally determined priorities. Individual departments would be obliged to subjugate their individual policies and aspirations to the wider collective goals.

Political events have conspired to increase the move towards centralism with the drive towards securing economies in public spending. A task force was established in early 1985 by the new Conservative government to consider ways to eliminate waste and inefficiency, and it set about its task with zeal.

MANAGEMENT

Canadian social culture espouses the virtues of individualism and private enterprise. Consequently there has existed for some time a body of opinion holding that the agencies of public administration are, because of the absence of the profit motive, inherently inefficient and require a leavening of the commercially orientated managerial skill found in the private sector. Top civil servants, in what is seen as the traditional mould, are portrayed as being skilled in the arts of policy deliberation, regulation, communicating with ministers, and dealing with Parliament but lacking the talents necessary for the effective management of the large enterprises which their departments have become. It is a response to this managerialist position which produces the wide range of quasi-autonomous agencies of the public sector which exist in Canada outside the civil service.

It was the Glassco Commission, set up in 1960 to consider the organisation of government, which gave this view its most authoritative iteration. The report alleged that the existing system was 'costly, frustrating, and unproductive', and opined that the meticulous political controls characterising the modus operandi of the civil service were not really necessary for ensuring honesty, efficiency or attention to the public interest. It was argued that once the political goals had been established, the departments should be substantially freed from the apparatus of parliamentary control over the manner in which they were to be achieved.

The result was the reduction in the power of the Treasury Board discussed above. This had important managerial implications: the departments became free to determine their own staffing and equipment levels, and operate their own budgets. Co-ordination would be ensured through a Treasury Board

presence in each department. The message of the commission
has been widely quoted as an exhortation to 'let the managers
manage'. The intention was to promote strong managerial leadership from within the bureaucracy at all levels. The Commission also recommended a decentralised personnel management
structure with much autonomy for departments to determine and
implement their manpower policies. Subsequently the Public
Service Employment Act replaced the Civil Service Commission,
an independent body responsible to Parliament for a system of
appointment based on the merit principle, with a reformed
body, the Public Service Commission, with greater authority
to delegate.

The recommendations, and subsequent reforms, were not
received with unqualified approval from practitioners or academics. For some the report was more like that of a management
consultant than a royal commission. It was held to have
failed to reflect the crucial difference between the public
and private sectors, and to have undervalued the control
mechanisms arising from the democratic constraints upon public
administration.

Although many managerial reforms had been implemented by
the end of the 1960s, there were other developments taking
place which were to exert countervailing pressures on the
process, including the rise in the level of government
spending which was seen as a direct result of the greater
freedom accorded to the departments. The 1979 report of the
Royal Commission on Financial Management and Accountability
saw in the low level of accountability of departmental heads
a major cause of management failure, and declared the central
control systems inadequate. Its recommendations were intended
to redress the balance of control in favour of the centre.

There were further managerial pressures for centralisation, including the development of Programme Planning and
Budgeting Systems, collective bargaining reforms (the collective bargaining machinery established negotiating groups which
were not reflective of the departmental boundaries, so that
departmental managers were rendered ineffectual in a wide
range of personnel-related matters) and official languages
policy. Generally speaking, the advancement of a policy to
increase the proportion of French-speakers in the federal
bureaucracy has had the effect of placing the Treasury Board
in high profile, and involved it in the production of guidelines to further circumscribe the freedom, in personnel
matters, of the departments. Indeed, the role of the Treasury
Board was so expanded that its staffing level increased fourfold in a single decade.

A further factor was the movement for parliamentary
reform, which has laid some stress on the development of parliamentary committees to scrutinise more thoroughly the activities of the departments. In a democracy as well established
as that of Canada this proves a cause difficult to resist

legitimately, and the Glassco call for managerial autonomy
from Parliament had a rather undemocratic ring. The political
nature of public administration, with its stress on accountability and responsiveness, reasserted its demand from public
servants of the skills of communication, explanation, and
negotiation possessed by the more traditional senior civil
servant.

In spite of the centralising tendencies inherent in management patterns in the federal civil service there remains
an irreducible amount of day-to-day management within the departments which is the responsibility of the deputy ministers
and other senior bureaucrats. The deputy ministers form
three ranks of seniority termed Deputy Minister 1, Deputy
Minister 2 and Deputy Minister 3. Below this are five further
classes of senior executive.

A pervasive philosophy underlying departmental internal
management over the past decade has been planning, including
methods for establishing objectives, and the evaluation of
the effects of policies within a given time frame. Towards
this end departments have been reorganised and their mandates
redefined. Within departments much energy was devoted to the
development of new programmes and new services, often leading
to co-ordination and liaison between different departments.
In addition to these initiatives, certain management techniques, such as PPBS, management by objectives, and performance
measurement were introduced on an experimental basis. The
internal organisation of departments changed to reflect these
innovations in various ways. The developments created something of an employment boom, and it was the creation of the
planning units which largely accounted for the great rise in
the level of employment of senior executives in the federal
civil service. However, the organisation exhibited predict-
able signs of bureaucratic inertia in the face of change, and
the units have been adjudged most successful in those departments where they did not have to fight with established parts
of the machine in gaining recognition of their value.

In his managerial role the deputy minister must assemble
a team of senior administrators with the appropriate managerial skills, and these will vary with the kind of department;
whether it is orientated primarily towards policy-making,
regulation, or programme implementation. In spite of the
increasing importance of management at this level and the
significant growth in the senior executive ranks of the
service, there have been allegations of failure to create a
cadre of officials with suitable skills. The 1976 report of
the Auditor General, and the Lambert Commission, argued that
the Glassco recommendations for greater managerial expertise
in the departments had led to the promotion of civil servants
to senior executive positions for which they were ill-fitted.

As a means of improving career development and the advancement of management skills, the Advisory Group on Executive

Compensation argued in 1971 for the identification of a middle-management group. In order to facilitate this, the Treasury Board and the Public Service Commission created manpower inventories, and the Lambert Commission recommended that deputies played a greater role in developing career development plans. However, there are some who oppose career planning and managerial succession on the grounds that this will effectively close the senior ranks of the service to outside recruitment, and induce rigidity within. Consequently, at present only a small group of 'high-fliers' have directed career paths, permitting greater flexibility and choice in the general composition of the upper echelons of the service.

POLICY-MAKING

The Lambert Commission conducted a survey of deputy ministers' perceptions of their roles. The most important functions were held to be: management of the executive team, assuring economy and efficiency, supporting the minister, ensuring that the department is responsive to government policy, and providing policy advice. Broadly speaking the role might be defined as advising on policy and managing. The fact that policy cannot be formulated without a knowledge of the machinery which will be required in its implementation, means that the advisory role of the deputy will always be central, and that the federal bureaucracy will play an influential role in the policy-making process itself.

A number of factors serve to enhance the policy role of the civil servants. Ministers do not normally possess the necessary degree of technical expertise in the range of issues requiring decisions, and must rely heavily on the advice they receive from their officials. This has become progressively more important as the role of government has increased to encompass a wider range of technicality. Indeed, the advisory role of the civil servants is so well accepted in Canada that ministers have even been called upon to resign on the grounds that they have not consulted sufficiently with officials in the making of some particular policy.

The policy-making role of senior civil servants is recognised in the manner of their appointment. Unlike other members of the federal bureaucracy, who are appointed by the Civil Service Commission, deputy ministers are appointed by the Governor General on the advice of the Prime Minister. This means that a Prime Minister can accept the influential role of the deputy ministers because he is able to count on their political commitment. The political role of senior civil servants was illustrated strikingly in 1948 when Lester Pearson, who had been a civil servant working in the area of external affairs, was actually appointed to a Cabinet position. At this time the Prime Minister stated that the

civil service should be seen as a 'stepping stone to the
Ministry'. Although this view was regarded as too extreme by
most commentators, and has not become accepted doctrine, it
indicates the climate in which senior civil servants operate.
The longevity of Liberal governments may be a factor in
explaining why this system of appointment works in Canada,
for it certainly reveals its greatest difficulties when there
is a change of the party of government, as evidenced in the
behaviour of the 1984 Mulroney government.

It is openly acknowleged in Canada that civil servants
can have a momentous role in the shaping of policy. Dr
Clifford Clark, Deputy Minister of Finance in the years
immediately following the second world war, is famed for the
imaginative influence he exerted over almost all aspects of
social and economic policy. This view of the policy role was
reinforced in the Glassco Report which advocated its increase.
This contentment is typified in the view that the fact that
'economic policy is largely determined by professional
economists rather than by small-town lawyers from Lethbridge
who happen to be MPs is good, not bad' (Van Loon and
Whittington 1984).

Nevertheless, there are those who argue that the overt
involvement of senior bureaucrats in policy-making has
dangers. Of particular concern is the relationship which
develops between the officials and the representatives of the
leading interest groups. As an avowedly pluralist society,
Canada welcomes such groups into the decision-making process,
and the dominant ones regard the bureaucracy as the most
effective point of access to government. In such a favourable
ideological climate, the level of potential influence of the
groups can become a threat to the majoritarian principle of
the polity. Departments come to rely on the interest groups
for information, expertise, and indeed policy advice, and can
in effect be 'colonised' to the extent that they are little
more than official advocates of the interests with which they
are consulting. Dangers also arise from the fact that in
terms of social, educational, and ethnic background senior
civil servants are by no means representative of the population they serve.

There are, however, several factors which may serve to
reduce civil service influence. The first of these is the
fact, already mentioned, that there exist in Canada a large
number of agencies of public administration outside the civil
service itself. This is perhaps cold comfort to those who
fear the power of officials as such, because the very raison
d'etre of such agencies is a reduction in control and
accountability. Party politics can also serve to reduce bureaucratic power, through the increasing use of programmes,
manifestos, and the notion of the mandate, whereby politicians
are able to gain authority for their case by virtue of their
electoral commitments. Further resistance comes from an

increasingly alert intellectual community, which highlights
and rehearses various facets of the public policy debates in
a manner which can inform both politicians and the public at
large. Another factor is the development of systems of ministerial aides and advisers, who are able to provide an intellectual and ideological counterpoise to the bureaucracy
through the access they are granted to ministers. As a
further means of reducing the role of civil servants in crucial policy-making areas, recent observers have noted a tendency of the Prime Minister, and his office, to take on a
greater amount of work than is traditionally the case.

CONCLUSION

A number of the factors influencing the federal civil service
in Canada may be regarded as peculiar to the country and consequently of particular interest. These include the influence
arising from the colonial history, where the dominant constitutional and administrative heritage is clearly British, and
colours much Canadian public administration. However, as we
have seen, the French influence is sufficiently present to
demand attention at a number of political and governmental
levels, and justifies the view of Canada as a bicultural
society, and we have seen that there are implications for the
civil service in this.

Another important influence on the Canadian state comes
from the United States of America. We have noted that there
are a number of ways in which Canadian politics and public
administration reflect this divergence of influences in the
adoption of intermediate positions in a number of practices.
Also of importance is the federal nature of the state, which
makes intergovernmental relations an important aspect of
public administration, and can enhance the authority of the
bureaucrats at all levels.

Although we have noted a high degree of acceptance of the
legitimacy of public bureaucracy in Canadian society, there
is also a body of distrust. Generally speaking this comes from
the forces of the right, and the federal civil service in
Canada is presently the object of suspicion from the Conservative government. There are perhaps two reasons for this. As
a party the Conservatives tend to enjoy the fruits of office
rather less frequently than the Liberals, with the effect that
whenever they do form the government they are faced with a
bureaucracy which has been built up, albeit largely through a
process of natural wastage and replacement of personnel, under
a Liberal regime. The second reason is less contingent on the
Canadian experience, and relates to the characteristic ideological position of the Conservatives in general, which tends
to favour the operation of the free market in the private sector in as many areas of social and economic life as possible.

Canada

REFERENCES AND FURTHER READING

Adie, P. and Thomas, P. G. (1982) Canadian Public Administration, Scarborough, Ontario, Prentice-Hall.

Albinski, H. S. (1973) Canadian and Australian Politics in Comparative Perspective, New York, Oxford University Press.

Doern, G. B. and Phidd, R. W. (1983) Canadian Public Policy, Toronto, Methuen.

Doerr, A. D. (1981) The Machinery of Government in Canada, Toronto, Methuen.

Hockin, T. A. (1975) Government in Canada, London, Weidenfeld and Nicholson.

Kernaghan, K (1982) Public Administration in Canada, Toronto, Methuen.

Kernaghan, K. (1983) Canadian Public Administration, Toronto, Butterworth.

Mallory, J. R. (1971) The Structure of Canadian Government, Toronto, Macmillan.

Presthus, R. (1973) Elite Accommodation in Canadian Politics, Cambridge, Cambridge University Press.

Stewart, G. T. (1986) The Origins of Canadian Politics, Vancouver, University of British Columbia Press.

Van Loon, R. and Whittington, M. S. (1984) 'Alternative styles in the study of Canadian politics', Canadian Journal of Political Science, 7:1 (March), 132.

Winn, C. (1985), 'Cabinet control of the public service', Canadian Public Policy - Analyse de Politiques, 11:1, 126-8.

Journals

Canadian Public Administration (The journal of the Institute of Public Administration of Canada, published quarterly)

Policy Options (published bi-monthly by the Institute for Research on Public Policy).

Chapter 4

FRANCE

B. G. Owen

POLITICAL SETTING

In contrast to that of the United Kingdom, the political
history of France has been marked above all by turbulence.
If it is true that one of the great achievements of the
French Revolution - together with the American Revolution -
was to give firm grounding to the idea that men could work
out for themselves the kind of political system under which
they wished to live, it is no less true that, having established the principle, the French have been unable to agree
for any length of time on how it is to be best put into
practice.

Since the Revolution France has experimented with a
variety of political systems. It was only a few years afterwards that Napoleon was crowned as Emperor. There followed
kings, another Emperor, and a number of republics. The
French themselves date the definitive founding of the
Republic not from 1789, but only from 1870. Since then, it
is probably true to say, there has been widespread agreement
that the form of government would be republican. But the
Third Republic, although the longest-lived of French post-
revolutionary systems, lasted only 70 years, to be followed
by Vichy France, by the fourth Republic (1946-58) and, since
1958, by the Fifth.

However, if France has been unstable constitutionally
she has, at the same time, allowed the development of a
powerful and comprehensive administrative machine. The
concept of 'the State' plays a large part in French political
thought, so that it is thought of as being quite real, almost
tangible. In fact, of course, it is barely any less of a
reality in other countries. In Britain, for example, all the
necessary component parts exist, in the form of Parliament,
government, civil service, local government, and so on. And
yet it can be argued that the British have never - mentally,
so to speak, as an act of recognition - put the pieces together so as to form in their minds the idea of the 'British

State'. Possibly they have never felt the need to. But this is not the case in France, where one recent writer, Professor Burdeau, whilst admitting that nobody has ever actually seen 'the State', yet asks whether anybody can doubt its reality, and suggests that, without 'the State', continued existence of the nation would be put at risk. It may not be too fanciful to suggest that, for the French, 'the State' has provided the reassurance that shifting constitutions have been unable to give.

The origins of the French state machine can be traced back to before the Revolution. The history of the gradual establishment and consolidation of what we now think of as France inevitably involved extending royal authority more effectively over the country, and this needed an administrative apparatus. The royal officials known as Intendants were meant to alter the balance of power between the nobility and the king. Under Louis XIV, the Sun King, the energetic Colbert laboured to turn the whole economy into an engine of support for policies directed solely to enhancing the strength and grandeur of France, and it is hardly an exaggeration to say that by the eighteenth century French influence was dominant throughout Europe. In the process the seeds were planted of a centralisation and of a tradition of state intervention in economic life which have continued down to the present, and which both encouraged and required a powerful administrative apparatus.

Napoleon was able to build upon this. He was not interested in political democracy but in administrative efficiency, needing a system which would steadily supply the troops and the money he required in order to be able to pursue his foreign designs. Some of the bodies Napoleon established continue to exist today and, if the functions of the Council of State and of the prefectoral system have been modified over the years, they still retain their importance as parts of a system which has operated - at least until quite recently - in an essentially centralising fashion.

Political thought, too, helped. French concepts of liberty and sovereignty have not been so clearly directed towards the individual as has been the case in Britain. Freedom has been taken to refer to freedom for the community at least as much as freedom of the individual, and Rousseau's lasting influence has continued to stress the moral superiority of the General Will over the more selfish collection of individual ambitions and desires known as the Will of All. All of this has come together in a recognition of the importance of the One and Indivisible Republic. And all of this has been conducive to the continued development of a statist tradition made more real by the workings of the administrative machine - a machine which has often had to function in spite of ineffective political leadership, rather than in support of coherent political authority. Even when France

entered her capitalist stage of development, it was never the
laissez-faire activity that it was in nineteenth-century
Britain, and the state always had a part to play in setting
guidelines. Arm's-length government, where the state tries
to restrain itself to the role of impartial referee, does not
find favour in France. The officials who staff the French
administration believe that the state has a right to its own
point of view - again, echoes of Rousseau - and they are
willing to use the political, administrative and financial
resources at their command to advance what they see as the
state's legitimate interests.

Effective political leadership has, indeed, often been
lacking. The turbulent history referred to earlier contributed to a political community riven with cleavages and
with only a low degree of consensus. By the late nineteenth
century Frenchmen might be said to have been in broad agreement about the Republic, but not about much else. French
political culture was lacking in trust, so that co-operation
and association in support of common aims did not come easily.
And the vocabulary of French political life was often
intensely ideological, thus making bargaining and compromise
difficult. This has been reflected in the French trade union
structure. On another plane, whilst there is general acceptance that France has far too many local government units -
over 36,000 in all - efforts to persuade small and inefficient
communes to merge with one another have had only meagre success. And pre-eminently from the standpoint of national
politics, France for a long time suffered the detrimental
effects of a multiplicity of political parties. It was
unknown for a general election to return one party with an
overall majority in the Chamber of Deputies, and so construc-
ting a government was necessarily a matter of cobbling together a coalition. But the dissentious and ideological
nature of French politics meant that such coalitions fell
apart all too easily, as soon as a government proposed some
concrete response to the very real problems facing France
from the 1930s onwards. The alternative strategy, having
once formed a coalition, was for the government to become
immobiliste, to try to sit tight and do nothing; this at
least meant that the coalition partners were given no excuse
or occasion for desertion. But the problems - of Hitler,
Indo-China or Algeria - most unreasonably refused to go away.
Immobilisme could never hope to do more than postpone the day
of reckoning.

All this General de Gaulle saw. He was not alone in
this but, by the late 1950s, he was the one remaining person
who might be in a position to do something about it. In de
Gaulle's view the selfish and bickering parties had abused
their parliamentary function. They had refused to allow
strong government and so France had been unprepared for war
with Germany in 1939/40. After the war de Gaulle campaigned

for a new constitution which would provide a more stable
executive, but he was defeated in a referendum. The politicians of the old school were able to construct a new republic
- the Fourth - which differed little from the Third. Power
still lay with Parliament, which was itself split into competing factions. Presently the General left public life and
retired to Colombey to await the downfall of the Fourth
Republic. He waited 12 years. During this time the process
of economic planning for modernisation was started, and the
first steps were taken towards establishing the Common
Market, but some of the credit here must go to civil servants
or outstanding figures who were not involved in the party
political game. The politicians, for their part, proved
incapable of holding on to Indo-China, and the lost war there
left the generals feeling that they had been betrayed.
Algerian demands for independence again found the politicians
incapable of pursuing a coherent strategy, and by the time
the generals in Algeria threatened insurrection in 1958 the
Fourth Republic was thoroughly discredited. De Gaulle
announced that he was willing to return as Prime Minister,
but he made it clear that he would submit a new constitution
for popular approval. The parliamentarians really had
nothing left with which to fight de Gaulle - certainly the
mass of the French people were not willing to defend the
existing system. De Gaulle had no difficulty in agreeing to
demands that the new constitution should be both republican
and parliamentary; he had no wish for anything other than a
republic, and the parliamentary stipulation proved easy
enough to modify in practice. By the end of 1958 the Fourth
Republic had given way to the Fifth, with de Gaulle as its
first President.

THE EXECUTIVE

The fundamental concern of the 1958 constitution is with the
ability of the executive authority to promote and safeguard
the fundamental interests of France (cf. Rousseau's General
Will) and to ensure that these are given prime consideration
over more short-term and partial considerations (cf. the Will
of All). Thus, article 5 charges the President of the Republic with the responsibility for seeing that the constitution
is respected, for ensuring the continuity of the state and
that the public authorities are able to function regularly.
Further, article 16 gives the President wide-ranging emergency
powers when he feels that France or her institutions are
threatened, and allows him to take whatever measures he feels
the circumstances dictate.
    In practical terms what was required was the creation of
a constitutional structure capable of safeguarding France's
basic interests and, moreover, of doing so in the face of

67

partial interests - as represented by the parties - which
would try to divert the executive from its true role. De
Gaulle was no would-be dictator. He did not intend the Fifth
Republic to be other than a liberal democracy. But liberal
democracy means competing parties and, in the Gaullist view,
the parties' previous record suggested that, if given the
opportunity, they would soon revert to their old, parliamentary games, played out in what one commentator had called a
'house without windows'.

The answer to this dilemma - of allowing democratic
parties to operate whilst yet limiting their obstructive
tendencies - was to be found via an approach which had both
positive and negative aspects. Positively, as the articles
mentioned above imply, the Presidency was to be strengthened
and assigned a more positive role. Moreover, it was to be to
some extent separated out from the rest of the political
system by having its own democratic base. Initially the constitution provided that the President would be elected by an
electoral college of some 80,000 'notables'. However, by
1962, having settled the Algerian crisis, de Gaulle felt
strong enough to propose in a referendum a constitutional
amendment providing for direct election of the President by
universal suffrage. The people approved the proposal and de
Gaulle was re-elected in this way in 1965. Henceforth the
President would be able to claim a democratic legitimacy
emanating from the entire electorate - something to which no
other political actor could lay claim.

Negatively, the constitution placed restrictions upon
the ability of Parliament to obstruct the executive. De
Gaulle had agreed, in 1958, that the new system would be a
parliamentary one and, in keeping with this promise, the
executive was to consist of more than just the presidency.
There was, in addition, to be a government, composed of a
Prime Minister and other ministers, and the government was to
be constitutionally responsible to the National Assembly.
However, domination of the government by the Assembly was to
be avoided by means of a number of provisions, amongst the
most important of which were the following:

1. membership of the Assembly was to be incompatible with
    holding ministerial office, and so a deputy who becomes a
    minister must resign his parliamentary seat;
2. the government was now to control the Assembly's time-
    table, and the number of committees was reduced so as to
    allow the more expeditious transaction of parliamentary
    business;
3. the government was given the right to demand bloc votes
    on its proposals and, specifically, if the Assembly did
    not approve the budget within 70 days it was to come into
    effect anyway;
4. although it was to be constitutionally possible for the

Assembly to pass a motion of no confidence in the
government, a number of procedural hurdles were designed
to make this difficult to do in practice.

In sum, the new constitution was meant to effect a shift
in the balance of power away from the parties in Parliament
and in favour of the executive. The result is that France
now has what has sometimes been termed a 'two-headed executive', consisting of the President on the one hand, and the
Prime Minister and the other ministers (the government) on
the other. In other countries it is much easier to locate
the centre of executive authority. In Britain and West
Germany, both parliamentary systems, the head of the executive is the Prime Minister or Chancellor, whilst the Queen
and the German President enjoy very little direct power. In
the United States, with its presidential system, federal
executive authority lies with the President. But in France
this authority is divided and shared. The system is a hybrid,
part-parliamentary and part-presidential. The parliamentary
aspect is found in the fact that the Prime Minister, although
appointed by the President, is responsible to the National
Assembly and needs to have the support of a majority of its
members. The presidential aspect is found in the fact that
the President, and he alone, is directly elected by the
French people and, although he needs the co-operation of the
Prime Minister or another appropriate minister for his
proposals to be made effective, securing this co-operation
has not been a problem - at least until 1986.
Between 1958 and 1986 the voters have always ensured
that the occupant of the Elysée Palace could rely upon a sympathetic majority in the National Assembly. Consequently,
Presidents have not found it difficult to appoint Prime
Ministers and governments acceptable to both themselves and
the Assembly, and this undoubtedly allowed for the presidentialisation of the system during its first 28 years. During
this period France was, to a considerable extent, governed
from the Elysée and the hybrid system worked substantially in
the President's favour, so much so that commentators have
sometimes talked of a 'republican monarchy'. But we must be
careful not to forget that the Prime Minister and government
continued to exist. Prime Ministers were not necessarily
non-entities and sometimes had their own sights fixed on the
presidency. Prime Minister Pompidou, after a short period in
the wilderness, actually became President, and Prime Minister
Chirac was unwilling to be no more than President Giscard d'
Estaing's assistant. Throughout the whole period, whilst
Presidents have grabbed many of the headlines, the other half
of the executive has continued to be a necessary part of the
constitutional structure. Nevertheless, and in spite of what
has been said about the government being responsible to the
Assembly, it is no longer subordinate to it in the way that

it was during the Third and Fourth Republics. During those
years governments were under the continuous control of the
legislature, but this has changed since 1958. Although no-
where in the constitution is it actually written down, at
least until 1986 governments owed their existence to the
President. Meetings of the Council of Ministers are chaired,
not by the Prime Minster but by the President. After the
events of May 1968, when it is arguable that it was Prime
Minister Pompidou's efforts, rather than those of President
de Gaulle, which avoided the toppling of the Fifth Republic,
de Gaulle nevertheless felt able to dismiss M. Pompidou quite
abruptly. Again, when Pompidou was President and M. Chaban
Delmas was his Prime Minister, the latter compared their
positions to those of captain and first mate, and agreed that
in the event of fundamental disagreements between them, it
would be the Prime Minister who would have to go.

By way of comparison, it is worth remarking that French
governments are smaller than British governments, and this in
a country where the weak local government system means that
the central state has, by way of compensation, very wide-
ranging responsibilities. British governments can easily
have a total membership in excess of a hundred. In France,
however, the number of governmental posts is usually less
than half this figure; in May 1981 Prime Minister Mauroy's
government numbered 43, and M. Chirac's government in May
1986 contained 38 members. But within the government considerable structural flexibility is possible, since the legal
basis of internal arrangements is simply the presidential
decree nominating the members of the government, followed by
further decrees which describe the various responsibilities
of those members. Beyond this, British observers can sometimes be confused by the different titles within government,
since the same ones are sometimes used differently in our two
systems. In France a minister is generally the political
head of a department (ministry), such as the Ministry of
Defence, of the Interior or of National Education. The title
of Minister of State - of whom M. Chirac named only one in May
1986 - does not prevent the minister concerned assuming specific responsibilities (in 1986 M. Balladur was named Minister
of State for the Economy, Finance and Privatisation), but its
essential significance is in underlining the importance of
the member of the government to whom the status is given.
Below the rank of minister there are also ministers-delegate,
and these may be described as being delegates either of the
Prime Minister or of other ministers; a minister-delegate
takes over, in effect, some of the functions for which a full
minister remains nominally responsible.

Beyond this there are three kinds of secretaries of
state - those who assist the Prime Minister, those who assist
other ministers, and those (created for the first time in
1974) who control a government department in much the same way

as does a full minister but who only attend meetings of the
Council of Ministers when matters relating to their responsibilities are under discussion.

If we try to translate this into British terms, we could
say that the Cabinet (i.e. Council of Ministers), chaired by
the President, consists of the Prime Minister, Ministers of
State and ministers. Outside this there are some non-cabinet
ministers (secretaries of state), and then there are junior
ministers (ministers-delegate and secretaries of state) who
assist full ministers. There are far fewer junior ministers
in French than in British governments, and most French
ministers are more poorly provided with such assistance than
are their British counterparts. At the same time, on the
administrative side, most French ministerial hierarchies do
not lead, pyramid-fashion, to a position of permanent secretary, and so a French minister does not have a single, official counterpart. Instead, most French ministries are organised into directions, each headed by a director, and it is
with his directors that a minister will deal. But if this
absence of a single, formal point of contact, between minister
as political head and permanent secretary as official head of
the department, leads us to expect problems for the minister
in co-ordinating the work of his ministry, the French response
would be to point out that their ministers possess a device
which British ministers lack, in the form of the ministerial
cabinet. Each minister is entitled to a cabinet of personal
assistants to help him in the running of his ministry and, in
practice, cabinets have come to be staffed more and more by
civil servants. Today, secondment for a few years to a ministerial cabinet is a good indication that the official in
question is seen as a potential high-flier.

It is possible to exaggerate the extent of governmental
instability during the Third and Fourth Republics. Although
the 12 years of the Fourth Republic saw 24 Prime Ministers,
the same faces frequently appeared and reappeared in different
governments. Nevertheless, the 1958 constitution was concerned to strengthen the executive. The Fifth Republic, which
has lasted more than twice as long as the Fourth, has so far
had less than half as many Prime Ministers. But there is the
argument that, given the existence of the powerful administrative machine referred to in the previous section (and whose
origins go back well before 1958), the 1958 constitution, in
changing the power relationship between the legislature and
the executive (to the benefit of the latter), has allowed the
development of a 'Civil Servants' Republic'. This is an
argument we shall return to later. First, however, it is
necessary to look at the administrative machine itself more
closely.

STRUCTURE

The French civil service is recognisable within the terms outlined by Max Weber for his ideal-type bureaucracy. That is to
say, it is organised hierarchically, its members receive a
salary and a pension, and admission to membership usually requires evidence of competence gauged by the possession of a
qualification and/or success in an examination. In common
with other countries French government is organised into ministries, and the individual official will occupy a position
within a particular ministry. This does not, of course, mean
that he or she will necessarily work in Paris. The general
weakness of the French local government system is compensated
for by the fact that many ministries have extensive networks
of deconcentrated field services, operating locally, some of
which carry out functions which in Britain would be the responsibility of local authorities.

Judged simply by numbers of personnel, the French civil
service appears much larger than the British - approximately
four times as large, in fact. The deconcentration referred
to above explains some of this difference; the French service has responsibilities which the British does not have. But
the more important explanation of the difference in size lies
in a different basis of classification. About two-thirds of
French civil service posts are to be found in the Education
Ministry and the Post Office whereas, in Britain, teachers
and postal service employees are not civil servants.

The service is divided into four grades - A,B,C and D -
distinguished by different levels of responsibility, complexity of work, and of course salary and conditions of service.
Grade A is the uppermost grade, numbering some 300,000-plus
employees; but, here again, about two-thirds of these are
university lecturers and senior secondary teachers. Even of
those remaining, whilst they are undoubtedly senior officials,
they could not realistically be described as belonging to the
inner administrative elite. These latter form a much smaller
group, each of whom is distinguished by the fact of having
gained membership of one or other of the great <u>corps</u> of the
state via a rigorous process of preparation and examiation.

The service as a whole is, in fact, organised through the
phenomenon of the corps. Upon joining the service the new
official becomes a member of a corps, which consists of all
the officials of a ministry recruited at a given level and
carrying out similar functions. And it is his corps which
provides the official with his career. Although some corps
only have one class (e.g. teachers), most are divided into a
number of classes, each class being further divided into a
number of salary levels. The normal career route is to progress up through the salary levels within a class; on reaching
the top salary level of his class the official may find
opportunities for progression to the next class, but still

within the same corps which he originally joined. This is
not to say that it is impossible to move out of a corps and
into a more senior one, but it is not usual. For the typical
civil servant the corps which he joins will provide him with
his career.

French civil servants enjoy considerable safeguards relating to conditions of employment. The official occupies a
grade rather than a particular post. This means, for example,
that if a post should cease to exist, the official who had
occupied it would retain his grade and attendant conditions,
even if he had to be moved to less responsible work. Further,
where an official is offered a period of service in another
part of the government machine (perhaps working with a minister in his cabinet) he retains his membership and position
within his corps, and he can always return there later.

The French civil service, then, is organised vertically
according to ministries, and horizontally according to grades.
But this matrix exists, in a sense, primarily as an organisational blueprint and as a way of calculating salaries. Super-
imposed upon it is the reality, that a French official belongs
to a corps, that it is his corps with which he primarily
identifies, and that it is within his corps that he expects
to make his career. From amongst all the corps a very few
may be termed 'great' (the grands corps of the state), and it
is their members who constitute the elite at the pinnacle of
the administrative pyramid.

THE BUREAUCRATS

As in any large public bureaucracy, the overall structure of
the French civil service is pyramid-shaped, as well as being
hierarchical. This means that as we ascend the pyramid we
find that the more senior (and powerful) the posts, the fewer
they are in number. Most civil servants are engaged in relatively routine clerical and executive tasks, and the number
involved in overall direction and management, not to say as
contributors to policy-making, is small by comparison. It is
these latter officials who constitute what is often termed
the 'administrative elite', and it is these in whom we are
mainly interested, particularly as it is often claimed that
the French administrative elite embodies features which make
it sensibly different from its counterparts in other
countries.

Already, by using the term 'elite', we have moved away
from the formal categorisation of grades described in the
previous section, and this suggests that unlike most members
of the civil service, it is not sufficient to identify members
of the elite simply as those occupying positions above a certain grade. More real than the badges of rank attached to
different officials is the shift in emphasis, as we climb the

pyramid, from work which is largely routine to work which is hardly at all so. The content of the work done by a member of the elite, and the surrounding ethos which forms the background to his work, mean, in effect, that he is a very different kind of animal to those lower down the hierarchy. To the extent that this is usually true of public bureaucracies, France fits in with the general rule that higher standards and more stringent qualifications are demanded of would-be recruits to the administrative elite. The requirements differ in detail from country to country. In West Germany a legalistic preparation is favoured, whilst Britain still prefers the generalist approach. However, differences apart, it remains true that those being recruited to the elite will need special preparation and, as Armstrong has shown, this is no new thing.

There is, in addition, a further feature of the French bureaucracy, in respect of which categorisation purely by formal grades is insufficient explanation. This feature is the phenomenon of the grands corps, to which reference has already been made. Membership of the elite means, first and foremost, gaining membership of one or other of the grands corps. Consequently, to understand just what membership of the elite means, we must first seek an appreciation of the role and significance of the corps, and then see how they connect with the French educational system, as well as relating this to the social (and, indeed, geographical) distribution of the French population.

The corps are not new, and the term grands corps de l'Etat has been in use for well over a century. For the young men and women graduating from the National School of Administration, to go into one of the grands corps means having done sufficiently well at the School to be able to choose from amongst a restricted number of vacancies, such as that of auditor in the Council of State or the Court of Accounts, or assistant inspector in the Finance Inspectorate. The most prestigious and powerful career avenues in the administration run through the grands corps, and the most strategically crucial sectors of the administration are - if not in law then certainly in fact - the property of those corps.

Looking at it from the standpoint of the individual recruit to the administrative elite, we can say that having decided that he wishes to make his career in, say, the Finance Inspectorate or the Prefectoral service, then he will need to join either the corps of Finance Inspectors or the Prefectoral corps. Of course, this will mean joining a ministry - say, the Finance Ministry or the Ministry of the Interior. But the significance of the corps phenomenon is that, in the recruit's own mind, he is primarily joining a corps, and the fact that the post he fills is located in this or that ministry is a secondary consideration. In any case, there is a good chance that the corps member will spend a fair amount of

his career working somewhere other than in his own ministry.
The prestige of the corps is such that their members are in
frequent demand for service throughout the public sector.
And, more than this, there are attractive opportunities in
the private sector, which is also anxious to attract corps
members, so that it is not uncommon for such officials to
leave the public sector for the private after some 10 to 15
years' service.

And the public sector in France is wide ranging and varied. As well as the nationalised industries one would expect
to find in an advanced economy, the state also controls a
sizeable proportion of credit and investment, not to mention
the tobacco monopoly. As mentioned previously, laissez-faire
capitalism never took the same doctrinal hold that it did in
Britain, and there are deep-rooted dirigiste traditions of
economic intervention by the state. But if it is true that
much of the public sector is legally distinct from central
government ministries, so that, for example, Gaz de France is
a distinct entity and not just part of a ministry, such distinctions are blurred by the fact that it is by no means uncommon to find the senior positions in such enterprises occupied
by members of the grand corps who are, after all, senior
civil servants. It is arguable, further, that this has contributed to the success of French economic planning, since
there exists a network of members of the grands corps, some
working in ministries, some in senior positions in the public
sector, some now in the private sector, and others in the
Planning Commissariat which is responsible for drawing up the
national economic plans, all of whom share similar training
and experience and have similar perceptions of the legitimacy
of the state's interventionist role in economic affairs.

The grands corps, then, are associations of elite administrators within the civil service. They may be divided into
the technical corps (such as Mining Engineering, Rural Engineering, Bridges and Highways), and the non-technical (such as
the Council of State, Court of Accounts, Finance Inspectorate,
the Diplomatic corps and the Prefectoral corps). Within a
given corps the members share a common preparation and
training and a common career grade structure. At any one
time, many of them will be working in the same administrative
area (e.g. most of the members of the Prefectoral corps will
be working in prefectures and sub-prefectures), whilst some
will be on detached service in other parts of the public
sector, some may have gone into politics (whilst still
retaining their corps membership), and some will have gone
into the private sector. Taken collectively, the members of
the various grands corps constitute the French administrative
elite.

That recruitment into this elite falls far short of being
socially representative is beyond doubt. It is skewed in
favour of those from middle-class backgrounds and above, who

often have parents in the 'liberal' professions (frequently including the administrative elite itself), as well as favouring those with a Parisian background. This is France's equivalent to the public school/Oxbridge bias which is so often criticised in Britain. Against the allegations of bias it can be argued that it is only a by-product of a wholly laudable desire to recruit the best as measured in terms of academic qualifications, but we are then brought up against the correlation between academic achievement and social background. Put simply, children from middle-class backgrounds tend to do better at school and university than those from working-class homes. The argument that recruitment is biased is, in the end, difficult to get away from, but it probably causes less heart-searching in France than in Britain because, whilst France is undoubtedly a highly elitist society, she is at the same time much less of a snobbish society. Frenchmen are less worried about the fact that an elite exists, so long as they can believe that its members are competent.

France, like Britain, was swept with a desire for reform and renewal in 1945 - although this did not extend so far as to include the constitutional reform urged by General de Gaulle. Arguably the need was even greater in France than in Britain, after the years of German occupation and a war which had actually been fought on her soil. And one of the reform measures instituted was the establishment of the National School of Administration (ENA). The aim here was twofold - to broaden (or democratise) recruitment to the grands corps, and to provide the recruits with a programme of training peculiarly suited to their needs as future occupants of senior posts in public administration. Specifically, it was felt that these goals could only be achieved through the establishment of a new institution capable of breaking the stranglehold over recruitment which had previously been enjoyed by the old Ecole Libre des Sciences Politiques. Interestingly enough, the British Civil Service Commission provided some inspiration, if not an actual blueprint here, particularly in its independence from the ministries for which the recruits were eventually destined. Through the Ecole Libre, many of whose lecturers were themselves civil servants, the grands corps, in effect, controlled recruitment to their own ranks, and it was felt that this had created and perpetuated a mentality which put the corps' own interests first, if necessary at the expense of those of the state. Thus, a recruiting and training institution independent of the corps was needed.

The aims were never completely realised. Much of the teaching at the ENA is still in the hands of civil servants who are themselves graduates of the School, but it is argued that after all these are the very people best suited to know what preparation is needed by the recruits who will later join them. Nor has recruitment been democratised. As mentioned above, it is still socially and geographically biased.

However, it is at least no longer so directly under the
control of the corps themselves. The School constitutes a
rite of passage which would-be entrants to the grands corps
must first complete and, in the seriousness with which the
two-year training period is thought out, there could hardly
be a greater contrast with the British Civil Service College.
In order to gain entrance, it is necessary to pass the
School's own examination. Although special arrangements
exist for a small number of candidates who are already Grade
B civil servants, most will be coming straight from full-time
university education. The School's entrance examination is
rigorous. It is difficult to pass without a special prepara-
tory course which, in effect, means reading for the diploma of
an Institute of Political Studies (IEP) - hence, the middle-
class bias. A number of Institutes exist at provincial universities, but it is the Paris IEP which provides most of the
successful entrants to ENA - hence the geographical bias.
Consequently, in any given year the class of entrants will be
mostly from Parisian, middle-class backgrounds, although
there may be a few from the provinces, and a few - slightly
older - who have previously been occupying Grade B posts.
After only a few weeks at the School the new entrants
are sent away for a year on placement, often in a provincial
perfecture. This gives them first-hand experience of what
senior officials actually do. It is also arguable that
working in proximity with members of grands corps constitutes
a socialising experience. The placement period is followed
by further study back at the School, in Paris, but the content
of the studies undertaken is far removed from British ideas
of the sufficiency of a rather general education to produce a
well-rounded intellect. Bearing in mind that the School is,
in effect, a postgraduate institution (since the students are
already university graduates), the aim is to provide training
particularly suited to the needs of the non-technical administrator. Its concerns are not primarily with economic or
political theory, but with decision-making, problem-solving,
and using quantitative research techniques. In addition,
European - including French - conceptions of government are
still strongly legalistic, and many of the training exercises
will consist of appraising a problem, arriving at a decision
or a policy recommendation, and embodying this in a draft
regulation or a note to a minister. Much of the work is done
through seminars, and this too reflects the fact that, in
practice, officials will work to a considerable extent through
consultation with other officials and with outside interests.
The aim is not to produce a generalist, in the British sense
of the word; indeed, the French would reject such a label.
The aim, rather, is to produce a non-technical administrator
whose training has equipped him specifically with the skills
needed by a senior public official in a country which is still
highly centralised and where the state plays a clear and

admitted part in guiding socio-economic development.

Gaining entrance to the School is so selective that success or failure at the School is not seen in terms of passing or failing at the end of the day. Few students fail to complete the course. However, most students, on leaving the School, do not join one of the grands corps. Typically, the number of grands corps vacancies will only be sufficient to provide positions for about a third or a quarter of the students graduating. The student who has performed best of all can take his pick from amongst the vacancies - and he or she will almost certainly choose a position with one of the grands corps; the student who came second chooses from amongst the remaining vacancies, and so on down the list in descending order of merit until all the grands corps vacancies have been filled. The remaining students - say, the bottom two-thirds - are still assured of positions, but not in one of the grands corps; instead, they will join the corps of civil administrators, assigned to positions across the whole range of ministries. Civil administrators are senior officials; they occupy positions in the upper reaches of the administration, but not at the very top; for our purposes, they cannot be described as members of the administrative elite. And this system of job selection, whilst it does ensure that the grands corps receive none but the very best (at least as measured against its own criteria of excellence), also has the effect of creating a virtually unbridgeable chasm between the very few right at the top and the rest who are below them. Failure, not to pass out of the School but, rather, to pass out sufficiently well, effectively guarantees that the official concerned will never climb to the very top of the administrative tree, and the knowledge that this is so has understandably adverse effects on the morale of the less successful.

The National School stands as a clear manifestation of the French belief that it is possible to take individuals of high potential and give them a course of preparation which will peculiarly fit them to occupy a variety of senior posts in the non-technical administration. But the School is not unique. It is one of a number of so-called 'great schools', the implication of the adjective being that they offer superior preparation more directly relevant to the posts their students will eventually occupy, than do the universities.

Students who wish to enter one of the technical grands corps follow a path which differs somewhat in detail, but not in principle, from that followed by the non-technical recruits. Rather than seeking entrance, after university, to the National School of Administration, technical aspirants instead take an entrance examination for the Ecole Polytechnique (known generally as 'X'). Thus, they do not first go to university. Instead, two years spent at X provides them with the equivalent of a first degree in general science,

during which period they are, officially, military cadets (X
was originally established by Napoleon to provide engineer
officers for the army). After X, the top stratum, of a
quarter or so, take up vacancies in the technical grands
corps, and this involves further, more specialised training
provided by the various corps themselves at their own schools.
Those who do not make it into one of the technical grands
corps become army officers although, since a military career
was not generally the original intention, most soon resign
their commissions.

Both the grands corps and the institutions which prepare
the entrants to them are part of a larger pattern and yet, at
the same time, they have a particular and elitist distinctiveness which sets them apart. There are many corps in the
French civil service, but only a few can legitimately be
termed 'great'. Similarly, many young Frenchmen and women go
to university, but only a few enter a great school. Having
admitted the necessity for an adminstrative elite, the state,
through the great schools, tries to ensure that its members
will be very good at their jobs. Undoubtedly, a side-effect
of the system is to perpetuate a clear division between the
minority who belong to the elite, and the majority who do not.
If being in the elite means that you matter, then the corollary is that not being in it implies that you do not really
matter. Few of those who enter the civil service straight
from school, or even from university, can realistically hope
that they carry field-marshals' batons in their knapsacks.
And yet, it can be argued, that having accepted the existence
of an elite as an organisational reality, it is shortsighted
not to ensure that its members are of the first quality.
There was a time when the accepted view was that civil servants had nothing to do with policy-formulation – that was,
after all, the task of the elected politicians. But that
time has long passed. It is now accepted that senior officials are inevitably involved – in collaboration with the
politicians – in the policy-making process. And further, if
it is true that the electoral hurdles imposed by liberal
democratic politics are not primarily designed to ensure that
it is the administratively capable who always achieve high
political office, then it might be even more important for
the administrative elite to supply that omission. Certainly
it can be argued that at a time, during the Fourth Republic,
when the politicians were out of touch with the needs of
France, the grands corps at least were able to act as agents
of change and innovation.

It has sometimes been suggested that preparation for and
entry into the grands corps creates a body of officials who
are very conscious of their distinctiveness and their superiority. And it would be surprising if this were not the case.
From the moment of entry to a great school all the messages
received are variations on the theme of excellence. However,

it is perhaps too easy to move from this into an assumption
that the corps amount to, in some way, quasi-monastic commun-
ities of philosopher-kings. There are other factors at work
as well. Kesler argued, over 20 years ago, in his study 'Les
anciens eleves de l'Ecole Nationale d'Administration', that
whereas the commonly shared experience of having passed
through the National School did go some way towards imparting
a collective consciousness, countervailing influences also
operate. There is, after all, some - albeit limited - diversity in the socio-economic origins of the students. That
minority of students who are already serving officials, in
particular, are likely to see the School in less idealistic
terms, more as just a necessary step in career advancement.
And in any case, after leaving the School, its graduates -
even those who enter one of the grands corps - will actually
find themselves working in considerably varied administrative
areas. There are, in other words, forces at work to prevent
them becoming too divorced from the real world.

Nevertheless, it would be surprising if there were not
identifiable a certain style amongst members of the grands
corps. Their self-confidence has been remarked upon by numerous observers, and they are often said to have a technocratic
or managerial approach to decision-making. They believe that
problems exist to be solved. They were sure that it was possible to modernise and improve the efficiency of the French
economy, and they were proved correct. In a great many sectors the France of today is a quite different place to the
France of 30 or 40 years ago. What is more, they believe
that the state could and should take a leading part in
stimulating and guiding the process of modernisation. This,
of course, is in line with French traditions of dirigisme.
More specifically, after 1945, new economic planning machinery
was established. It was the civil servants who actually put
the planning machinery to work, and they began to do so under
the Fourth Republic, when strong political leadership was
lacking. All of this seems to fit in with Kesler's
observation, that the graduates of the great schools are not
primarily interested in 'isms', but with achieving results.

POLICY-MAKING

From all that has been said, it might be thought that civil
servants in France are peculiarly equipped to occupy a dominant position in the policy-making process. It is common knowledge that senior civil servants do play a part in policy-
making. The old, Wilsonian dichotomy, which saw policy-making
as the preserve of the politicians, whilst the role of the
administrators was confined to the implementation of policy
is too simple. The factors which lend strength to civil servants in their dealings with ministers are just as applicable

in France as in other liberal democracies. In addition, in France, it is arguable that the rigourousness of the processes of selection and training provides a body of self-confident - perhaps even brashly so - officials, who are quite capable of running the machinery of the state without the assistance (or interference) of the politicians.

That the French administrative elite is confident is beyond doubt. Equally, there have been periods in the past when the elected politicians were unable to provide leadership. But much has changed since 1958. Between 1958 and 1986, at least, France has had stable governments. If the years of governmental instability increased the policy-making opportunities of the officials, then the years since 1958 should, logically, have seen those same officials being put back into something more like their 'rightful' place. We should not forget that, in spite of the constitutional provisions designed to lessen the ability of the legislature and the parties to hinder the executive, France still remains a lively democracy, where those with political ambitions tread the electoral rather than the administrative road to power. If we are not careful, too much talk of the civil servants' republic can lead us to dark conspiracy theories for which there is little direct evidence. French civil servants contribute to policy-formulation, as do senior civil servants elsewhere; to say that they dominate it is quite something else.

Some commentators, pursuing a slightly different line, have suggested that France provides an example of pluralism giving way to neo-corporatism. In other words, there has grown up a relationship network between the state and a number of monopolistic groups which speak for various sectors of French society. Policies are formulated via this network, and the democratically elected parliamentarians, together with those groups which are not favoured as interlocutors by the state, are left out in the cold. But, persuasive as this scenario might appear, it ignores the fact that the state itself is not a monolith. The state might be more real to French than to British political thought, but it is still, in the end, a collection of ministries, agencies, central and local authorities. And the French universe of interest groups is, for ideological and cultural reasons, much less cohesive, and much more divided within and against itself, than a corporatist arrangement would require. It is true that French public life is studded with a multitude of commissions and committees on which both interest groups and the state (in the persons of civil servants) are represented, but many of these meet only rarely, and the contribution of many of them to policy-making is marginal at best.

The Fifth Republic has brought changes. The fact that the presidency is now a prize worth the capturing has stimulated the parties, on both the left and the right, to move closer to co-operation. The executive is more stable, and is more able to develop consistent policies over time. The locations of political power, and the relationships between those locations, are easier to discern. There is now much less excuse for the immobilisme of the Third and Fourth Republics. France herself has changed considerably but, if the part played in this by the civil servants has been important, they have not done it all by themselves.

ACCOUNTABILITY AND CONTROL

France is a liberal democracy in the Western European mould. She also has a public bureaucracy recognisable in Weberian terms. These two facts mean that in common with those of other liberal democracies, the French civil service is subject to a variety of controls.

Although a bureaucracy without power would be, if not a contradiction in terms, then at least a pointless waste of money, it is not in keeping with democratic notions that the bureaucracy should be too powerful. And yet there are features of bureaucracy which sometimes appear to give officials the advantage over elected politicians when differences of opinion arise. The permanence and longevity of the bureaucracy, the familiarity of officials with the working of the administrative machinery, possibly the superior training of senior officials, mean that we do not have to go so far as to propose a conspiracy theory to see the importance of effective controls over bureaucratic activity.

Some of the controls to which the French bureaucracy is subject are familiar territory. Allowing for some differences of detail, they are controls with which any European civil servant would be familiar. The fact that the service is hierarchically organised means that subordinate officials are subject to control by their superiors. There are also internal financial controls, and there are central financial organs which keep a check on the whole bureaucracy.

Still in keeping with liberal democratic ideas, we should not forget that France remains, at least in part, a parliamentary system. Notwithstanding the effective presidentialisation of the system since 1958, the government is still accountable to the National Assembly, and the elected deputies naturally take an interest in the activities of the bureaucrats in the various ministries. And so, all in all, there does exist, both within and outside of the civil service, a network of controls which may be seen as quite normal for a modern liberal democracy.

However, especial attention should be drawn to some additional control mechanisms which may be less familiar to British observers. Three control agencies in particular should be mentioned - the Council of State, the Court of

Accounts and the Finance Inspectorate – whose members, significantly, each belong to their own great corps; finally, we
shall also look briefly at ministerial cabinets – whose members, again, are mostly civil servants.

From the standpoint of control of the administration, the
origins of the Council of State do not appear, at first
glance, to have been propitious. Having replaced the ancien
régime, it was a prime concern of those who led the Revolution that the courts should not be able to place obstacles in
the way of the changes they wished to introduce and so, as
early as 1790, a law was passed which provided, quite simply,
that the actions of the administration should be beyond the
control of the courts. The adminstration was to be free of
all judicial control; any complaints against the administration would be looked into by the administration itself.
However, it was not long before there began to emerge within
the administration itself a body particularly concerned with
the handling of such complaints. Under the Consulate, and
with Napoleon as First Consul, the Council of State was established as the government's own judicial and legal adviser,
and it quickly adopted the function of preparing, for the
government, suggested solutions for cases where complaints
were being made against the administration. This function
continued, so that the Council came to act – to borrow
Waline's comparison – something like the legal division of a
private company. By 1806 the Council contained a section
specifically concerned with claims and complaints, which
increasingly acted judicially, hearing both sides of a case,
and whose recommended solutions tended to be accepted by the
Head of State, both under the Empire and afterwards. If, in
retrospect, this development was not surprising – since no
chief executive could possibly spare the time to investigate
personally the complaints made – it means, nevertheless, that
during the nineteenth century an appropriate jurisdiction was
born and grew within the heart of the administration itself.
It only remained to put this on a more formal footing and,
under the initial liberal impulses of the Third Republic, a
law of 1872 gave legal basis to the Council's judicial
functions, allowing it to render judgements 'in the name of
the French people'. Today, the Council still retains its
role of legal adviser to the government; indeed, in certain
areas the government is obliged to consult it. But it also
acts as judge in administrative law cases, that is, cases
between an individual and the administration, or between
different parts of the administrative machine (say, a local
authority and a central ministry), and the dual nature of the
Council's function was reaffirmed as recently as 1963.
Furthermore, and staying true to its origins, the Council
itself remains a part of the administration. Members of the
Council are civil servants. Among the great corps, theirs is
one of the greatest – although part of the explanation for

its prestige and its importance lies in the fact that its
members are to be found, on detached service, occupying positions in the upper reaches of the whole state administrative
network. The position was summed up by Michel Debre in 1958,
when he explained to the Constitutional Consultative Committee, that as he saw it, an administrative magistrature as
such did not exist, only administrative officials carrying
out judicial functions.

In practice, most administrative law cases are heard in
the first place not by the Council but by locally based administrative tribunals, but the Council remains the keystone of
the whole administrative justice structure, acting as a court
of appeal from the local tribunals (and so contributing to
the existence of a coherent body of adminstrative law) and
hearing at first instance particularly important or urgent
cases. In the field of administrative law it would be difficult to exaggerate the Council's importance, and Marcel
Waline has commented that without the Council there would be
no administrative law worthy of the name.

In so far as the French administrative courts invalidate
governmental action on the grounds that the official or the
authority has exceeded his substantive powers, or else has
failed to follow required procedures in exercising those
powers, they are not doing anything remarkable. In Britain,
where there are no specialised administrative courts, the
ordinary courts recognise these defects as being ultra vires.
However, where the French administrative courts are particularly effective is in controlling the use of power for the
wrong reasons. There is a general assumption - in Britain,
too - that, where powers are conferred, they are conferred
for a purpose (such as, for example, powers of compulsory
purchase of property for the purpose of facilitating a slum
clearance programme) and that the use of those powers for
another purpose (such as, for example, to enable the authority
to compulsorily purchase a property, hold on to it until it
has risen in value, and then sell it at a profit) is illegi-
timate. But, whereas it might be relatively easy for a court
to determine whether an official actually had the substantive
power to do what he did, or whether he followed the correct
procedures, his motives or reasons for doing what he did might
be more difficult to ascertain. They might be less obvious,
they might not be stated anywhere, and he might even lie
about them. Moreover, unless the relevant legislation makes
it clear, it might not be easy to decide or discover just
what was the original purpose for which the power was created
and conferred. And it is precisely here that the French
administrative courts benefit from the fact that they are
still a part of the administrative machine. The administrative judges hearing the case are civil servants. They are wise
in the ways of the administration. They act as advisers to
the government in the drafting of legislation. Additionally,

the court itself actively investigates the whole case, rather
than just arriving at a decision on the basis of presentations
by the two sides to the case; the procedure, in other words,
is inquisitorial rather than just adversarial. For these
reasons the administrative courts, under the inspiration and
leadership of the Council of State, have been able to build
up and apply a strong and relevant body of administrative law.
The basic reasoning behind all this is simple. The state is
not just another citizen writ large. The state is different
and special. Special considerations apply. And so, within
the general principles of the rule of law, it is seen as
being no less than appropriate that cases involving the state
and its officials should be handled by special - and specialised - courts.

The appropriateness of specialisation is seen again in
the Court of Accounts. The origins of the Court can be traced
back to the initial creation of a financial jurisdiction in
1318 but, in its present form, it was another Napoleonic institution. As with the Council of State, the Court has both
advisory (to the government) and judicial functions. It,
too, constitutes one of the grands corps; its members are
mostly graduates of the ENA, although the government can
appoint to vacancies outsiders whose services are considered
to be both valuable and validated by virtue of experience
elsewhere in the state system. However, if the dual functions
of the Council of State are more or less evenly balanced, the
Court of Accounts is primarily - as its name implies - a
specialised, judicial tribunal, and its members enjoy a judicial status intended to safeguard their independence.
Furthermore, the Court has closer relations with Parliament
than does the Council; its annual report is submitted to
Parliament as well as to the President of the Republic, reflecting the traditional interest of parliaments in financial
matters. Also, members of the Court participate on a regular
basis in the activities of a wide range of bodies concerned
with the financial performance of different parts of the
state machine. Judicially the Court is concerned not only to
ensure that money has been raised and spent legally, but that
it has been used efficiently as well. The Court is quite
willing to point out that a particular policy is being applied
in a way that is wasteful of resources, and the fact that its
officers are members of one of the most prestigious of the
corps, and that some of them have had direct experience of
public administration, make their comments and recommendations
both more realistic and weightier. Understandably, the
Court's activities have become more important as the state has
extended its own socio-economic intervention, particularly
since 1945.

Further control - again financial - is provided through
the Finance Inspectorate, originally established in 1831.
Unlike the Court and the Council, the Inspectorate does not

have a judicial status. Organisationally it is simply a
central government inspection service, but it, too, is one
of the grands corps, with all that that implies for the
importance of its function and the status of its members.
The distinguishing feature about the Inspectorate's financial
control is that it is exercisable at any stage of the public
expenditure process, rather than being confined to an audit
of accounts relating to completed operations. This in itself
might be enough to lend importance to the Inspectorate, since
money is at the heart of government. And the inspectors,
here too, are interested in administrative efficiency and
value for money. However, it is at least arguable that the
real importance of the corps stems only secondarily from its
immediate financial role, and that its members are primarily
noteworthy for the considerable influence they wield through
the wide range of posts which they occupy which have nothing
directly to do with financial inspection as such. We have
already come across detached service, whereby members of the
grands corps fill posts in other parts of the state apparatus,
whilst at the same time retaining membership of their corps.
In the case of the Finance Inspectorate, detached service has
become almost a way of life. At any one time, it is probable
that there will be more members of the corps on detached
service - in nationalised industries, in ministerial cabinets,
or in the private commercial and financial sectors - than
there will be actually working as finance inspectors in
central government. Paradoxically, then, as Pierre Escoube
has pointed out, the status of the Inspectorate among the
grands corps has grown commensurately with the extent to
which its members have lessened their concentration on financial inspection per se, and have instead colonised the administration in a more widespread manner. The prestige attached
to membership of the corps can hardly be overstated, so that
one could almost say that membership is in many cases a
stepping-stone to other things - not excluding the presidency
of the Republic. As Escoube remarks, it is important to
enter the corps, but it is more important to leave it. In
France, colonisation by the grands corps is not unusual.
What is marked in the case of the Finance Inspectorate is the
extent to which its original function seems to have become
little more than a means to this end.

Lastly, under the heading of control, some mention should
be made of ministers' cabinets. Each minister is entitled to
a cabinet, although the size of cabinet tends to vary with
the importance of the ministry and the largest cabinets are
those of the Prime Minister and the President of the
Republic. The cabinet is, in effect, a ministerial entourage,
and ministers have considerable discretion whom they appoint
to membership. A cabinet's functions go beyond control of
the bureaucracy; they include political responsibilities,
helping the ministers to maintain a good public image, nursing

the constituency to which he may wish to return one day, and keeping on good terms with deputies and senators. But the cabinet is, too, concerned with the minister's relationship with his ministry. It acts as his eyes and ears, as a progress-chaser on his behalf, and tries to see that the ministry's work is effectively co-ordinated in support of the government's and the minister's policies. Most French ministries do not have any administrative equivalent to the British permanent secretary, and so the cabinet is especially important as the institutional link between the minister and the ministry under him, concerned with what the French call the animation of the administrative machine. It is in this sense, then - somewhat less specifically than for the Court of Accounts or the Council of State - that the cabinet may be seen as a control device.

As the range of government has grown, so too has this administrative side of the work of cabinets. And so, too, has the extent of the penetration of cabinet membership by civil servants. Increasingly, cabinets are coming to be staffed by senior officials, in their late thirties or a little older, for whom a period in a ministerial cabinet is a necessary (albeit not officially so) stage in their career progression. If we ask why this is so, the answer lies in two parts. One is the sheer prestige of the graduates of the ENA and the other great schools who then go on to membership in the grands corps. The second is more nebulous, and has to do with a conception of government as being a non-political activity, perhaps even a technocratic one instead. Certainly the founder and inspiration of the Fifth Republic saw party politics as detracting from good government. Jean-Louis Quermonne argues that one of the most important changes in governmental structure since 1958 has been the emergence of a network of strategic staffs, including the Secretariat-general of the Government and the Secretariat-general of the Elysée, and to which may be added ministerial cabinets, all of which are staffed largely by members of the grands corps.

CONCLUSION

In recent years there has arisen in France a fashion for combing through the collected speeches of politicians, counting up how many times they use certain key words or phrases. In this way, it is thought, the deepest and most abiding concerns of the person whose utterances are being analysed will be brought to the fore and made obvious. Thus, General de Gaulle was found - to nobody's surprise, really - to have frequently used such words as state, patrie and France.

In so far as this technique has any validity, its application to this present chapter would surely highlight the frequency with which the phrase 'grands corps' has been used, or the phenomenon of the corps has been referred to, and this may be thought to reflect back upon their importance. Such a conclusion would be correct but, at the same time, it is important to keep this in proper perspective.

It is worth remembering that there is more to the government of France than just the administrative elite. It may be necessary to remind ourselves of this, partly because of a temptation to give too ready credence to the idea of the 'civil servants' republic', and partly, too, because this book and this chapter are essentially about civil servants, and we can too easily lose sight of the fact that other actors also have their places on the stage.

Within the civil service, however, the role of the grands corps continues to be of fundamental importance. They constitute, very definitely, an elite. Perhaps, given that any civil service contains an elite, we should say that they are a super-elite. Some of them may be seen as the contemporary equivalents of the grands commis of the ancien régime. And their impact is undoubtedly widespread, because of the practice of borrowing members of the grands corps for detached service, and through the operation of pantouflage. It has been argued that French economic planning could not have been so successful were it not for the fact that many of those involved in the planning process, both as civil servants and as ex-civil servants now in the private sector, shared a common background in the great schools - something which was lacking in the British attempt at economic planning. But then it has equally been argued that planning could not have been so successful without firm backing at the political level - something, again, which was lacking in the British case.

Like other European countries, the French state is interventionist. Where France differs from some other countries is not in the fact that the twentieth century, and particularly the years since 1945, have seen new techniques and greater state intervention. France differs in that the principle of state intervention goes back a long way, certainly to before the Revolution. Napoleon innovated, but equally he built upon foundations already laid. The result is a state which, compared, say, to Italy or West Germany, continues to be highly centralised. The state is important, and is appreciated as being important, in France. The administration plays an important part in French life and, within the administration, the grands corps occupy a vital position.

REFERENCES AND FURTHER READING

Aberbach, J. D., Putnam, R. D. and Rockman, Bert A. (1981) Bureaucrats and Politicians in Western Democracies, Harvard, Harvard University Press.

Armstrong, J. A. (1973) The European Administrative Elite, Princeton, Princeton University Press.

Burdeau, G. (1970) L'Etat, Paris, Editions du Seuil.

Escoube, P. (1971) Les Grands Corps de L'Etat, Paris, Presses Universitaires Francaises.

Gladstone, David (1986) 'The Role of the Three Civil Services', in R. Morgan and C. Bray (eds) Partners and Rivals in Western Europe: Britain, France and Germany, Aldershot, Gower.

Hayward, J. E. S. (1983) The One and Indivisible French Republic, London, Weidenfeld & Nicolson.

Howarth, J. and Cerny, P. G. (eds) (1981) Elites in France, London, Frances Pinter.

Kesler, J. F. (1964) 'Les anciens élèves de l'Ecole Nationale d'Administration', Revue Française de Science Politique, 14(2), 245.

Quermonne, J. L. (1980) Le Gouvernement de la France Sous la 5ieme Republique, Paris, Dalloz.

Stevens, A. (1978) 'The role of the E. N. A.' Public Administration, 56, 283-96.

Suleiman, E. N. (1974) Politics, Power and Bureaucracy in France, Princeton, Princeton University Press.

Suleiman, E. N. (1977) 'The myth of technical expertise', Comparative Politics, 10(1), 137-58.

Suleiman, E. N. (1978) Elites in French Society, Princeton, Princeton University Press.

Suleiman, E. N. (1978) 'Higher education in France: a two-track system', West European Politics, 3, 87-114.

Waline cited in Weil, P. (1975) Le Droit Administratif, Paris, Presses Universitaires Françaises.

Chapter 5

IRELAND

M. Mc Manus

THE POLITICAL SETTING: INSTITUTIONS

It should be clear from the start that this chapter is
concerned with the system of central administration that
exists in the Irish Republic (or Eire) and does not deal with
the administration of Northern Ireland, which since 1922 has
been a constituent part of the United Kingdom. For the sake
of convenience we shall refer to the state as 'Ireland' and
to the people as 'Irish'.
      Ireland is a small country on the edge of Europe, tied
to England for much of its history and like Wales and
Scotland treated as a province. In 1922 it achieved
independence from Britain though still remaining in the
Commonwealth. This link was loosened somewhat by de Valera
when he came to power in 1932, and was finally broken by the
Republic of Ireland Act 1948 which formally constituted
Ireland as a republic. Despite this repudiation of English
political control the major influence on Irish political
thought and practice has been British and this is manifested
quite clearly in much of the system of government as it
exists today.
      The population of Ireland is small, in 1981 it was
3,443,405, making it one of the smallest members of the EC. It
is also the least densely populated country in the EC with 47
people per square kilometre, and still basically a rural
nation heavily dependent on agriculture, although there have
been determined efforts in the last 20 or 30 years to increase
the industrial base of the country. The agricultural
population is made up primarily of owner-occupiers of small
farms, who constitute an important part of the political scene
in both local and national government. A. J. Humphreys noted
that 'the small farm families, taken collectively hold and
exercise the largest measure of power in the rural community'
(Humphreys 1966). The importance of this for the political
culture is that it has encouraged the dominance of static
conservatism within Irish society. Thus if you tie this with

the normal reluctance of most bureaucrats to adopt change it
is easy to see how for a long time after independence there
was the continued existence of what Chubb has called the
'dying pre-industrial society' (Chubb 1982).

Another feature of the Irish population which is
important in terms of political values is the fact that 95
per cent of the population are Catholic, and by this one
means that they are practising Catholics, with 90 per cent of
them attending Mass at least once a week (Irish Episcopal
Commission for Research and Development 1974). The Catholic
Church is obviously influential in all areas of Irish life
and affects the formation of public opinion, not least
through its control of education. However, it is easy to
overestimate the power of the Church, and although the
Catholic Church cannot be regarded as just one of many
pressure groups in Ireland, it would be wrong to regard the
country as a theocratic state. Girvin suggests that it is
the society that is theocratic not the state, and that the
state has accepted and developed this special relationship
between the Church and society since independence (Girvin
1986). It should be noted that the rapid industrialisation
of Ireland has severely affected the traditional hegemony of
the Church and recent surveys have discovered a weakening of
the old values of conservatism and authoritarianism, especially amongst the urban populaton under 30 (Foggarty 1984).

One further aspect of the Irish political culture that
might be relevant is the value placed upon loyalty. This
springs from several sources, among which are the agrarian
struggles of the past and the obvious ties resulting from the
fight for independence and the ensuing civil war. This
loyalty was manifested by de Valera in his choice of
ministers and colleagues and is also shown in the voting
habits of the electorate, although the floating voter is now
more common among the young. This loyalty leads in turn to
another aspect of the culture that affects the administration,
namely the tendency to secrecy. Lee argues that this is due
to the 'peasant residue in the Irish psyche', though to what
extent Ireland is any more secretive than Britain it is hard
to say (Lee 1982). It is said by some that the desire for
secrecy on the part of the civil service is because of the
fear that public knowledge might limit their own freedom of
action, and whilst there is some truth in the charge that
information is difficult or even impossible to obtain,
whether this is due to some 'conspiracy of silence' or just
to inefficiency is difficult to say.

Ireland has a written constitution, the **Bunreacht na
hAireann**, passed in 1937, which replaced the Constitution of
the Irish Free State of 1922. The 1937 Constitution was the
culmination of several years of constitutional reform
following de Valera's succession to government in 1932. It
was in some ways a radical departure from 1922 and in other

ways a confirmation of existing practice and principle, its
main difference being the repudiation of formal Commonwealth
links and the elimination of the role of the Crown in the
constitution, so as to stress the republican nature of the
new state. This process was finally completed in 1948 when
Ireland was formally declared to be a republic. The machinery
of government enshrined in the Bunreacht na hAireann is based
very firmly on the early twentieth-century Westminster model,
to a large extent confirming the existing structures. As de
Valera explained to the Dail in 1937, 'What is being done
here is to translate into practice what has been done in the
past ... making explicit what was implicit all the time'.
Following to some extent the British tradition the Bunreacht
provides for a bicameral system of government consisting of a
House of Representatives, known as the Dail Aireann, and a
Senate known as the Seanad Aireann. The members of the Dail
are referred to as TDs (Teachta Dala, the Irish for Members
of the Dail) and are the equivalent of the British MP. The
Irish Parliament is called Oireachtas and constitutionally
consists of the President as well as the two Houses.

HISTORICAL BACKGROUND

The development of the civil service in Ireland is obviously
linked to the development of the British administration, and
indeed until 1922 the country was run as a part of the United
Kingdom. This was done both by departments based in
Westminster and also by specific Irish departments based in
Dublin. There seems to have been no overall strategy for the
development of departments and functions in the nineteenth
century, the government's approach being an essentially
pragmatic one with newly discovered problems being tackled on
an ad hoc basis. This led inevitably to a confusing number
of bodies being involved in the administration of Ireland,
with varying amounts of central control over their actions,
though this was mitigated to some degree by the relatively
compact nature of the Dublin administration and the close
personal contacts of senior officials.

The reforms of the Northcote-Trevelyan Report in the
nineteenth century affected the Irish civil service as much
as the British, transforming it from a patronage-appointed
body into a service appointed by open competitions related to
the current educational system. The importance of this was
that since educational standards were approximately the same
in both England and Ireland, Irishmen were able to join the
civil service and serve in both countries. Moreover they
were able to rise to the most senior positions, such that an
analysis of the 48 most senior civil servants in Ireland in
1914 showed that they were 'overwhelmingly Irish', only ten
having come from England (McDowell 1964). To this must be

added the fact that of the 48, 28 were Protestants and 20
Catholics, showing the advantageous position of the
Protestant community in social and educational terms, yet
also showing that it was not a religious monopoly.

The move to independence was helped by the nature of the
Irish civil service and there was no administrative vacuum as
experienced by some later ex-colonial states. The situation
is clearly described in the 1935 Report of the Commission of
Inquiry into the Civil Service.

> The passing of the State services into the control of a
> native Government, however revolutionary it may have
> been as a step in the political development of the
> nation, entailed, broadly speaking, no immediate disturb-
> ance of any fundamental kind in the daily work of the
> average Civil Servant. Under changed masters the same
> main tasks of administration continued to be performed
> by the same staff on the same general lines of
> organisation and procedure (Chubb 1983).

When the new state was set up in 1922, 21,000 of the
existing 28,000 civil servants transferred to the new
administration, bringing with them all their expertise and
knowledge and a large measure of continuity. A few hundred
of them chose to transfer to the Northern Ireland administration and less than a thousand opted for premature retirement in the first few years of the new state.

The legislative basis of the new service was laid down
in two acts, the Civil Service Regulation Act (1923), and the
Ministers and Secretaries Act (1924). The Civil Service
Regulation Act set up the Civil Service Commissioners to
examine and certify the qualifications of entrants into the
civil service, very much as in the British system. The
Ministers and Secretaries Act created 11 departments out of
the 47 departments, boards and other bodies that had existed
prior to 1922. It set out the boundaries of tasks for each
department and established the statutory framework for the
organisation of the civil service. One of the significant
features of the act was that it created the minister as the
'corporation sole' of the departments; that is, the minister
is legally responsible for all the actions and decisions of
his department and officials, no matter how small the issue
involved. It is argued by some writers that this helps to
account for the concern of the Irish civil servant with the
minutiae of administration rather than with the broader
issues of policy-making (Barrington 1980).

As in Britain the sixties were a time of re-assessment
for government, and the first major look at the civil service
since the founding of the state took place in 1966 when the
Public Services Organisation Review Group was set up by the
Minister for Finance in order to 'examine and report on the

organisation of the Departments of State at the higher
levels, including the appropriate distribution of functions
as between both departments themselves and departments and
other bodies' (Devlin 1969: 3).

The Group is better known after its chairman, Liam St J.
Devlin and the final report which appeared in 1969 is commonly
referred to as the Devlin Report. It diagnosed two main
faults in the civil service as it existed: an inadequate
emphasis on policy-making and a lack of co-ordination within
the service as a whole. It stated its views on the role of
the public service in the following section:

> It is of the essence of government to act development-
> ally and acceptably and the machine to serve it should,
> therefore, provide for an input from the people. In
> each functional area, this machine should provide for
> the appraisal of policy proposals by competent staff who
> can devote their whole time and energies to such
> appraisal. A third desideratum is that the instruments
> of government should be efficient. This efficiency will
> depend on the way in which the public service is
> structured, organised and operated.
>
> The first role of the public service is to serve
> the government in a policy-advisory capacity, by
> sifting and recommending major policy alternatives, by
> collecting the public input, through appellate,
> consultative and research systems, and by assisting in
> the preparation of new legislation and in advice to
> Ministers.
>
> The second role of the public service is executive.
> Its task is to assist the government in the running of
> the country under the roles laid down by the Oireachtas
> and to implement its policies. The question of what
> the government should do itself and what it should
> delegate to others to do under a comprehensive code of
> instructions is central to our enquiry and has been one
> of the most intractable problems in the organisation of
> the public service (Devlin 1969: 144).

In order for government to fulfil these roles the report made
several major recommendations for the civil service as a
whole, as well as a number of specific recommendations for
particular departments. Its basic suggestion was that there
should be a separation of policy-making and the execution of
policy, which would be accomplished by establishing in each
department, an 'Aireacht' or policy-making section that would
be the core of the department, comprising the minister and
the top civil servants. This was to be separated from the
'executive offices' which would administer the various
services for which the department was responsible, and the
'executive agencies', which would be mainly the existing non-

commercial state-sponsored bodies within the remit of the
department. These executive units would have considerable
powers devolved to them so that ministers and senior civil
servants would be taken away from dealing with the day-to-day
concerns, including much of the trivia, so as to concentrate
on long-term policy issues. Secondly, it suggested that each
department should have an internal structure of separate
staff units responsible for planning, finance, organisation
and personnel, and that these units should be co-ordinated
through the Finance Department and a new Department of Public
Service. In order to assist with the public input into the
service it also suggested that a Commissioner for Administrative Justice be set up. The aim of the new system was to
ensure a more efficient and co-ordinated government service
based on the prevailing orthodoxies of the day in management
theory, namely systems theory and a federal decentralised
model that was thought to be appropriate to the management of
large organisations.

The response to the Devlin Report has been mixed, with
many of the main recommendations not being implemented or
only being partially carried out. The Department of Public
Service was set up in 1973 and the Public Service Advisory
Council, which was to monitor the progress on the reorganisation and report annually on it, was established shortly
afterwards. The enactment of legislation to provide for an
Ombudsman in 1980 is also a direct result of the report. In
general, however, response to the report has been
disappointing and there are perhaps several reasons for this.
First, the intellectual foundations upon which the report was
based have been criticised on the grounds that structural
solutions do not necessarily solve organisational problems
and that some of the solutions, while having much managerial
logic and combined wisdom as their basis, could, perhaps, be
regarded as too technocratic and neat for their effective and
immediate application to the democratic institutions and
processes of contemporary Ireland. Secondly, the political
will to effect the changes has been absent on the part both
of ministers and of TDs. Ministers saw it as a limiting of
their powers in that the executive units would have more
power devolved to them than in the existing systems and their
knowledge of day-to-day activities would be limited. Though
this was seen as desirable by Devlin, the political culture
is such that ministers are expected to deal with individual
complaints, and a knowledge of executive issues is thus
important for a minister in electoral terms. Similarly, TDs
saw that if executive matters were removed from the ministers
they would lose their right to question them in the Dail and
would also lose their control over the executive agencies.
Thus Devlin questioned deep-seated values relating to accountability and the role of the parliamentary representative, and
judging from the response of TDs in the debate on the

creation of the Public Services Department, when there were only six speakers to the Bill in the whole debate, it was a subject which was not high on the political agenda.

The reaction of senior civil servants was also important in ensuring a muted reaction to the Devlin proposals, as Patrick Lynch, a member of the Public Service Advisory Council said: 'We achieved nothing whatever in promoting reform because of the absolute resistance to change among senior civil servants' (quoted in Chubb 1982: 246).

THE EXECUTIVE

The system of government has been described by Chubb (1983:56) as 'early British Commonwealth' in that it is parliamentary with a Prime Minister and cabinet government. The Head of State is the President, who is elected every seven years, though only on four occasions since 1937 has the post been contested by more than one candidate, the various parties usually coming to some agreement beforehand. He is usually a nominee of the party in power, the choice being ratified formally by the Dail. The role of the President is largely that of a figurehead rather than the active political one we are familiar with in the United States or in France. Effective political power resides in the Taoiseach (the Prime Minister) and the government of the day.

The Dail is the more important of the Houses of the Oireachtas and its composition is fairly conventional, in that its members are elected by adult franchise based on geographical constituencies. The elections take place by means of the single transferable vote system of proportional representation, introduced just before independence in order to safeguard the interests of the Protestant minority and kept by the Irish electorate despite several referendums to try and abolish it. The Dail reflects the influence of England on Irish political structures, since it operates in much the same way as the British Parliament, with many of the same problems. Essentially, with a secure Taoiseach, a comfortable majority and voting on party line, the role and effectiveness of the Dail is limited.

There are at present 166 Deputies or TDs. There are three main political parties, though a new party, the Progressive Democrats (launched in December 1985), may upset the established trio of Fianna Fail, Fine Gael and the Labour Party. Fianna Fail was founded by Eamon de Valera in 1926 as the anti-Treaty party, while the pro-Treaty party Fine Gael, established in 1933, was the successor to the Cumann na hGaedheal, the original pro-Treaty party. The Labour Party was founded by James Connolly in 1912.

The second House, the Seanad, is part elected and part nominated in an attempt to provide both a balance and a check

to the first House and a different kind of representation. A
continuing problem has been to arrive at a satisfactory
method of constituting a second House that is both democratic
and yet different in kind to the Dail. The solution proposed
by de Valera still holds today with minor changes. The Seanad
is composed of three groups selected as follows. First there
are six Senators who are elected by the two universities and
the other institutions of higher education as specified by
law. Secondly, 43 Senators are elected, using the single
transferable voting system, by an electoral college of 900,
consisting of members of the Oireachtas and county and county
borough councillors. The candidates for this election are
nominated by five panels representing different groups of
interest (education and culture, agriculture, industry and
commerce, labour, public administration and social services)
and also by members of the Oireachtas. The remaining 11
Senators are nominated by the Taoiseach himself to give
representation to any groups neglected by the rest of the
process, and as de Valera himself admitted, to ensure a
government majority. Despite this attempt at wide and non-
political representation, the reality is that the Seanad is
still composed mainly of party politicians and offers a
limited check or challenge to the Dail. However some Seanad
committees do have quite wide-ranging powers to investigate
mis-spending and misconduct by the government, so it would be
wrong to dismiss totally its power and effectiveness. With
that proviso in mind the Seanad is inferior and subordinate to
the Dail, and is treated as such in both the Bunreacht and
political life.

STRUCTURE

The 47 boards and departments that existed before 1922 were
rationalised into 11 by the Ministers and Secretaries Act
(1924), with most existing departments being transferred en
bloc as functioning units. Over the years the names, responsibilities and functions of the various departments have
changed to some extent, normally to cope with the expansion
of government control. In common with the British system, on
which it is obviously modelled, the structure is not permanent and can be changed by order of the Taoiseach, though
the main departments, such as Finance and External Affairs,
have remained relatively stable. The main Departments of
State are shown in Table 5.1.
    The allocation of functions to departments in 1924 was
not carried out according to any overall plan but mostly on
the grounds of common-sense groupings based on past
experience and guided by the desire to make the minister
individually responsible for all the business conducted by
his department. To this end each minister was declared to be

TABLE 5.1 Expenditure and staff in main departments of state

Name of Department	Expenditure (£m)	Staff in Post (Jan. 1985)
Agriculture	393.9	4,677
Central Services	81.8	3,100
Communications	196.2	1,285
Defence	253.4	634
Education	1,005.1	1,069
Energy	12.9	233
Environment	769.4	971
Fisheries and Forestry	68.8	1,213
Foreign Affairs	44.9	780
Gaeltacht	14.0	72
Health	1,170.8	365
Industry, Commerce and Tourism	300.3	744
Justice (incl. Gardai and Prisons)	324.2	15,719
Labour	170.6	830
Public Works	109.3	1,010
Revenue Commissioners	92.5	7,026
Social Welfare	1,360.6	3,470

(Source: 1985 Government Estimates)

a corporation sole by the Ministers and Secretaries Act (1924) in the expectation that all the executive power of the state would flow directly through the members of the government. There was no investigation into the allocation of departmental functions until the Devlin enquiry in 1966, and any changes that have taken place have tended to be carried out on ad hoc grounds, either to cope with the expansion of government business, as in the case of the growth of welfare services after the second world war, which necessitated the setting up of the Departments of Health and of Social Welfare, or to serve political convenience, as in the case of the Department of Economic Planning and Development, which was set up in 1977 and disbanded in 1979. As in many other countries it seems that the distribution of functions to departments and ministers has more to do with the management style of the Taoiseach and political considerations than with any functional logic.

The attempt to reduce the administrative units of government to either ministerial departments or local authorities did not last too long, and within a few years of the existence of the Republic new public authorities began to emerge, the first of which were the Electricity Supply Board and the Agricultural Credit Corporation in 1927. These organisations are generally known as 'state-sponsored bodies', a term which has no exact meaning either in law or official parlance and about which 'there is a certain looseness' as the Devlin Report said (Devlin 1969: 29). They are generally bodies set up to carry out specific functions on behalf of the government. The Devlin Report defines them as 'any autonomous public body with a Board appointed by the Government to discharge those functions assigned to it by the Government' (Devlin 1969: 29). The Minister for Public Services said in 1976 that 'generally the term may be taken to include bodies established by or under statute and financed wholly or partly by means of grants or loans made by a Minister of State or the issue of shares taken up by a Minister' (Chubb 1982: 270). Universities, judicial bodies and purely advisory bodies are excluded from the definition, but according to Chubb, that still gives an approximate total of 100 state-sponsored bodies in 1979, employing 54 per cent of public sector staff and 9 per cent of all workers (Chubb 1982: 271, 354-5). Each organisation has a sponsoring minister who is ultimately responsible for it and there is a broad functional grouping of the state-sponsored bodies around the relevant departments. 'The overall picture is of a central core of Departments with their associated fringe of agencies reporting to those Departments with which they are functionally connected' (Devlin 1969: 30). However, since the growth of these bodies has been on an ad hoc basis there has been no serious attempt to work out the distribution of executive functions in the public service nor to work out a comprehensive system of communication and control either between the various bodies themselves or between the Oireachtas and the state-sponsored bodies.

The significance of the growth of state-sponsored bodies lies in the fact that it represented a 'conceptual change', as Devlin put it. First, it marked the abandonment of the concept of the minister as the corporation sole, in that certain boards were delegated some executive powers of state. Secondly, it united elements from both the public and private sector in the management of government enterprises, and thirdly, it opened up a new way for the exercise of the executive functions of government, one that was inherently freer and less subject to interference and control by the central bureaucracy.

Despite the use of state-sponsored bodies to carry out executive functions of the state that might have been carried out by civil servants, the latter's numbers grew from 21,035 in 1922 to 60,463 in 1980. The growth has not been constant; indeed in the first ten years of the state there was no growth at all, and the major increase took place in the 1970s, when the civil service increased by two-thirds, from 36,388 to 60,463 (Chubb 1982: 256).

Ireland

The organisational structure of the Irish civil service
is modelled fairly closely on the British system, with a
departmental secretary as head of each department, with
deputy and assistant secretaries supported by principal
officers and assistant principal officers. Below these are
the administrative and clerical grades which form the bulk of
the manpower. There are in general two main classes of civil
servant, the general service class which performs the general
administrative duties of the department from the clerical
level to the highest policy-making level, and the specialist
officers who may be divided into two types. First, there are
the officers who are recruited on general educational
standards but who work in a specialist department or section
of a department and acquire certain skills as a result of
their work experience. Secondly, there are officers who are
recruited because of the specialist qualifications they have,
which relate to the specific function or work of the department. The role of specialists and generalists in the civil
service will be discussed later in the chapter and the debate
parallels in many ways that held in the British civil service
over the same issue.

One of the features of the civil service that illustrates
the extreme centralisation running through Irish life is the
fact that there is no dispersal of government offices
throughout the country. Unlike successive British governments
which have adopted a deliberate policy of distributing major
departments throughout the country, Irish governments have
done nothing in this way. All departments are still situated
in Dublin, although some, for example the Department of
Social Welfare, have a more developed field agency structure
than others.

THE BUREAUCRATS

As is common in most other systems of central government the
terms 'civil servant', 'public servant' and 'bureaucrat' are
not rigidly defined and the terms tend to be used in a fairly
loose manner, especially in the case of the latter two. In
this work we are concerned with those officials who work for
the departments of central government, rather than administrators in public utilities or state-sponsored bodies, who
might sometimes be referred to as public servants or
bureaucrats.

The social and educational background of the top civil
servants in Ireland prior to the Treaty mirrored that of the
English civil service in many respects and especially in
terms of the upper-class nature of the higher ranks. This
situation changed after the move to independence and has
continued to change in the ensuing years so that the present
civil service differs markedly in its social composition from

the English one, especially in terms of the higher echelons. The major difference lies in the fact that there is no aristocracy or 'establishment' in the British sense in Ireland, and consequently the senior civil servants tend to come from middle-class backgrounds. Work by Mathuna (1955) and Cohan (1972) has shown that the higher civil service in Ireland is a relatively homogeneous group which reflects the non-stratified structure of Irish society. For example, of 64 secretaries of government departments, 97 per cent were Roman Catholic, 82 per cent came from urban areas (49 per cent of the whole population was then urban), and 26 per cent had a university degree. The small proportion of senior civil servants with a university education is a result of the small number of graduates entering the service in its early days and the policy of opening up jobs to higher executive officers. This is in sharp contrast to the pre-Treaty civil service where of the 48 top officials in 1914, 43 of them had university or professional education or training. By the late 1960s perhaps 90 per cent of the posts of assistant secretary and above were filled by people from secondary school and 4 of the 15 heads of departments had entered as clerical officers. Chubb states that by 1980 'the service, if not open to all classes, was within wide limits classless'.

One interesting feature of the educational background of the top civil servants is the proportion of them who were educated in Christian Brothers' schools. The Christian Brothers were founded in 1808 to provide education for poor boys but grew to provide education for all classes and especially at the secondary level. This is perhaps the nearest equivalent of the 'old school tie' factor in Ireland, and Mathuna in an article examining this aspect of the civil service suggests that the type of education received from this schooling, an intensive, over-academic and narrow one in the main, helped to shape the civil service and its traditions. The Christian-Brothers-school stereotype tended to be intellectually able and hard working but overly practical and concerned with short-term objectives. A reluctance to look critically at the system they were working in, coupled with the traditional civil servant's distrust of external advice, meant that although they were capable of running the civil service as an efficient administrative machine they were not capable of dealing with the demands of a modern state and the long-term vision and planning that that required.

Since the mid-1960s there has been increasing change in the civil service, especially in the education and character of its recruits. The number of entrants from Christian Brothers' schools has decreased and the nature of those schools has also evolved with the changes in Irish society. Thus the narrowness of approach and the reluctance to look at long-term goals and plans has receded to some extent, though there are still some (Barrington 1980) who are pessimistic about the changes that have been achieved.

The general picture of the civil service personnel, then, is of a relatively homogeneous group with no major divisions on the grounds of class or education within the service. This picture has held true for a long time, but if the civil service continues to be an accurate reflection of the social structure then it might be expected that its higher reaches would reflect the growth of a new native elite, and entry to it would become restricted. The fact that a large number of civil servants are recruited directly from school has obvious implications for training and education within the service. The intellectual calibre of school entrants was high due to the standards of the entrance exam, which was intensely competitive, as a result of the limited access to university and the absence of alternative employment for many bright pupils who, in a different education system, would have gone on to university or higher education of some sort. Many of these entrants obtained university or professional qualifications while working in the civil service and so were ultimately no less qualified than their counterparts in other civil services. At the time of writing the problem of recruiting graduates into the civil service is again becoming acute, with the increasing tendency for the higher-qualified graduates to emigrate to better paid posts overseas.

The fact that most higher officials have worked their way up the system means that there is a common assumption that the work of the administrative classes is the same as that of the executive classes, with the obvious effect on policy-making and long-term planning which was noted before. There is also a positive side to this, in that it is claimed that this system of promotion ensures that the top civil servants are aware of the work that is done by the lower grades and are more in touch with their problems and with the day-to-day mechanics of administration.

One problem faced by most administrations is the relationship between the specialist and the generalist administrator. In the Irish system there are two types of specialist administrator. First, are those officers who are recruited with a general education, like general service officers, but who are allocated to work which is specific to a department or section of a department. Examples of this would be officers in the Office of the Revenue Commissioners involved in tax matters or the Customs and Excise section. As a result of their intensive on-the-job training they become specialists whose career will be contained in the relevant department. Secondly, specialist officers are recruited to the civil service for performance of specialised work with a qualification related to the work to be performed. These professional and technical officers tend to remain in the same department with little mobility either in terms of promotion to senior posts or in terms of horizontal moves to other departments. This lack of mobility was commented upon in the Devlin Report but it would seem that little has been done to remedy the situation. The traditional belief still holds that management of the service is best carried out by generalist staff rather than specialists, presumably on the basis that they can provide a more objective and broader appraisal of policy proposals than specialists. There is a tendency then to regard professional staff as consultants to the service rather than as an integral part of the policy-formulation machinery in a department, which is a major cause of dissension between generalist and specialist staff.

POLITICAL ACCOUNTABILITY

The concept of political accountability that is applied to both the executive and the central bureaucracy in Ireland owes much to the British origins of the administrative system. As Chubb says, 'the Irish state adopted in toto these constitutional and legal principles, myths and all, and the procedures and inhibitions to which they gave rise' (Chubb 1982: 314). The principle of legal control was deemed to be effected through the normal legal channels using the ordinary courts. Moreover, the main concern of these courts was held to be the enforcement of legal rights and obligations, not the fulfilling of public policy. The principal means of political accountability was the doctrine of ministerial responsibility, the legal concept of the minister as the 'corporation sole' in the department, responsible for every action taken in his name by any of his officials. Responsibility, in this sense, is taken to mean answerability to an elected body and in the Irish Constitution the principle is expressed in the following clauses:

> Article 28.
> 4.1 The Government shall be responsible to Dail Eireann.
> 4.2 The Government shall meet and act as a collective authority, and shall be collectively responsible for the Departments of State administered by the members of the Government.

The constitutional principle is put into effect by the practice of members questioning the appropriate minister about the conduct of his department. This appraisal may range from the general conduct of services and broad outlines of policy to specific, minor points that concern the handling

of an individual case by an individual officer. This
responsibility for the actions, or inactions, of the staff
extends to the details of operations where central government
departments are concerned, but in the case of local
authorities or state-sponsored bodies the minister only has an
overseeing role and thus the responsibility is more general.

The duties and powers of each department are formally
assigned to the minister, as the Devlin Report put it:

> ...normally all the Department's acts are the acts of its
> Minister . . . With the complexity of administration
> and the mass of detail to be covered, it would be
> impossible for any Minister to have direct personal
> knowledge of all the operations of his Department . . .
> Nonetheless he is not empowered by statute to delegate
> his power to his civil servants . . . The modus operandi
> which has been adopted is to issue letters, minutes and
> instructions in the name of the Minister. An official
> signing the letter expresses himself as having been
> 'directed by the Minister to say' . . . the personal and
> final responsibility of the Minister is in every
> instance stressed (Devlin Report 1969: 61).

The reality of the situation differs somewhat from the
constitutional theory as it is obviously impossible for one
person to be held responsible in practical terms for all his
subordinates' actions or inactions. Thus although the legal
responsibility is still his, in political terms a minister
may decide what he shall be held responsible for and what
shall be attributed to others. By this means he may use
nameless civil servants in order to deflect criticism of his
department or of his actions. Even where there have been
cases of wrong decisions, incompetence and misbehaviour there
have been no occasions on which ministers have been forced to
resign. Equally cases of civil servants being forced to
resign because of maladministration and incompetence are
rare, though presumably inside knowledge of their performance
would have affected their promotion chances.

Following the British tradition the main method of
appraising the actions of the central bureaucracy is by means
of the parliamentary question. As an objective method of
checking on the effective working of the bureaucracy this
leaves much to be desired, since the political atmosphere in
which questions are asked may make the occasion more a gladiatorial one than a seeking after the truth. The fact that
the content of the questions is uncertain may help to prevent
arbitrary action by officials and departments, and the
ability to raise issues in the Dail does help to maintain an
environment of questioning and criticism which reinforces the
subordinate status of the civil service. The usefulness of
the question is blunted to some extent by the fact that the

minister need only reveal what information he considers to be necessary in answer to the enquiry and that, coupled with the traditional secrecy of the civil service, may make it difficult to obtain a satisfactory reply.

Parliamentary questions are useful weapons in the armoury of inter-party warfare and are frequently used for that purpose, but they are also important to individual citizens, especially in Ireland, since they enable them to take their case directly to the policy-makers and bureaucrats. It also means that deputies and senators communicate directly with officials in departments in pursuance of individuals' requests for help. Deputies may address their requests for information either to the relevant minister or to the permanent secretary of the department, and to some extent this seems to depend on whether the minister is of the same party as the deputy, with government deputies tending to communicate with the minister and opposition deputies addressing themselves to the permanent officials.

The picture of the deputy as a person who goes about persecuting civil servants springs from the long tradition of 'service' in the Irish political system, whereby the representative is seen to be at the beck and call of his electors and his function is thought to be that of adviser, contact man, expediter and intercessor at both national and local level. This function of the deputy is in many ways peculiar to Ireland, but is deeply embedded in the political consciousness. All deputies will have regular correspondence with those departments which are most concerned with services to individuals, and the matters most frequently dealt with will include housing grants, agricultural grants, entitlements to welfare benefits and even such routine matters as old-age pensions. Whether the intercessions of deputies actually speed up decisions or bring about a resolution of a matter in favour of the constituent is not always clear, but it is the perception of the power of the deputy that is important, not necessarily the reality.

The impact of this activity by deputies on a government department can be considerable. First, it affects the administrative procedures of departments, such that some departments adopt the policy of always sending a reply to a deputy complete with a carbon copy, which can then be sent by the deputy to his constituent. As Senator Michael Hayes put it 'members of the Dail are treated rather as intermediaries or messengers between their constituents and the state itself, the civil service and the various state bodies' (Chubb 1963: 279). There is also some evidence, says Chubb, that sometimes ministers ask their officials to provide them with advance copies of letters to deputies so that the minister can inform his party colleagues in the area, in order that they may forestall any advantage the enquiring deputy may have had, especially where they belong to a different party.

Secondly, the pressure of this type of work on a department may mean that other more important tasks are left aside.
If a department has to deal every day with 40 or 50 requests
for information on detailed individual cases, it will consume
an inordinate amount of staff time. Moreover, since the
requests are often addressed to the departmental secretary or
other senior officials it diverts them away from the task of
long-term policy-making, forcing them to concern themselves
with day-to-day issues of administrative minutiae.

The darker side of this activity is the possibility of
representatives using their influence unfairly or even
illegally. Accusations of jobbery are common at local
government level, and although opportunities for special
pleas for jobs only arise in a few departments, where the
work is at labourer level, when representations are made the
following phraseology is commonly used: 'I will bring the
representations to the engineer in charge for his favourable
consideration' (Chubb 1963: 278). More recently much more
serious charges have been made that involve representations
about the outcome of appointments made by the Civil Service
Commission, a body set up purposely to stamp out such illicit
pressures on government appointments. Moreover in 1980 the
president of the Association of Garda Sergeants and
Inspectors complained that politicians were trying to use
their influence to have prosecutions quashed, a charge backed
up by the general secretary of the Association of Customs and
Excise Officers. This involvement by politicians in the
administrative process is all the more unusual for the fact
that, although it is seen as a major part of the deputy's
role by both politicians and public, it has no underpinning
in the constitution. When in 1961 the Minister for Local
Government said that he 'thought it was in the very nature of
a Deputy's work to interview Departmental officials on behalf
of constituents', the following legal response came from Mr
Justice Budd in giving his verdict on the case. He declared
that:

> most important functions were positively assigned to
> Deputies by the Constitution, the paramount duty being
> that of making laws for the country. The Constitution
> did not anywhere in the Articles relating to the
> fuctions of Deputies recognise or sanction their
> intervention in administrative affairs (Chubb 1963: 286).

There is obviously a gap between the constitutional niceties
and the political realities for there is no evidence that
deputies have changed their role or their relationship with
civil servants since that judgement was made. Indeed they
have been anxious to keep the role of 'go-between', even when
changes might have meant a lightening of the caseload and
more opportunity to become involved in policy-making at the

macro level. Moreover, the public faced with the ever-
increasing complexity of the modern welfare state also seem
reluctant to give up their traditional channel to the
bureaucrats.

In most parliamentary states one of the other methods of
holding the bureaucracy accountable is through the
deliberations of committees, which have specific briefs for
particular areas of policy and which are empowered to
investigate anything and anyone they deem relevant to their
area. Despite the strength of this system in the United
States, from where the Irish have borrowed other administrative ideas, in this case they have chosen to keep to a pale
version of the British model. The Oireachtas has chosen to
adopt the select committee system but without the means to
make it effective. Moreover the terms of reference are
usually such that they preclude the questioning of government
policy and the committees lack the professional staff needed
to provide the research support. This means that usually the
only people who actually know anything in detail about the
subject being considered are the minister and the civil
servants who briefed him.

It can be argued that the single transferable vote
system of proportional representation has contributed to this
lack of emphasis on the overall control of the bureaucracy,
since it favours the election of representatives who see
their role as consumer representatives rather than
legislators. As a result most members of the Oireachtas do
not see themselves as committee men, since that activity does
not receive much public recognition and politicians can only
survive in the Irish system if there is public awareness and
recognition of their work. One of the other reasons for the
reluctance of any government to adopt a fully fledged committee system, and perhaps also for the lack of support from
senior civil servants for such a system, is the fact that
committees may be seen as inhibiting the government's freedom
of action through the creation of alternative centres of
information, expertise, prestige and power within the same
legislature. Given the predisposition to secrecy among civil
servants it is unlikely that they would relish the open
government that would emerge with a well-organised committee
system.

A less formal means of holding the administration
accountable is the attention paid to it by the mass media,
including the press, the radio and television. In Ireland
the press has a relatively free hand to report as it pleases,
within the normal confines of libel legislation and other
basic judicial restraints. Thus ministers and officials find
it difficult to restrict the content of papers, and even if
they succeeded with the Irish papers, British papers
circulate freely in the country and a large proportion of the
television sets in the country can receive both BBC and ITV

programmes. The ability to control the content of the press lies solely in the reluctance of official sources to release information, a situation which contrasts with the availability of material in a country like Sweden, where the Freedom of the Press Act guarantees access to state and local authority documents.

The radio and television stations in Ireland are viewed rather differently from the press, in that there is a belief among politicians that they ought to be more socially responsible. To this is added the fact that they are state monopolies, owned and operated by a state-sponsored body, Radio Telefis Eireann (RTE). They are thus reliant on the government for finance, although the advertising that they carry generates some of their income. Moreover their governing body is appointed by the government and on one occasion, in 1972, a dispute between government and broadcasting authority was resolved when the government dismissed the whole body.

Views on the role of RTE range from the belief of programme makers that it should be an independent service free from government interference, to the idea that it should be an instrument of public policy as expressed by Sean Lemass in 1966, when he was Taoiseach:

> Radio Telefis Eireann was set up by legislation as an instrument of public policy and as such is responsible to the Government. The Government have overall responsibility for its conduct and especially the obligation to ensure that its programmes do not offend against the public interest...To this extent the Government reject the view that Radio Telefis Eireann should be, either generally or in regard to its current affairs and news programmes, completely independent of Government supervision (Chubb 1982: 80).

The troubles in Northern Ireland have tended to exacerbate the friction between broadcasters, politicians and officials, but perhaps the Irish experience is no different from that of other democracies where the rights of the media are not laid down in law or official guidelines, but rely on a more-or-less agreed code of conduct.

The newest form of political accountability has been the establishment of an Ombudsman in 1980 following the recommendations of an All-Party Committee on Administrative Justice which reported in 1977. The Ombudsman actually took up office in January 1984. An important difference between the working of the Irish Ombudsman and that of the French and British is that people in Ireland may invoke his help directly, without having to direct their complaint through a parliamentary representative. Moreover, if he thinks it proper, the Ombudsman can initiate an enquiry himself, thus making him a much more active agent of accountability than in

some other countries. In his first report he commented on
the relations between the Ombudsman's office and the civil
service in the following terms:

> The response of many civil servants to the creation of
> the Ombudsman's Office has been most encouraging. They
> recognised the need for the Office and co-operated whole-
> heartedly in its enquiries. There was evidence, however,
> that some senior civil servants had considerable
> suspicions about the new institution and resented its
> intrusion, particularly when their decisions were under
> scrutiny (Report of the Ombudsman 1984: 3).

In some cases there was actually a legal challenge by the
civil service to the powers of the Ombudsman, but in all
cases his authority was justified and it is anticipated that
as the service becomes more accustomed to the working of the
system such challenges, and the suspicion that creates them,
will die out.
    The means of political accountability in relation to the
central bureaucracy are varied both in their scope and
effectiveness, but gradually the power of the individual voter
to influence the enormous state machinery that now exists is
growing, and the bureaucracy is having to become more aware
of the impact of its decisions.

INTERNAL CONTROL

Political Control

The control which politicians exercise over the civil service
is obviously related to the issue of accountability and as
was apparent when discussing that issue, the relationship
between the civil servants and their political superiors, the
ministers, is not as simple as it first seems. The control
that ministers can exert is limited by a number of factors.
First, the complexity of a modern state means that there is
now a mass of legislation, all the details of which no
minister can be expected to be aware of. The implications of
the application of legislation may also be outside his
knowledge and as a result the minister may be at the mercy of
his civil servants for help and information. The short length
of stay of most ministers in their office means that only the
civil servants are capable of a long-term overview of policies
and legislation, because of their stability and access to the
bureaucracy's information sources. As a result of this their
role as gatekeepers to the minister assumes great importance
in terms of policy-making, and partly as a response to this
there is the increasing practice of ministers appointing their
own political advisers. Secondly, the enormous increase in

the business of each department means that it is virtually
impossible for a minister to exercise effective control over
his civil servants. All of this raises questions about the
role of civil servants in the making of legislation and policy
and shows what great reliance is placed on the traditional
objectivity and impartiality of the civil servant.

Financial Control

Within the structure of the Irish civil service the Department of Finance has tended to develop into an elitist corps
and has exerted considerable influence over the activities of
the whole bureaucracy. This it does by entering into
negotiations with each of the ministries over their budgets
and thereby controlling the nature and direction of the
policies promoted by the spending department. In the past it
tended to take the majority of the graduate intake and to pay
a higher rate of pay, which inevitably militated against any
mobility of its officers and caused ill-feeling vis à vis the
other government departments. The Secretary of the Department
of Finance was always recognised as the Head of the Civil
Service, and although the reorganisation of the civil service
has led to the creation of a new Department of the Public
Service, this was formed by hiving off a section of the
Department of Finance, so it will presumably still be imbued
with its ethos and values.

The stringent economic policies of recent governments
have increased the power of the Finance Department, since the
major objective of successive executives has become the
controlling of inflation, particularly by means of
controlling public expenditure. The major criticism of this
development is that it leads to the dominance of short-term
economic goals over any long-term ones, a failing which
successive governments since the 1960s have sought to redress
in the push for economic growth.

Judicial Control

As a constitutional republic the powers of the government and
its agencies rest upon the constitution, the Bunreacht na
hAireann, which means that public bodies can exercise no
powers except those they derive from the law and the
constitution and they can only exercise them within those
limitations. The constitution provides for courts whose
jurisdiction extends to the question of the validity of any
law having regard to the constitution. The legal route is the
normal court system, since in Ireland, as in Britian, there
is no special droit administratif and there are no specific
regulations for the day-to-day operation of public bodies.

Ireland

The success of this system depends on there being relatively easy access to the courts for the ordinary citizen, both in physical and financial terms, and it was not until the late 1970s that a general system of legal aid was introduced in Ireland, easing the path for the ordinary citizen.

In the early days of judicial involvement in constitutional matters the judges tended to take a fairly conservative line in interpreting the constitution, as there was a lingering regard for the old principle of the immunity of the Crown, which had been translated into the immunity of the state with the coming of independence. Since the mid-1960s, however, judges have been far more bold in their treatment of the constitution, to such an extent that Mr Jack Lynch, when he was Taoiseach, made the comment that 'it would be a brave man who would predict, these days, what was or was not contrary to the constitution'. As the courts have become more adventurous they have also become more impatient with attempts to sustain departmental secrecy and ministerial privilege. This has implications for the growth of more open government and it highlights the natural tension that exists between the desire of administrative bodies to preserve secrecy and the practice of courts to argue all aspects of a case out in the open.

This change in judicial attitude towards the constitution and the actions of the administration has serious implications for administrators which they do not seem to have grasped totally. First, the administrator needs to understand the relationship between the courts and the administration. Secondly, the insistence of the courts on the concepts of human rights and natural justice as standards by which to judge the actions or inactions of departments means that administrators must be more aware of these concepts and their implications. Thirdly, there must be a change from the view that every judicial comment is an attack on the bureaucracy, which leads to departments always adopting defensive attitudes, sometimes over things which are indefensible. Unfortunately the reaction of some departments to investigations by the Ombudsman has shown that this attitude still exists.

The main challenges to the bureaucracy concern the validity of actions in terms of constitutional powers, the question of whether actions are _ultra vires_ or not. This however still leaves open the area on _intra vires_, where an agency is within its powers and commits no breach of natural justice, but where someone thinks that it is acting foolishly or unreasonably in the exercise of its discretion. This area of complaint has now been dealt with to some extent by the setting up of the Ombudsman, described in the previous section, but the fact that there is no compulsion on the agency or department to follow the advice of the Ombudsman limits the effectiveness of the system as a means of redress for the ordinary citizen.

The other avenue open to a citizen appealing against an
action by a government agency is the tribunal system which
exists in some departments. There are a total of about 80
such tribunals, some of which are used very rarely and others
of which handle a substantial amount of business. In 1982,
for example, the Department of Social Welfare received 13,663
appeals. However, these appellate tribunals do not exist for
all areas of public service and they vary in nature from
commissioners who are independent of, but appointed by,
ministers, to special external tribunals, staffed from outside the public service. The varied nature of these appeal
bodies has generated a correspondingly varied set of problems,
amongst which are the status and knowledge of the tribunal
personnel and the quasi-judicial nature of many appeal
procedures which tends to inhibit the citizen who is making
the appeal. The more complex the legislation, the greater
the need for appeals procedures and also the need to review
these very procedures to ensure their efficiency and
effectiveness.

MANAGEMENT

As well as control by outside bodies the civil service has
the task of controlling itself through its internal management
procedures. These were identified by the Devlin Report as an
area of considerable weakness. As it put it, 'the lack of an
overall organisation and management service is the first and
most serious defect in the management of public service
institutions' (Devlin 1969: 140). The problems derived from
several sources: the emphasis upon day-to-day work in
departments, the lack of training amongst senior officers,
the reluctance to share information between departments and
the general lack of information about the performance of the
civil service. It seemed, for example, that when Devlin
looked at the civil service the only current source of
information on the state-sponsored bodies was the Yearbook
and Diary published by the independent Institute of Public
Administration. 'It is a simple fact that nobody knows,
today, where to go to find out what are the total organisational and manpower requirements of the public service'
(Devlin 1969: 140). It seemed to Devlin that the essential
unity of the civil service had been lost and that the crucial
functions of planning, finance, organisation and personnel
were less than perfect, with the result that the organisation
was not capable of dealing effectively and efficiently with
the demands made of it.

The solutions proposed by Devlin have been mentioned
before, but in essence he suggested three fundamental reforms:
first, the establishment of a policy-making Aireacht in each

department, which would consist of the minister and his top
civil servants; secondly, the executive officers of a
department would have considerable legal authority devolved
onto them, so as to lessen the responsibility of the minister
for every action taken by his department; and thirdly, all
executive bodies would be controlled by means of four units -
finance, planning, organisation and personnel - which would
be co-ordinated by the departmental secretary. The heads of
these 'staff units' would be included in the Aireacht, so
that the management implications of policy decisions could be
seen and co-ordinated. It could have been argued that these
proposals were the product of the management ethos of the
time, which was based upon the systems approach and the
concept of federal decentralisation. Both of these
approaches stressed structural answers to organisational
problems, an approach that has now fallen out of favour to
some extent, since where it has been employed it has not
necessarily produced the desired results. The successive re-
organisations of the National Health Service in Britain are
an interesting example of the pursuit of the notion that
organisational changes by themselves improve the quality of a
public service.

The government accepted the Devlin Report in principle
but progress towards its implementation has been slow. The
Department of Public Service was set up in 1973 to direct the
changes but without a sufficiently clear mandate or a clearly
defined role in relation to the other departments. Moreover,
it was not given any new powers over the other departments
and therefore had to implement the reforms by means of
exhortation, negotiation and compromise. The new structure
was initially introduced into the Department of Transport and
Power and then into one or two other departments, but it was
1977 before the government gave permission for it to be
introduced into all departments. Even now it is still not
functioning in all departments, and where it has been implemented it seems that there has been little visible impact on
the working practices or attitudes of most staff.

The reasons for the tardiness in changing the management
structure of the civil service can be explained by pointing
to several factors. First, and perhaps most important, was
the hostility of most senior civil servants to the proposed
reforms. Secondly, there was the reluctance of ministers to
release control of all aspects of the work of their departments, to take their fingers out of the pie so to speak.
Thirdly, there was the reluctance of the Dail to free large
areas of government administration from day-to-day control.
It would seem that in general there was a lack of political
will to implement the reforms which transcended party
boundaries.

One of the positive results of Devlin is that there is
now an increased awareness within the civil service of the

need for education and training of officers, and it is
perhaps on the personnel front that the greatest advances
have been made. However, as Kevin Murphy, the Deputy
Secretary of the Department of Public Service said, 'training
and staff development...are not a high priority with senior
management in most Departments' (Murphy 1982: 13).

As in several other countries where there have been
attempts to reform the central bureaucracy, the quest for
administrative efficiency has encountered the competing
demands of public accountability and the politicisation of
administrative tasks, which seem to render it somewhat akin
to the pursuit of the Holy Grail.

POLICY-MAKING

As we have explained already, the model under which the Irish
bureaucracy works is basically the British one, in which the
government makes the laws with the advice and consent of the
representative assembly. Moreover, in this model, the
ministers are regarded as the initiators of policy who are
responsible for all that goes on in their name, and as we
have seen this latter is something of a fiction. The reality
of policy-making in Ireland, as in other modern parliamentary
democracies, is much more complex and difficult to untangle.
There can be little doubt that the bureaucracy has always
participated in the policy-making process and that it is
difficult if not impossible to make a neat dichotomous
division between administration and policy-making, especially
at the senior levels of the civil service.

This influence of senior civil servants has grown in
recent years as a result of several factors, amongst which
are the increasing complexity of the legislative process, the
relative job stability of civil servants vis-à-vis ministers,
the increasing workload of ministers and the exhortations to
the central bureaucracy by successive Irish governments to
become more involved in the development of policy, especially
in relation to increasing national economic growth. Added to
these proximate policy-makers are the political advisers who
have been appointed by some ministers in recent years, some
of whom have been civil servants transferred from other
duties or departments and others outsiders appointed as
temporary civil servants for the duration of the minister's
stay in office.

It is difficult to say exactly what role bureaucrats
play in the policy-making process. Peter Self suggests that
'climate setting' and the identification of major objectives
are ministerial functions, but the role of T. K. Whitaker,
Secretary to the Department of Finance in the 1950s, in
promoting and organising the growth of state planning and
economic development shows that civil servants can, on

Ireland

occasion, make major contributions to policy initiation and
implementation.

Peter Pyne in an article entitled 'The bureaucracy in
the Irish Republic' suggests several ways in which the Irish
bureaucracy participates in and influences the political
system. First, the administration function may inevitably
involve policy formulation as the implementation of a policy
is not a simple application of rules but quite often
involves discretion in interpreting general rules to specific
cases. Secondly, the decisional function of the bureaurcracy
means that it increasingly makes decisions which count,
either by deciding what to recommend to a minister or by
deciding what he should attend to in terms of priority. This
is not to imply that ministers are at the total mercy of
their advisers, but the gatekeeper function of civil servants
is an important and influential one. The formulation and
preparation of measures requires the collection and appraisal
of data, the analysis of problems and the identification and
evaluation of possible courses of action, all of which are
the tasks of the bureaucracy. Thirdly, following on from
this the bureaucracy acts as a communication bridge between
the government and organised pressure groups and so acts as
an input channel into the formulation of policy. A large
part of the day-to-day contact of a senior official will be
with representatives of various pressure groups and
legitimated groups will be contacted as a matter of course
for their opinion on matters which involve their interests.
Fourthly, as a result of this contact with pressure groups,
the bureaucracy also exercises an aggregation or conflict
resolution function. Fifthly, bureaucrats exert a considerable indirect influence over the semi-state sector by their
representation of the boards of state-sponsored bodies and
the advice they tender to ministers as a result of these
contacts. Lastly, the growth of judicial functions in the
civil service, through the large number of tribunals that now
exist, means that decisions made by such bodies may affect
the implementation of existing policy and determine the shape
of future policies.

It can be seen from the foregoing analysis that the work
of the bureaucracy is so varied that it covers large areas
which might be deemed to be political rather than administrative, and that by the very nature of the tasks they carry out
civil servants, and especially senior ones, are inevitably
involved in policy-making at some stage or other. What is of
special interest in the analysis of policy-making in Ireland
is the small number of people who are involved in it. Chubb
has estimated that the total number of the proximate policy-
makers is 350-400, of whom 100-150 are senior civil servants.
The whole process is far from open and democratic, though
whether that is a criticism of the bureaucracy, the
politicians or the general culture is difficult to say. The

only way to change the situation would be for a government to
introduce legislation to eradicate the weaknesses, which would
actually have the effect of imposing more controls on itself
and creating better informed and more effective opponents.

It is no surprise to see that such reforms do not
command the immediate attention of political parties, except
when they are in opposition, and are resisted fiercely by
civil servants whenever they are proposed.

CONCLUSION

The origins of the Irish civil service lie in the British
administration which was set up to govern the country when it
was still a colony, and those roots have influenced the
subsequent development of the service. It inherited many of
the traits of the British service which were of great use in
the early days of the republic, when a measure of stability
and continuity was needed. Whether those same traits are as
useful in the present economic and social climate is an issue
which has been raised since the 1960s but which has yet to
reach a satisfactory conclusion.

The innate conservatism of bureaucracies is heightened
in Ireland by the basic values that pervade the society and
tend to encourage the preservation of secretive and closed
government. The small number of people involved in policy-
making adds to the rather claustrophobic and parochial
atmosphere that some have detected in the upper reaches of
the civil service. The conversion of senior staff to any
reform of the organisation has thus been severely hampered,
though it is probably true to say that this merely mirrors
the attitude of the majority of the population towards major
social change, as evidenced by the recent referendum on
divorce.

The reactions to the Devlin Report and the subsequent
work of the Department of Public Service in trying to
implement the reforms have highlighted several interesting
aspects of the central bureaucracy in Ireland. First, it has
illustrated the immense problems involved in trying to change
not only the structure, but also the concomitant attitudes,
in a large, well-established organisation. Secondly, it has
shown that the intertwining of political and administrative
functions is such that reform of one necessarily entails
reform of the other, and that unless this nettle is grasped,
no amount of departmental name changing and internal reorgan-
ising will bring about the desired improvements.

This leads on to the third facet of the bureaucracy, the
part played by role expectations in its work. The
expectation of the electorate that ministers will be know-
ledgeable and helpful about executive decisions affecting
individual citizens imposes severe demands on the civil

service, especially in terms of information processing and
retrieval, such that policy formulation becomes a minor
function even at senior levels of the service. Moreover, the
doctrine of ministerial responsibility imposes role demands on
the minister which his civil servants need to be constantly
aware of, and which severely affect the managerial responsibility and accountability of the departmental managers.
This role conflict seems to be inherent in the way jobs are
structured in the civil service and the move to implement the
Aireacht structure in all government departments is seen as a
way of reducing this conflict.

The state of the civil service in Ireland at the present
time is probably best described as unsettled after a long
period of gradual but unsystematic reform. Opinions range
from the pessimism of T. J. Barrington (1980: ch. 8) to the
relative optimism of Basil Chubb, who thought that by the
late 1970s the civil service 'had adapted or was in the
process of adapting to the needs of the time'. It had
adopted a more professional and modern approach to its work
and was gradually becoming more open, under the demands of a
modern welfare state and the constant prodding of the
judiciary. Membership of the Common Market had also forced
the bureaucracy to look beyond Britain to the mainland of
Europe, forcing wider horizons on departments and officials
whose perspective had previously stopped at the coast.

The processes of change and reform have affected the
Irish civil service as they have the bureaucracies of all
countries and shown that no matter how small or large the
state many of the problems are common and as insoluble in a
small state as in a large.

REFERENCES

Barrington, T. J. (1980) The Irish Administrative System,
  Dublin, Institute of Public Administration.

Bax, M. (1975) 'The political machine and its importance in
  the Irish Republic', Political Anthropology, 1, 6-20.

Chubb, B. (1963) 'Going about persecuting civil servants:
  the role of the Irish Parliamentary Representative',
  Political Studies, 11, 272-86.

Chubb, B. (1982) The Government and Politics of Ireland,
  London, Longman.

Chubb, B. (1983) A Source Book of Irish Government, Dublin,
  Institute of Public Administration.

Cohan, A. S. (1972) The Irish Political Elite, Dublin, Gill

and Macmillan.

Devlin Report (1969) <u>Report of the Public Services Organisation Review Group, 1966-69</u>, Dublin, Stationery Office.

Foggarty, M. (1984) <u>Irish Values and Attitudes</u>, Dublin, Dominican Publications

Garvin, T. (1974) 'Political cleavages, party politics and urbanisation in Ireland: the case of the periphery-dominated centre', <u>European Journal of Political Research</u>, 2, 302-27.

Gibbon, P. and Higgins, M. D. (1974) 'Patronage, tradition and modernisation: the case of the Irish "Gombeenman"', <u>The Economic and Social Review</u> 6 (1), 27-44.

Girvin, B. (1986) 'Social change and moral politics: the Irish constitutional referendum 1983', <u>Political Studies</u>, 34, 61-81.

Humphreys, A. J. (1966) <u>New Dubliners: Urbanisation and the Irish Family</u>, London, Routledge and Kegan Paul.

Kelly, D. (1979) 'The Public Service Reform Programme', <u>Administration</u>, 27(4), 399-407.

Kelly, J. M. (1984) <u>The Irish Constitution</u>, Dublin, Jurist Publishing.

Lee, J. (1982) 'Society and Culture', <u>Administration</u>, 30 (2/3), 1-18.

McDowell, R. B. (1964) <u>The Irish Administration 1801-1914</u>, London, Routledge and Kegan Paul.

Mathuna, S. O. (1955) 'The Christian Brothers and the civil service', <u>Administration</u>, 3 (2/3), 69-74.

Murphy, K. (1982) 'Raising productivity in the civil service', <u>Seirbhis Phoibli</u>, 3 (1) (Meitheamh 1982).

Office of the Ombudsman (1984) <u>The Report of the Ombudsman</u>, Dublin, Stationery Office.

Pyne, P. (1974) 'The bureaucracy in the Irish Republic: its political role and the factors influencing it', <u>Political Studies</u>, 22, 15-30.

Chapter 6

ITALY

R. E. Spence

HISTORY

The most striking feature of the civil service in Italy is its
remarkable continuity. Many of the characteristics of the
present civil service evolved during the period immediately
after unification and have endured, with only slight modifications, to the present day. Perhaps the most interesting fact
is that changes in political regime have had relatively little
impact upon the service. In the period 1921-3 and again in
1945-8 the political leadership of the country changed quite
radically but the structure and function of the service was,
by comparison, hardly changed at all. This is not intended
to imply that the civil service has not changed with the
expansion of government activity over the last century or so,
but rather that the changes which have occurred have been
gradual and have, on the whole, been independent of changes
in the political regime.
    The origins of the present civil service are to be found
in the structure created by Cavour when, in 1853, he introduced radical reform of the Piedmontese civil service, providing the first steps on the road to a 'constitutional bureaucracy'. Prior to the Cavour reforms the administration of the
state was divided between government ministries and special
agencies. The former were responsible for the administrative
management and the latter for economic management, or to put
it another way, the ministries had responsibility for the
direction of policy and not its execution, which was the responsibility of the special agencies. The intentions of the
reform were to unify the whole of the administrative system,
to place the ministries at the centre of the system and to
place government ministers at the apex of the structure. The
Cavour reform also introduced the role of secretary general
in order to provide a clear line of authority between the
bureaucrats and the politicians by co-ordinating and controlling their activities. The most important change with regard
to the creation of a 'constitutional bureaucracy' was that of

placing the activities of the ministries under the direct
supervision of Parliament.

Modifications were made to the structure created by
Cavour by another major reformer, Francesco Crispi. He abolished the position of secretary general and replaced it with
the office of under-secretary along the lines of the British
example of the parliamentary secretary. This was considered,
both then and now, to have been a mistake, since it left a
void between the political heads (the ministers) and the various divisions within the ministries. The gap was later to
be filled by the 'Directors General', a fact which has led to
a good deal of fragmentation inside the individual ministries
(see below).

Apart from the inevitable changes in the dimensions of
the civil service resulting from the rise of collectivism in
Italy, its basic structure has remained largely unaltered
right up to the present day.

Though the organisational model of the civil service has
changed little since the middle of the nineteenth century,
the dimensions of the service have changed dramatically. In
the years immediately after unification there were only seven
ministries, today there are 20. The period which witnessed
the greatest expansion was that which coincided with the
first world war, when the number of ministries increased from
11 to 16.

The growth of government in total can be judged from the
fact that immediately after unification the state employed
50,000 people. By 1910 the figure had risen to 376,777. By
1941 it had risen to a figure in excess of one million:
1,139,774. 1975 witnessed a total of almost two million:
1,995,834. The present figure is in excess of two million:
2,145,960. Obviously not all these are classified as civil
servants, since the total is made up of teachers, the military
workers employed by the central departments and the 'autonomous bodies'. The actual number of civil servants is about
861,126, of which 406,549 are employed by the central ministries and the rest by the autonomous bodies.

THE POLITICAL CULTURE

Bureaucracy does not exist in a vacuum. The degree to which
the bureaucracy can influence the political process is clearly
dependent upon the way in which the other principal actors
within the political system - Parliament, the Cabinet, political parties, interest groups, etc. - are able to create and
maintain their own sphere of action. Similarly, how these
bodies interrelate with the bureaucracy will be determined by
the nature of the political culture. Without entering into
the debate over the causal relationship between culture and
structure within the political system, there are without

doubt aspects of the Italian political culture which have had
a major influence on the Italian bureaucracy.

The problem that faces the student of modern Italy is one
of reconciling what he knows about modern Italy with what the
literature dealing with Italian political culture tells him.
After reading the literature one is left with the impression
that Italy has more in common with modern Lebanon than with
the more stable regimes of the rest of Western Europe.

If we accept the standard definition of political culture as being a complex of values, attitudes and beliefs towards politics which are accepted by the entire population, we
can say that though the Italian political culture is becoming
more homogeneous there are still quite significant subcultures
which influence the nature of the political process. Here we
shall concentrate upon what we might call the 'ideological
subcultures' and the influence of the uneven development
between the north and the south of Italy.

The ideological subcultures tend to manifest themselves
through three broad political traditions: the liberal, the
Catholic and the communist. The liberal subculture has, until
quite recently, been seen as the weakest of the three. There
appears to be widespread agreement amongst historians that,
unlike the situation in many other countries, the Italian
bourgeoisie never succeeded in creating a unified social
class. Instead it consisted of myriad conflicting groups
which reflected the many different interests which arose
within the process of industrialisation. Because of its
failure to establish a cultural hegemony over the emergent
state, the rise of working-class and socialist organisations
left the bourgeoisie in an almost total state of paralysis.
The lay liberals left the defence of the state against
socialism firstly to the Catholic organisations and, when
they failed, to the fascists.

At the foundation of the state the term 'lay' referred to
the liberals' anti-Catholic stance; in other words, their
opposition to the increasing Catholic domination of the
state's affairs. In more recent times the term has taken on
a much broader meaning and has come to denote a stance not
just in opposition to the principles of Catholicism but
against those of the communist 'church' also. The Communist
Party (PCI) in Italy is considered to many within the lay
culture to be tied to ideological constructions and administrative practices which reproduce the coercive mechanisms of
the Catholic Church (Rusconi 1981). The modern epithet 'lay'
has come to denote modern 'progressive' values which fall
outside the ambit of the two dominant subcultures of Catholicism and communism. In organisation terms the liberal/lay
culture finds expression in the small centre parties such as
the increasingly conservative Socialist Party (PSI), the
Social Democratic Party (PSDI), the Republican Party (PRI)
and the Liberal Party (PLI).

The Catholic subculture has undergone a whole series of changes since the foundation of the Italian state. From an initial position in which the Church's hierarchy refused to recognise the very existence of the state, the Catholic Church has, through its various organisations, come to dominate much of the state apparatus. The Catholic subculture is concerned with the ideal of the family and lessening the impact of class conflict through lessening the impact of capitalist competition and thereby eroding the support for socialism. The first and clearest exposition of the Church's position is to be found in the papal encyclical of 1892 entitled 'Rerum Novarum'. Despite recent updating its fundamental principles remain the same.

Whilst the Christian Democratic Party (DC) has been the one to give high priority to the concerns of the Church it would be a mistake to totally equate the party with the Catholic subculture, since many Catholics do not support it and many non-Catholics do. Over recent years, due to the setbacks it experienced in the referendums on divorce and abortion, the party has been attempting to present itself as a mass conservative party which speaks for, though is not dominated by, the Church. Many people believe that the existence of a non-Italian Pope has helped the party adapt itself to an increasingly secular society.

The Marxist subculture increasingly finds its expression in the PCI. The other heir to the socialist tradition, the PSI, has in recent years been abandoning the socialist subculture and become more a party of the petit-bourgeoisie. The PCI has, since the second world war, given expression to both the urban and rural socialist traditions. It finds its major areas of support in the 'red-belt', the agricultural centre of the country. During the 1960s and particularly the early 1970s the party's support grew rapidly in many areas, especially the south, bringing the party a share of power in many of Italy's large urban centres. Though the party is the main vehicle of working-class protest, its support is by no means confined to the working class. Its expansion in the late 1960s and early 1970s was largely due to increased support from amongst the middle classes.

The PCI has in recent years been going through an identity crisis. Its commitment to the 'Italian road to socialism' has involved the party in making a number of compromises. The party leadership has for some years been stressing its attachment to the social democratic traditions of Western Europe in an attempt to divest itself of its more 'authoritarian' images. Whether the party will be able to make such changes and avoid factionalism, so much a part of the life of the other parties, is a matter of opinion.

The division of the Italian political culture into these three broad subcultures hides much important detail. Many authors prefer to stress the dualism of Italian political

culture, emphasising the gap between the progressive culture
of the north with its northern European influences, and the
backward south, with its Mediterranian influences. Here the
contrast is drawn between the advanced north, where political
advancement is made on the basis of achievement, where universal rules are followed in judging the rights of individuals
before government agencies and time-honoured customs and traditions are easily set aside, and the south which is viewed
as being dominated by particularistic and ascriptive attitudes in its political and administrative practices, and where
family ties are more important than personal achievement.
These aspects of the culture cut across those outlined above,
creating an even more complex and fragmented picture. This
image of the southern culture is something of a caricature
since the south has changed dramatically in recent years.
Nevertheless, the relative economic backwardness of the south,
as we shall see, does have a disproportionate effect on bureaucratic behaviour, since it is from the south that the majority of bureaucrats are drawn (see below).

THE EXECUTIVE

The fragmented nature of the Italian political culture
described above has had a profound effect on the nature of the
Italian parties and through them on the executive. In many
ways the divisions represented in the political culture are
magnified by the Italian electoral system. Based on the
principle of strict proportionality, the electoral system
ensures that even the very smallest parties have parliamentary
representation. There are very rarely fewer than 10 parties
represented in Parliament and often as many as 11 or 12. As
a consequence of this, coalition government is the norm.
  Italian governments are notoriously unstable. Since
1948, the year of the first election held under the new constitution, Italy has had no fewer than 49 different governments, each lasting on average about ten months. However,
one should not accept such figures at face value, since much
of the instability is more apparent than real. It is not an
insignificant fact, for example, that one party, the DC, has
played a dominant role in every post-war government. It has
likewise provided, on all but four occasions, the Prime Minister, and has sought to ensure that certain key ministries
are allocated to the party, such as Agriculture, the Interior
Ministry and the Treasury.
  Closer scrutiny of the personnel who make up the Cabin
ets also reveals a good measure of continuity, with the same
names appearing time after time. Alcide De Gasperi, for
example, was Prime Minister on no fewer than eight occasions.
Likewise, Moro, Rumor and Andreotti have each held the post
on five occasions. To give an individual example of the

longevity an Italian politician can enjoy, Giulio Andreotti
has been in the government for each of the last 29 years.

The Italian coalition system has often been likened to a
game of musical chairs, but there is one significant difference: in the Italian example the number of chairs remains the
same, with the result that there is a great deal of movement
but very little change.

The instability of the Italian coalitions has given rise
to a number of explanatory models, not to mention a whole new
political vocabulary. The Italian mass media is replete with
terms such as centre-right, centre-left, organic centre,
convergence, limited-spectrum, enlarged-sprectrum, total-
spectrum and so on. The formula at the time of writing is
the pentapartito or five-party coalition comprising the DC,
PSI, PSDI, PLI and PRI.

The two models which have dominated academic debate more
than any others were developed by Sartori and Galli in the
1960s (Galli 1966, Sartori 1966). The model developed by
Sartori is the now famous one of 'polarised pluralism'. This
is quite complex and describes a situation in which a plural-
ity of parties are involved in a form of 'centrifugal competition'. The essential features of the model are:

1. a highly polarised political system in which the gap
   between the left and the right is great;
2. the existence of a large number of parties represented in
   Parliament;
3. the existence of one or more political parties permanantly
   occupying the centre of the political spectrum;
4. the existence of anti-system parties;
5. the dominance of centripetal tendencies within party competition as manifested by irresponsibility of the anti-
   system opposition and immobilism and factionalism within
   the centre parties.

Sartori contrasts the model of polarised pluralism with those
of moderate and simple pluralism. In the latter there are
not the extremes formed by anti-system parties. A form of
centripetal politics emerges in which the parties seek to
occupy the centre ground of politics. In the case of polarised pluralism the centre is either vacated, as in Weimar
Germany or Fourth Republic France, or becomes an arena in
which small factional parties produce an almost total political immobilism, as in Italy's case.

The model has come in for a good deal of criticism in
recent years, partly because it has been overtaken by events.
Whilst the immobilism and factionalism of the centre remains,
the PCI can no longer be seriously considered as the 'anti-
system party' the model requires. The PCI, as we have already
noted, has undergone a process of 'social-democratisation' in
recent years to the extent that many people believe it to

have become little more than a 'catch-all' party, willing to
make any compromise necessary to gain votes.

The Galli model of 'imperfect bi-partism' concentrates
upon this change in the Communist Party's image and highlights the increasingly bi-polar nature of the party system
as witnessed by the increasingly dominant position of the two
largest parties, the DC and PCI. The system is referred to
as 'imperfect bi-partism', because, unlike the situation in
either Britain or West Germany, there is no alternation of
government. Instead one pole of the system, the DC, is able
to stay in office thanks to the efforts of the small centre
parties. The exclusion of the communists from government has
now more to do with tactical than ideological considerations,
since the smaller centre parties gain a good deal from the
status quo. The result is a 'blocked democracy' in which
there is no mechanism for punishing or rewarding parties on
the basis of their achievements or failures.

Both models serve to highlight certain aspects of the
Italian political culture and party system, but neither is
able to explain the full complexities of the situation. A
slightly more eccentric view of the instability of Italian
coalitions is that which views government collapses as being
beneficial to the political system and the only way in which
government can be disciplined. This view overlooks two
important facts; first, that the same coalition tends to re-
emerge after a crisis and secondly, that government crises
are often the result of factional infighting and not disputes
over public policy.

Executive power in Italy is fragmented amongst a large
number of separate centres of power. The Prime Minister in
Italy does not enjoy the power and prestige afforded to his
British counterpart. This is despite the fact that the
constitution clearly states in Article 95 that 'the president
of the council conducts, and is responsible for, the general
policy of the government' and that, 'he maintains unity in
general political and administrative policy, and promotes and
co-ordinates the activities of the ministers'. In reality
the Prime Minister is hostage to powers which lie well outside his control. All Cabinet ministers owe their position
to a number of factors amongst which are:

1. the strategic position of their party of origin. The more
   central the party is to the coalition formula being used,
   the greater is the number of ministries to which the
   party can lay claim;
2. their own position within the party, that is, whether
   they are leaders of the dominant 'correnti' or faction;
3. their region of origin, since, like the situation in
   Canada, each region of the country must find expression
   within the Cabinet. In other words the Prime Minister's
   role in forming the Cabinet is extremely limited.

In general Cabinet members are drawn from Parliament,
but there are occasions, such as when a government crisis is
proving difficult to resolve, when 'experts' are co-opted.
However, in a country where party considerations are of paramount importance, these occasions are extremely rare.

Italian Cabinets tend to be unwieldy instruments for
policy formulation for two reasons. First, within the
Italian constitution there is no distinction made between
ministers within the Cabinet and those outside, as is the
practice in the British political system. Article 95 estab-
lishes the principle of collegiality between all ministers.
Secondly, there is a political difficulty in reducing the
size of the Cabinet, which stems from the need to ensure the
parties as much government representation as is possible.
Alongside the ministers who are departmental heads, there are
a number of ministers without portfolio. The legitimacy of
such appointments has been questioned by a number of constitutional lawyers who argue that since they are not specifically mentioned by the constitution, unlike the departmental
heads, they are unconstitutional. Despite such opinions the
practice of creating ministers without portfolio has been
common to every post-war administration. Under recent administrations ministers without portfolio have been allocated
the tasks of civil protection, regional affairs, the co-
ordination of European Community policy, technology and
scientific research, ecology and relationships with Parliament. Italian Cabinets rarely, if ever, contain fewer than
30 members.

In 1983 the practice was established of creating an
'inner cabinet' or consiglio di gabinetto consisting of the
Prime Minister, the Deputy Prime Minister and seven ministers.
Though the seven most important ministries are represented
(Foreign, Budget, Treasury, Defence, Industry and Labour),
the major consideration in determining membership is the
minister's role in representing his party in the coalition.
The first such inner cabinet contained the party secretaries
in the case of the minor parties and four important leaders
of the DC (the secretary of the DC refused to take part).
The inner cabinet's role is that of setting the direction of
the government and warding off possible coalition breakdown
by gaining the prior approval of the party secretaries to
policy initiatives. In this respect it has almost replaced
the Cabinet as the major decision-making forum. Although in
recent years there has been a slight strengthening in the
power of the Italian Prime Minister, the style of government
remains neither prime ministerial nor cabinet government, but
government by ministries. The level of co-ordination between
ministries is often woefully inadequate and individual
ministries consider attempts by other ministries to affect
their policy as unwarranted meddling. It is also not
uncommon for conflicts between ministries to become personal

attacks by ministers on each other. The Prime Minister's
ability to discipline such behaviour is limited, given the
fact that the ministers owe their position to external power
sources. An attempt to discipline the minister may result in
the withdrawal of his party's support for the coalition and
produce a government crisis.

The role of the Cabinet is also somewhat reduced by a
'leakage' of some of its functions to outside bodies. These
public bodies, though connected with the ministries, enjoy a
good deal of autonomy in decision-making and absorb not
insignificant amounts of departmental finances. Almost every
ministry has at least one such body. The Ministry of
Commerce for example has the ICE – The Institute for Foreign
Trade. The Ministry of Labour's responsibility for pensions
is carried out in the main by INPS – The National Institute
for Social Insurance. Apart from those which undertake
functions on behalf of single ministries there are also
others which perform an inter-ministerial function such as
CIP (the Interministerial Committee on Prices), CIPE (the
Interministerial Committee for Economic Planning), and CPD
(the Supreme Council of Defence). The existence of these
bodies and the independence of the individual ministers serve
to weaken the Cabinet's position as the major forum for
policy-making.

STRUCTURE

The Ministries

The number and internal organisation of the ministries is
rigidly determined by law, as is the role of the civil
servants working within them. The highly legalistic environment stems from the tradition of the stato di diritto (state
based upon law) in which the organisations and individuals
who exercise public powers are subject to the tightest possible legal controls.

The ministries themselves are a very heterogeneous group.
Half employ fewer than 5,000 people. The five smallest have
fewer than 500 employees. The Ministry of Education, the
largest, employs about 50 per cent of all state employees.
The ministries and their areas of concern are as follows:

ORDER
Foreign Affairs
Defence
Interior
Justice

ECONOMIC ISSUES
Finance

Treasury
Budget and Economic Planning
Agriculture and Forestry
Trade and Industry
Labour and Social Security
Foreign Trade
State Holdings

INFRASTRUCTURE
Public Works
Transport
Merchant Shipping
Post and Telecommunications

SOCIAL AND CULTURAL
Public Education
Health
Tourism and Entertainment
Culture and Environmental Heritage

Unlike the situation in many other countries there has
been no move in Italy towards creating amalgamated ministries.
Instead the number of ministries has increased to keep pace
with the growth of government, with the result that Italy has
more ministries than most other comparable democracies.
Unfortunately the growth in the number of ministries has not
been paralleled by a similar rationalisation of functions.
The examples of overlapping responsibility are legion.
Italy's attempt to form a coherent energy policy, for example,
is severely hindered by the fact that responsibility for
energy matters is shared between State Holdings and Budget
and Economic Planning. Similarly, responsibility for financial policy is shared between the Ministries of Finance and
Budget and of Economic Planning. The possibilities for con-
fusion are clearly demonstrated if one considers the fact
that 25 divisions (see below) of the Ministry of Industry, 16
of the Treasury and six each of the Ministries of Finance and
Trade and Industry have responsibility for foreign affairs.
Considered against the background of the lack of 'collegiality' of Italian Cabinets the consequences of such fragmentation can be quite alarming as demarcation disputes between
ministries delay the application of legislation (Cassese
1983).

Another factor to which the structure of the ministries
has not responded has been the devolution over recent years
of many functions to the organs of regional and local government. Yet the ministries have remained unscathed. They have
done so because of the vital role they play within the coalition system. Without the 20 ministries the political parties
would have no vehicles for their game of party and factional
politics.

The Internal Structure of the Ministries

The internal organisation of the ministries appears to be based upon a principle of maximum fragmentation. Each ministry is divided into functional directorates of which there are more than a hundred throughout the 20 ministries. The smaller ministries such as the Budget contain three such directorates; some of the larger ones, such as the Ministry of Finance, contain 12 or more. Each of the directorates is headed by a director general. The fragmentation, however, does not end there. Each directorate is further subdivided into 'divisions', presided over by the head of division, and each division further subdivided into sections, each with its own sectional head.

With the exception of the Ministries of Defence and Foreign Affairs, the co-ordination of the activities of the various divisions is left rather vague. Within the Defence and Foreign Affairs Ministries a post of secretary general has been maintained in order to co-ordinate activities. Elsewhere the lack of such a co-ordinating role leads to a good deal of uncertainty and overlapping of function between the sections and, as we have already observed, between sections in different ministries. Some co-ordination is carried out by the under-secretaries, but this in itself can be problematical, as they are drawn from different parties within the coalition and inter-party rivalries between them are not uncommon. The growth of ministerial cabinets on the lines of the French model has provided some opportunities for greater co-ordination, but the overall pattern remains one of uncertainty.

Much of the work undertaken by the ministries is devolved to units of field administration. Prior to the creation of the regional governments, 14 of the 20 ministries had had field agencies at the regional, provincial and communal level. The only ministry to lose all its decentralised agencies to the regions has been the Ministry of Agriculture. The degree of decentralisation varies from ministry to ministry. The Ministry of the Interior has 84 per cent of its personnel located at the periphery, the Ministry of Labour 87 per cent, the Ministry of Education 88 per cent (the vast majority of whom are the teachers). The least decentralised is the Ministry of Health, with about 18 per cent of its personnel at the periphery (the figure is so low because health care since the 1978 reform is the responsibility of the regions and local health authorities, the Unita Sanitaria Locale).

The decentralisation of the ministries has led to its own problems. The ministries have tended to decentralise their tasks in a highly incremental fashion and without reference to the decentralising activities of the other ministries. As a result there is a great deal of overlap of responsibilities, not just amongst the ministries, but

between the ministries and the units of local government.
Attempts to create a body capable of co-ordinating the activities of the ministries at the periphery have so far come to
nothing.

No description of the Italian administrative system
would be complete without an account of the system of
'parallel administration'. The system takes two different
forms, the network of 'autonomous administration' and public
boards or enti pubblici.

There are five autonomous agencies, all of which are
separated from normal administration in order to subject them
to market pressures and limit ministerial intervention. In
reality their relationship to the central departments is not
dissimilar to that of the public corporations in Britain.
The five autonomous administrations are:

Administration of State Monopolies
State Railways
National Road Building Agency
Post and Telecommunications
State Agency for Telephone Services

The last two of these agencies, both of which are under the
control of the Post and Telecommunications Ministry, perform
almost all the ministry's functions.

It is, however, the existence of the enti pubblici that
more than anything else distinguishes the Italian administrative system from that of its European neighbours. The system
is very complex, so much so that there is a good deal of disagreement as to just how many such organisations exist. Some
estimates have put the figure as high as 60,000, though this
includes those which also come under the tutelage of the
local authorities. For those under the direct supervision of
the ministries the figure has been estimated to be around
40,000. The enti pubblici differ enormously in size, legal
status and in the functions they perform.

Some, like the Istituto Nazionale per la Previdenza
Sociale (INPS), are responsible for the provision of public
services, in this case the administration of the state
pension system. Others, such as the Ente Nazionale per
l'Energia Electrica (ENEL), which has a monopoly on the production and supply of electricity, perform an essentially
entrepreneurial function. By far the largest in this category
is the Istituto per la Ricostruzione Industriale (IRI), which
owes its origins to the crisis of 1929 when the banking col-
lapse forced the government to take over the banks, and with
them a vast proportion of Italian industry.

Apart from these high-profile bodies there are a large
number of other, much smaller ones, dealing with welfare
services, educational and cultural affairs, sport, leisure
and so on. There is almost no area of Italian life which is

not influenced by one or more of the enti pubblici.

The obvious question which comes to mind is: why have successive governments chosen to create these organs of 'parallel administration' rather than grant the services they perform to the central administration proper? Part of the answer lies in the reluctance of governments to tackle the problem of bureaucratic reform head on, choosing instead to by-pass the normal bureaucratic apparatus and to set up new bodies for new tasks. The enormous growth of the enti pubblici in the early 1950s was due in no small measure to the desire of the Christian Democratic regime to prevent the responsibility for major acts of reconstruction being thwarted by a bureaucracy which was at best inefficient and at worst hostile to the very essence of democratic procedures. One can see ample evidence for both these views if one looks at the debates preceding the creation of the (recently abolished) Casa per il Mezzogiorno, the body charged with the industrial-isation of the south of Italy.

With the passage of time the enti pubblici came to form part of the Christian Democratic regime's system of political patronage. Both existing and new bodies were created to pro-vide jobs for the regime's supporters, and to buy electoral support through public works and welfare projects. Very few appointments were made to, or services provided by, the enti pubblici without party consideration being paramount (Serrani 1979).

THE BUREAUCRATS

In 1980 the number of people directly employed by the central ministries amounted to 1,692,683, excluding those involved in the 'autonomous agencies'. Of this figure, by far the largest group is that formed by the teaching profession, as can be seen from the list below.

Teachers	881,978
Civil Servants	383,329
Armed Forces	340,241
Manual Workers	43,336
Others	37,036
The Judiciary	7,673

Since 1956 the civil servants have been divided into four categories: carriera direttiva, carriera di concetto, carriera esecutiva and carriera ausiliaria. The first three categories are roughly similar to the administrative, execu-tive and clerical classes of the British civil service. The fourth is made up of manual occupations. A reform of 1972 further divided the carriera direttiva into three managerial categories: primo dirigente, dirigente superiore and diregente generale. The importance of the 1972 reform lay in the fact that it was the first attempt to create a new class of 'managers' at the apex of the service, as well as attempting to include the top civil servants in the decision-making process (see below).

Of the 383,329 civil servants about 6,700 are members of the administrative class. The higher echelons of the civil service remain a predominently male preserve. The proportion of women employed in the administrative class in the Ministry of the Interior, for example, is about 15 per cent and it is considered to be one of the more egalitarian ministries as far as the sexes are concerned.

One of the most striking features of Italian administration, at every level, is the extent to which the personnel are of predominantly southern extraction. Immediately after unification in 1861, the administrative apparatus of the newly created state was dominated by civil servants drawn mainly from the Piedmont ruling class. This situation remained unaltered until the first decade of the twentieth century, largely due to the lack of a strong administrative culture in the other states. By the 1930s the picture had changed dramatically, to the extent that over 50 per cent of the administrative class were now of southern extraction, with about 30 per cent originating from the central regions and less than 20 per cent from the north.

Table 6.1 shows the relationship between the number of civil servants drawn from the three regions and their populations as a percentage of the whole.

TABLE 6.1 Population and origin of civil servants by region (all figures are percentages)

Region	Population	Civil Servants	Direttiva	Concetto	Esecutiva
North	44	37	19	34	41
Centre	18	20	21	21	21
South	36	42	59	43	37

Source: Cassese (1977)

The table also demonstrates that the percentage of the personnel who are of southern extraction increases as one moves up the organisational hierarchy.

The reasons for the predominance of personnel of southern extraction within the administrative system are to be found in the relative economic backwardness of the south. Only fairly recently has Italian industry developed any base in the south but the gap between the north and the south has, if anything, continued to grow. The north is still the main producer of wealth and the south the main consumer. The consequences of this fact are that the main avenue open to those seeking employment in the south is the public sector. What is the first resort for the southerner is the last resort for their more fortunate countrymen in the north, since there are more highly paid and more prestigious openings in the industrial and commercial sectors.

The predominance of administrators of southern extraction has had, in the opinion of most observers of the Italian bureaucracy, a quite profound effect upon the nature of the service. The problems originate in the clash between the 'two cultures'. First, the fact that, until quite recently, the south was a basically agrarian society has meant that most administrators lack what one might define as an 'industrial mentality'. Secondly, there is an absence in Italy of what has been loosely defined as a tradition of public service, something which is said to be particularly strong in Britain and France. Research carried out in the 1960s by ISAP amongst the top administrators discovered that over 50 per cent of respondents to a questionnaire stated that their criteria for choosing public service as a career were either the lack of any alternative, or job security. The average bureaucrat is protected by a multitude of legally enforcable guarantees which render the matching of personnel to administrative needs almost impossible.

RECRUITMENT

Recruitment procedure within the civil service is surrounded by a highly complex series of legal regulations, the most fundamental of which was created by the constitution. Article 97 of the constitution stipulates that all appointments to the service should be made on the basis of open competition except in those cases laid down by law. The principle was established as part of a system of legal guarantees surrounding public service in order to ensure the recruitment of the most able candidates and to liberate the procedure from political interference.

The entry procedure consists of a series of written or oral examinations organised by the individual ministry and carriera for which the posts are available. The competitions for posts are advertised in a government publication known as the Official Gazette. The whole process is extremely long and tortuous. It is not uncommon for a period of three years to elapse between the announcement of the competition and the final results. The highly legalistic nature of the procedures leaves no room for the assessment of the candidates' personality or motivation.

To gain access to the competitions certain educational standards must have been reached, varying according to the carriera for which the candidate is applying. Access to

positions in the carriera direttiva is granted by way of a
university degree (in some cases with an added professional
qualification) or by having reached the top of the carriera
di concetto. Entrants to the latter must possess the
maturita or school leaving certificate, though over recent
years the increase in graduate unemployment has led to a
situation in which a large proportion of this class are also
graduates.

The inefficiency of the whole recruitment procedure means
that it is difficult for the administrative apparatus to
respond in a flexible way to the needs of efficient administration. Despite all the constitutional and legal safeguards
the recruitment procedure is not free from 'extraneous'
influences. The examiners enjoy a good deal of discretion in
making appointments, and pressure from above leads to that
discretion being used to particularistic ends. Though difficult to quantify, most civil servants believe this to be the
case. The research undertaken by ISAP demonstrated that over
50 per cent of members of the carriera direttiva believed the
recruitment procedure to be partial and over 60 per cent considered it inappropriate for the selection of the most able
candidates (ISAP 1965).

CAREER PATTERNS

There is no equivalent in Italy of the British civil service
commission, so that recruitment to the service is undertaken
on a departmental basis. Apart from adding to the ineffi-
ciencies indicated above, it also exacerbates the degree of
compartmentalisation to be found within the civil service
structure. Once employed by a particular department it is
very rare for a civil servant to move across departmental
boundaries. Until the creation of the regional governments
there was also a high degree of 'geographical compartmentalisation', little movement between the central departments and
the field agencies and vice versa.

These staffing rigidities have quite a severe impact
upon the efficiency of the service. Compartmentalisation has
led to a good deal of hostility and suspicion between departments, which often results in inter-departmental conflicts.
It has created enormous difficulties in transferring staff to
parts of the service where they are most needed and has
encouraged the development of quite powerful clientelistic
relationships between departments and interest groups within
their constituency. The only exception to this trend is the
transfer of top civil servants to the organs of 'parallel
administration', which are made on the basis of political
patronage and contribute more to the political manoeuvring of
the parties than to the dictates of administrative efficiency.

The job security which the Italian civil servant enjoys

is paid for at the expenses of his salary. Compared to his
European counterparts the Italian public administrator is
very badly paid. Whilst it is difficult to make direct
comparisons between the public and private sector employees,
the former are paid about one-third of the salaries of those
employed in broadly similar tasks in the latter. Whilst not
the only cause of the 'meridionalisation' of the bureaucracy,
the greater opportunities available to northern graduates
does help to perpetuate the process.

In recent years a serious effort has been made to improve
the quality of the higher civil service by expanding the role
of the Higher School of Public Administration (Scuola Superiore della Pubblica Amministrazione). The school has four
centres in Rome, Bologna, Reggio Calabria and Caserta and
makes use of the most respected teachers of public administration in Italy and Europe. The school provides in-post
training for members of the direttiva and dirigente. The
subject matter of the courses is of both a specialist and
generalist nature and includes a period of 'placement' in
other ministries and public agencies. A large part of the
school's resources are taken up by the provision of
recruitment courses which provide direct access for
university graduates into the direttiva. Entrants, who have
to be in the final year of their university study, gain
access to the school through a competitive examination and
are financed through grants made available by the school
itself. Recruitment through the school breaks the traditional
practice of recruitment by ministry. It is hoped that this
will resolve some of the problems of sectionalism and compartmentalisation described above. The school is seen by its
supporters as a long-term investment in the future, and as
such its effects are only just beginning to be felt.

ACCOUNTABILITY AND CONTROL

Accountability

Unlike the situation in many other countries Italy does not
place much importance on Parliament as an instrument for the
control of the bureaucracy. Instead the citizen is protected
against arbitrary government by a system of legal guarantees
which are enshrined within the constitution. As a result,
such parliamentary conventions as the collective and individual responsibility of ministers, so important to the British
system of government, are totally alien to the Italian political system. In any case, the functioning of the Italian
political system does not lend itself to such essentially
political practices. As we have already seen, ministers in
Italy owe their position within the government to a complex
system of coalition bargaining reflecting the strengths of the

parties and their factions and not to the confidence of Parliament as such. This gives the ministers a good deal of
protection, since any attempt to remove them may threaten a
delicately balanced coalition. Equally, the concept of collective responsibility only has any meaning if there is an
alternative to the government which has resigned. Because of
the restricted 'arc' from which government coalitions are
chosen and the rigidity of Italian voting patterns, the
chances of a government being 'punished' at the polls are
almost nil.

Another factor which separates the Italian Parliament
from many others with regard to the control of the executive
is its almost total lack of any real control over public
expenditure. Budgets are usually presented to a half-empty
assembly because, as estimates of government expenditure,
they are almost totally meaningless. Most government expenditure is predetermined by individual pieces of legislation
and the expenditure of the regions, provinces, communes and
many para-state organisations does not appear in the budget
estimates at all. The expenditure that does appear within
the budget is usually expressed in such vague terms as to be
almost useless. The task of presenting a budget that conforms
to reality is rendered more difficult by the fact that much
of the money allocated is never spent, so that individual
ministries build up massive passive reserves with the
consequent possibilities of malpractice. On the occasions
when parliamentarians do become preoccupied with the budget
they become so in order to protect particular clientelistic
interests rather than the broader general interest. Despite
the fact that Parliament is equipped with a large array of
standing committees their impact upon the executive and administration is slight.

Political Control

It is often argued that the similarity of backgrounds between
the political and administrative elites in countries like
Britain and France ensures a kind of meeting of minds, or
esprit de corps, over what one might define as the rules of
the game, the assumption being that regular contacts diminish
the possibility of the bureaucrats assuming too much power.
Whatever the merits of such an argument, the literature on
Italy would appear to suggest that such a meeting of minds
does not exist between the two branches of the Italian state.

The image of the Italian civil servant which emerged
from research undertaken in the late 1960s was one of
'...legalistic, illiberal, elitist, hostile to the usage and
practice of pluralist politics, fundamentally undemocratic'
(Putman 1975). The research which led Putman to these conclusions was carried out at a time when most leading positions

in the civil service would have been occupied by civil servants who formed their political attitudes during the fascist
period. As Putman himself observed, these officials will by
now have succumed to the 'ineluctable biological processes'
and will have been replaced by officials who have learned
their craft in a more democratic climate.

If the present administrative elite do now share with
their political masters a more democratic outlook on life
there still does not appear to have occurred the desired
meeting of minds. On the contrary there would appear to be
an enormous cultural gap between the personnel of the two
careers. First, the 'meridionalisation' of the bureaucracy
means that the members of the administrative elite are more
than twice as likely to originate from the south than are the
political elite. This is said to produce a conflict between
the legalistic culture of the southern civil servant and the
industrial culture of the politicians. Secondly, there is
almost no 'cross-fertilisation' between the two elites. In
contrast to their European neighbours in France where movement
from one role to the other is quite common, or in Germany
where 26 per cent of post-war ministers began their careers
as civil servants, no such 'osmosis' occurs in Italy. As a
consequence few ministers understand the problems of the
civil service and vice versa.

The clash of cultures between the two elites gives rise
to a situation in which the administrative elite places more
importance on career and job security than providing an efficient service to the public. The administrators are constantly
trying to shield themselves from political interference in
order to guarantee the predictability of their career
patterns.

The politicians, for their part, conform to the wishes
of the administrators in order to keep the administrative
machine working. The clearest example of this is the
politicians' aquiescence to the seniority rule, in which the
length of service of an administrator is more important for
promotion than qualifications or expertise.

In this way a modus vivendi is worked out between the
two elites in which the administrators exchange power for
security and the politicians exchange autonomy for loyalty
(Cassese 1983).

One indirect control which the politicians have over the
administrators is simply that of ignoring them. We have
already seen how successive governments have sought to circum-
vent the normal administrative process by way of the creation
of 'parallel' organisations in the form of the enti pubblici.
Another practice which has become increasingly important is
the creation of ministerial cabinets along the lines of the
French model. Their job is to help formulate policy and
provide direction to the work of the ministry. In so doing
they further limit the power of the administrators and

increase the powers of patronage open to ministers.

It is also true to say that one of the major reasons why the political elite has failed to control their administrative counterparts is due to the ephemeral nature of the governing coalitions. It is difficult to stamp one's will on a department when one is constantly looking over one's shoulder to see from where the next government crisis is coming.

Legal Control

The absence of strong political control over the bureaucracy places an even larger burden upon the system of legal protection than otherwise might be the case. Two major and quite separate institutions are at the apex of a system of legal safeguards against bureaucratic malpractice. The Corte dei Conti is the watchdog of public spending and the Consiglio di Stato provides a system of safeguards for the ordinary citizen.

The Corte dei Conti (the Court of the Exchequer) is responsible for a number of matters. Article 100 of the constitution states that it '...exercises preventative control on the legitimacy of government measures and successive control over the management of the budget'. Its preventative controls are aimed at ensuring the legality of proposed legislation. Its controls are particularly tight over presidential decrees which, because of their emergency nature, may not receive the careful drafting which will make them conform to the law.

The control of the court starts with the transmission of a piece of legislation from the sponsoring department to the court. If the legislation is properly drafted and in accordance with the law it is stamped and registered. If on the other hand irregularities are discovered it is sent back with its observations. The minister must then return it to the department for amendment or he can reject the court's verdict and leave it to Parliament to decide its legitimacy.

The court's major responsibility concerns the control of public expenditure; any organisation which is responsible for the utilisation of public funds falls under the court's jurisdiction. The court's workload has increased at the same rate as public expenditure has increased. It is, however, doubtful whether the court's facilities and practices have changed to enable it to keep pace with its workload.

The court's jurisdiction concerns both what we might call micro and macro issues. In the former it concerns itself with administrative justice on behalf of the individual, hears cases involving the mis-appropriation of funds by officials and cases involving such items as the pension rights of individuals. At the macro level it is involved in the task of deciding on the financial probity and legality of the whole of central government transactions.

In its capacity of controlling public expenditure the
court is directly responsible to Parliament. Unfortunately,
the relationship between the two bodies is not always harm-
onious. Quite often the court, in its annual report to
Parliament, has to condemn practices which Parliament itself
has initiated.

The Consiglio di Stato (the Council of State) is in fact
a constitutional court exercising four broad powers:

1. it judges the constitutionality of state and regional
   laws, and any act having the force of law;
2. it is the final arbiter in conflicts between the top constitutional organs of the national government, between the
   state and the regional governments and between regions;
3. it has the power to pass judgement on impeachments;
4. it decides on the admissability of referendums.

The court has become one of the most prestigious and highly
respected organs of the Italian state. In attempting to make
the law of the land conform to the spirit of the constitution
it has done a great deal to protect the ordinary citizen from
abuses of power and maladministration.

In comparison with some other European countries, Italy
is backward with regard to the establishment of a specifically
administrative form of redress. Some of the regional governments are experimenting with a form of ombudsman to protect
their citizens from unnecessary administrative delays and
inertia. Proposals for the creation of an ombudsman at the
national level have been made, but little has so far come of
them.

POLICY-MAKING

Many of the factors mentioned above concerning the separation
of politicians from civil servants obviously have a quite
profound effect upon policy-making. The top civil servants
in Italy are not entrusted with the same responsibilities as
their French or British counterparts. Italian civil servants
play at best a secondary role in the policy-making process,
and very often no role at all. The key role is played by the
increasingly important ministerial cabinets. The modern
Italian minister will surround himself with often as many as
a hundred advisers drawn from both the public and private
sectors. The creation of the ministerial cabinets serves to
further widen the divide between the top departmental
officials and their ministers. There are numerous stories,
not always apocryphal, of officials who have not seen their
own departmental minister for as many as four years.

Though the civil service lacks a dominant role in the
making of policy it does have a quite profound impact later

on. According to Cassese the civil service takes its revenge
upon policy-makers by acting as a brake upon policy implementation. Its ability to delay the implementation of legislation is notorious. One of the reasons for the build-up of
passive reserves within the bureaucracy is the failure of the
bureaucracy to implement legislation.

It would be a mistake to assume that the higher civil
service in Italy does not contain people of a very high
quality. There are a large number of top civil servants with
status at the national and international level on a par with
those of any other country. The problem is that there are
not enough of them to have an impact upon the nature of their
departments or they are pulled out of the ministries to run
other state organisations.

CONCLUSION

That the civil service in Italy is in urgent need of reform
is widely accepted right across the Italian political spectrum. Yet, despite this acceptance, a radical reform of the
service is still a long way off. The failure to reform the
service is certainly not due to a lack of understanding of
the problems, nor is it due to a failure to provide workable
solutions. In the last decade or so there have been numerous
commissions of inquiry and reports, of various kinds,
presented to Parliament which, if they had been acted upon,
would have greatly improved the quality of the service. The
failure to reform the central ministries is part of a broader
crisis of decision-making in Italy. The immobalismo for
which the Italian political system is noted ensures that
major problems are responded to in a partial and fragmented
fashion. Long-term problems are treated with short-term
emergency measures which serve to alleviate the symptoms
rather than the causes of the problems. The problem of civil
service reform cannot, in other words, be separated from the
much broader question of institutional reform as a whole.
This was certainly the view of the parliamentarians whose
efforts led to the establishment of the Bi-Cameral Committee
for Institutional Reform (known as the Bozzi Committee after
its Liberal chairman, Aldo Bozzi) set up in 1983. The committee inquired into every aspect of the Italian political
system in order to establish a blueprint for reform. The
result was not one, but several reports which reflected the
party grouping which made up the committee. It had itself
fallen victim to the disease it sought to cure. Without more
stable coalitions and a more powerful executive it is
difficult to envisage a reform as complex as that required
for the civil service being undertaken.

REFERENCES AND FURTHER READING

In Italian

Calandra, P. (1978) Storia Dell'Amministrazione Pubblica in Italia, Bologna, Il Mulino.

Cassese, S. (1977) Questione Amministrative e Questione Meridionale, Milan, Giuffre.

Cassese, S. (1981) 'Grandezza e miseria dell'alta burocrazia Italiana', Politica del Diritto, 2-3, 219-61.

Cassese, S. (1983) Il Sistema Amministrativo Italiano, Bologna, Il Mulino.

Ferraresi, F. (1980) Burocrazia e Politica in Italia, Bologna, Il Mulino.

Galli, G. (1966) Il Bipartismo Imperfetto, Bologna, Il Mulino.

Istituto per il Studio di Amministrazione Pubblica (1965) Archivi, Milan, Giuffre.

Serrani, D. (1979) Organizzazione per Ministeri, Rome, Officiana.

In English

Allum, P. (1973) Republic without Government, London, Weidenfeld and Nicolson.

Dogan, M. (ed.) (1975) The Mandarins of Western Europe, New York, Halsted Press.

Hine, D. (1979) 'Italy' in F. F. Ridley (ed.), Government and Administration in Western Europe, Oxford, Martin Robertson.

Putnam, D. (1975) 'The political attitudes of senior civil servants in Britain, Germany and Italy', in M. Dogan (ed.), The Mandarins of Western Europe, New York, Halsted Press.

Rusconi, G. C. and Scamuzzi, S. (eds) (1981) Italy Today: Special issue of Current Sociology 29(1).

Sartori, G. (1966) 'European Political Parties: the case of polarised pluralism', in La Palombara, J. and Weiner, M. (eds) Political Parties and Political Development, Princeton, Princeton University Press.

Italy

Spotts, F. and Wieser, T. (1986) Italy: A Difficult Democracy, Cambridge, Cambridge University Press.

Zariski, R. (1972) Italy: The Politics of Uneven Development, Hinsdale, Illinois, Dryden Press.

Chapter 7

SWEDEN

B. M. Jones

THE POLITICAL AND HISTORICAL SETTING

The liberal democratic constitution of Sweden has developed
steadily from the early nineteenth century. In the seven-
teenth century Sweden was a world power but since 1814 has
maintained neutrality. In the eighteenth century there was a
period of parliamentary government followed by a short spell
of royal absolutism, but the constitution of 1809 placed restraints upon the king and since 1975, although titular head
of state, his political powers have been nil. The government
has been responsible to the Riksdag (Parliament) since 1917
and in the case of deadlock it is the Speaker of the Riksdag
who assumes the initiative for policy and control.
    Sweden is a unitary state. The Riksdag's laws apply
throughout the whole state territory and can cover all aspects
of the affairs of the Swedish people. In practice there is a
degree of local autonomy which shows itself partly as freedom
of local authorities to interpret a skeleton or framework law
in ways appropriate to the locality, and partly as the freedom of local authorities to make their own regulations in
such matters as parking. It would be a mistake, however, to
suppose that local government in Sweden is nothing more than
this might indicate. Local government also has the freedom
to take initiatives in any way not specifically reserved to
another authority and proceed with those initiatives until
challenged successfully by a local resident through a quasi-
legal process. This major freedom arises from the constitution. Local government is a serious matter to the Swedes,
outspending central government in the ratio of two to one,
and this has implications for the nature and structure of the
civil administration, as will be described.
    The Riksdag itself has 349 members, 309 of whom are
elected from constituencies. The remaining 40 seats are allocated so that party proportionality is achieved. Any party
which gains at least 4 per cent of the overall vote or 12 per
cent in any one electoral district will be represented in the

143

Riksdag. In practice this has meant that a five-party system
has evolved at national level with seats being gained in such
a way as to keep the Social Democrats (a centre-left party)
in control from the early 1930s until today, except for the
period 1976-82. The Social Democrats are now (1988) in government in coalition with the Communists.

There is no Upper House. The government finds its support in the Riksdag and the constancy of the Social Democratic support over such a long period, set against the background of neutrality in international affairs, has meant that
Sweden is often held up as the model of a welfare state
created by popular will expressed through the parliamentary
process. With electoral turnout figures usually over 90 per
cent, the legitimacy of the government cannot be questioned
(at least not from liberal democratic premisses). The welfare
state provides protection 'from the womb to the tomb'. The
standard of living is the highest in Europe and indeed Sweden
is Europe's materialist counterpart to the USA, with the
added feature of a much more even distribution of income and
wealth.

The growth in the welfare state has, however, been at a
faster rate than industrial growth in recent years and this
has led to increasingly severe budgetary deficits. These in
turn have led to financial constraints being placed upon
welfare. This forms a major problem for the Swedes and has
led to the rather more precarious nature of the Social Democratic control. The Scandinavian states have been termed the
'Consensual Democracies': there is some evidence that the
liberal-left consensus is now weakening under the financial
difficulties. One sign of this in other Scandinavian states,
and indeed in other northern European polities such as West
Germany and the Netherlands, has been the emergence of
environmentalist parties - the Greens. Although Sweden has
such a Green Party, as yet it has made little electoral
impact. This can be interpreted as evidence that, in Sweden
at least, the consensus still holds.

The institutions of government and law are held in high
repute by the Swedes. Laws are not seen as an erosion of
civil liberty; the government is not seen as something to
be resisted. Rather the rule of law is seen as supportive
of the community and society in which individuals can seek to
express themselves. There is thus no formal mechanism of law
to restrain the government (as in the USA or West Germany).
Mechanisms do exist by which lawyers can advise the Riksdag
when constitutional change is proposed. Of course, as in
most western democracies, a good proportion of the Riksdag
members are lawyers, and the Swedes have procedures for
changing the constitution which involve the people. Either
an election must intervene between two successive Riksdags
passing a constitutional amendment or a referendum must
be called by the Riksdag to confirm such a vote. Any

other legal protection against the political aspect of the
state is given to the citizen via the normal courts.

The Swedes have been pioneers in developing ways of controlling the government, whether in its political or administrative form. These mechanisms will be described later, but
the Ombudsman (actually four ombudspeople) is a peculiarly
Scandinavian creation which has been imitated in various
forms in many parts of the world.

There is little direct democracy in Sweden. The Riksdag
can call for a referendum, but its status is only advisory.
The Swedes were given a choice between alternative pension
plans and their expression of choice was accepted. They were
also consulted on the change from driving on the left to
driving on the right, but although their clear preference was
to retain the former and their wish was respected for a time,
the government eventually ignored the referendum and changed
anyway.

Such is the constitutional, institutional and political
background against which Swedish bureaucracy must be
described.

THE POLITICAL EXECUTIVE

The Swedish monarch has no political power. The constitution
vests the power to govern in the political executive. The
cabinet government is drawn from and supported by the Riksdag,
presided over by the Prime Minister and serviced by civil
servants who also turn decisions into realities. If the
Riksdag withdraws its support (which normally happens only
when the electorate reconstitutes the Riksdag upon different
party lines) then the government falls. In short, Sweden has
a highly legitimate, parliamentary form of government.

The Prime Minister is appointed by the Riksdag. He or
she then selects a Cabinet drawn from the majority party or
coalition parties. This Cabinet has about 20 members of whom
about a dozen have responsibility for a 'ministry' or 'department' while the remainder have no fixed portfolio. The departmental ministers are responsible for introducing 'submissions' from their departments to the Cabinet. The Cabinet is
collectively responsible for the decisions that it takes.

So far there is nothing particularly unusual about this
account. In its essentials it conforms to the standard pattern of government by parliamentary executives in liberal
democracies throughout the world. The feature which makes it
distinctively Swedish is the thoroughness with which the
decision-making process has been delegated and streamlined.
There is a weekly meeting of the Cabinet chaired either by
the Prime Minister, the deputy or the longest-serving minister. At least five other ministers must be present for the
meeting to be valid. The meeting lasts about 40 minutes and

typically between 500 and 600 decisions are taken every week - an average of about 15 decisions per minute, totalling about 300,000 in a year.

Quite clearly there is little, if any, disagreement during the meetings. The agendas are carefully prepared, the submissions are listed department by department and the minister concerned will have taken care that any issue which impinges upon the work of another department will have been discussed at both ministerial and bureaucratic levels beforehand. If there is any degree of controversy about the submission it will have been discussed at a uniquely Swedish institution, the daily Cabinet lunch. Ministers are expected to put in regular and frequent appearances at this and use the opportunity to discuss any political problems in advance of the weekly meeting.

If there is any measure which is likely to lead to great controversy then it will not be dealt with in the regular meetings but will be discussed at special Cabinet meetings. It will also, of course, be the subject of party discussions, parliamentary discussion and, through the media, discussion by the electorate.

The Swedes can thus be seen to have drawn a distinction between the routine and the non-routine decisions and to have followed the distinction to its logical conclusions. The routine decisions are, in effect, made by the bureaucracy in consultation with the relevant minister. His or her job is to ensure that the submissions which go before the Cabinet are really routine and non-contentious. The Cabinet's task is merely to rubber-stamp the departmental decisions. The measure of success can be seen in the fact that only one minister since 1945 has resigned over a disagreement.

The non-routine decisions are made in consultation with the Riksdag either formally or informally. They are set in the political process, whereas the routine decisions are set in the administrative process. The measure of success here is the stability of Swedish government. Since the early 1930s Sweden has had an almost continuous centre-left government. Only from 1976 to 1982 have there been non-socialist governments and these, it must be admitted, have not had much stability - indeed four governments in the six years could be held up as a model of instability! But this period is so obviously exceptional in the Swedish context that no general conclusions can be drawn from it.

The stability which has characterised Sweden is based on an efficient civil service which enjoys a good rapport with the political government, and sensitive politicians who have enjoyed, on the whole, a good relationship with the Riksdag and the people. The extent to which at the interface between politics and administration the senior Swedish civil servant behaves like a politician is an important and interesting question, which we shall return to in due course.

THE STRUCTURE OF THE BUREAUCRACY

Turning now to the structure and functions of the bureaucracy
itself, two further points must be made before considering
the central government apparatus. First, local government in
Sweden is both strong and extensive. It has the power to
raise its own revenue through a local income tax and out-
spends central government by a ratio of more than two to one.
Included in local government's purview are both school education and the health services (both extensive and expensive),
and so the size and power of central government are correspondingly reduced. Secondly, Sweden would count, alongside
Austria, as Europe's most developed corporate state. Many of
the arms of government are designed to promote this corporatism: the harmony between the private and the public, between the individual and the state.

TABLE 7.1 Ministries and their responsibilities

Ministry	Responsibilities
Agriculture	Agriculture and forestry, pollution, conservation, food control, sport
Defence	The total defence system, fire safety
Education and Cultural Affairs	Cultural affairs, schools, radio and television, international cultural co-operation
Finance	Economic policy guidelines, budgets, taxes, domestic trade, consumer affairs
Foreign Affairs	Foreign relations, foreign trade, assist-ance to developing countries, disarmament issues
Health and Social Affairs	Child and youth care, welfare and treat-ment of alcoholics, national insurance system, public health and medical care
Housing	Residential construction, construction industry, national physical planning
Industry	Industrial policy, energy supplies, tech-nology, regional development
Justice	Courts, police, correctional treatment, public order and safety, freedom of the press
Labour	Occupational safety, unemployment insur-ance system, immigration
Public Administration	Civil service employment, county administ-rations, municipality and county councils
Transport and Communications	Roads, aviation, railways, shipping, postal services, telecommunications

In 1983 there were 12 ministries with functions as listed
in Table 7.1. The total number of civil servants employed
directly by these ministries was approximately 3,000, of whom
more than half can be classified as administrators. The
great majority of these work in Stockholm, the major exceptions being the field staff of the Foreign Affairs Ministry
which has about 1,000 employees stationed at about 100 overseas postings.

The organisation of ministries was extensively revised
in 1965 and a standard structure for organisation emerged to
which most ministries conform closely. This standard scheme
is shown diagrammatically in Figure 7.1.

FIGURE 7.1   Ministerial organisational structure

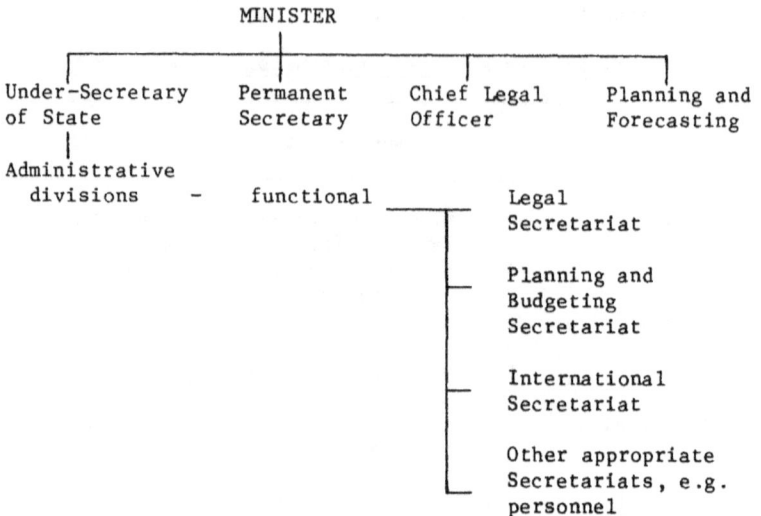

MINISTER

Under-Secretary   Permanent   Chief Legal   Planning and
of State   Secretary   Officer   Forecasting

Administrative
   divisions   —   functional   Legal
                                             Secretariat

                                             Planning and
                                             Budgeting
                                             Secretariat

                                             International
                                             Secretariat

                                             Other appropriate
                                             Secretariats, e.g.
                                             personnel

The major exceptions to this structure are the Ministry for
Finance and the Ministry of Foreign Affairs, which because of
history and function cannot conform to the standard pattern
which has proved acceptable elsewhere. The Finance Ministry,
for example, has a statistical section, while the Foreign
Ministry has political, protocol and press/information units.

In addition to the civil servants employed in the ministries there are also some in the Cabinet Office which exists
to service the government itself, particularly the Prime
Minister and the ministers without portfolio.

The under-secretary of state is a political appointment.
That is to say, he or she is appointed by an incoming government and is expected to resign when a government falls. The
other officers at all levels are permanent appointments and
remain in office whatever the political complexion of the

government. All civil servants at whatever level are entitled to participate fully in the political life of the
state - centrally or locally.

The secretariats are self-explanatory. They provide
services available to all the administrative divisions which
are organised on a functional basis. In the case of the
Ministry of Agriculture, for example, the administrative
divisions in 1983 were fourfold:

A   Agriculture, Horticulture, Emergency Food Supplies
B   Forestry, Fishing, Reindeer Herding, National Disaster
    Grants, Water Rights
C   Environmental Protection, Environmental Protection
    Reserves, Radiation Safety
D   Services and Monitoring, Higher Education and Research,
    Sports and Outdoor Relaxation, Hunting and Wildlife
    Management

It is clear that such a small number (3,000) of civil
servants cannot run a state apparatus as extensive as that of
Sweden. The actual detailed delivery of the service is done
by the extensive network of agencies. There are three main
divisions of agencies:

1. between 70 and 80 which are directly responsible to
    individual ministers of state;
2. county agencies which liaise between the 24 county
    councils and the government;
3. about 100 miscellaneous agencies, responsible to the
    government but not necessarily to any individual ministry.

A complete list of the ministerial agencies would be
unnecessarily long and not particularly helpful. Table 7.2
sets out as examples the largest agencies associated with the
ministries listed in Table 7.1. The total number of administrators employed by such agencies is in excess of 35,000, but
it should be pointed out that many of these boards are substantial employers of labour, for example 18,000 police personnel, 35,000 service personnel and 15,000 road construction
personnel are employed by the relevant agencies.

Approximately 9,000 administrators are employed by the
county agencies, the 24 authorities (one for each county)
which are responsible for co-ordinating activities on two
fronts:

1. central and local activity;
2. the activities of different branches of central
    government.

The county agencies are an important feature of Swedish
government from the point of view of both the central

TABLE 7.2 The largest ministerial agencies

Ministry	Example of agency
Agriculture	National Board of Agriculture
Defence	Material Administration of the Armed Forces
Education and Cultural Affairs	National Board of Education
Finance	Central Board of Statistics
Foreign Affairs	Swedish International Development Authority
Health and Social Affairs	National Social Insurance Board
Housing	National Land Survey Board
Industry	Geological Survey of Sweden
Justice	National Police Board
Labour	National Labour Market Board
Public Administration	County agencies
Transport and Communication	National Road Administration

administration and local government.

The third group of agencies includes such bodies as medical institutions (e.g. for research), cultural institutions
(e.g. The Royal Opera or the National Museum), public enterprises (e.g. the Post Office or the railways) and finally
government-owned business companies (e.g. mining, steel or
tobacco).

Before moving to a consideration of the functions of
these bodies it will be interesting to look at the typical
structure of the first type of agencies, those agencies which
relate directly to a central government department. It must
be stressed that any account must be of the principles of
organisation. There are too many agencies for a detailed
look at each and there is an ongoing process of agency reorganisation. The main thrusts of this reorganisation have been
in four directions:

1. an increasing emphasis on the role of lay boards in the
    management and decision-making processes;
2. the rationalisation of lines of command in the larger
    agencies, interpolating several layers of authority
    between the top management and the, often diverse,
    functionaries;
3. the increasing decentralisation of agencies. This
    includes both the physical decentralisation - more than
    half the agencies are not located in Stockholm - and
    decentralisation by the delegation of authority;

4. the rationalisation of functions, combining overlapping
agencies and splitting agencies which have more than one
role which do not really harmonise.

The most basic model that has emerged is now the board
structure. In this model the director general of the agency
chairs the lay board to which he or she is responsible. The
various branches of the agency are responsible to the director general. The effect of this organisation is to place the
responsibility for the day-to-day running of the agency
fairly and squarely with the director general while the major
policy decisions can be taken by the board. It should be
noted that the board often contains parliamentarians, which
helps the processes of control and accountability.
The agency structure may be simplified by removing the
Agency Board. This, of course, has the effect of increasing
the authority and decreasing the accountability of the
director general. It corresponds to the historical situation
and fewer agencies each year remain without the oversight of
a board. An agency which functions without a board is sometimes said to have a unitary structure.
The board structure may be complicated by interposing a
layer or layers of divisional heads between the director
general and the functionaries. This is purely a management
device and no political significance should be attached to
it. The director general will keep in touch with the
divisional heads more efficiently than he or she might previously have kept in touch with the many diverse functions.
This situation (which may or may not operate with a board) is
termed the corporate structure.
The major point to realise when discussing the functions
of ministries and agencies is that Sweden has accepted the
distinction between routine and non-routine decisions and
pursued it to its logical conclusion. The ministries are
responsible for the policy decisions; the agencies are responsible for the routine execution of the policies. This has
the effect of removing political responsibility from the minister for the routine decisions taken by agencies under his
or her charge and absolves him or her for responsibility for
maladministration by minor functionaries. The ministries
themselves are free for major decision-making and policy
development. The public are protected by the appeal system
which usually gives any dissatisfied individual the right of
appeal to the government itself.
The functions of the ministries and the agencies are
thus quite distinct. The only area of ambivalence is the
role played by director generals. These are persons of some
prestige and, particularly in the situation where there is no
board, quite clearly have scope to go beyond their brief.
Even where there is a board the director general will have
access to the ministry and can thus feed ideas into the

decision-making processes. These ideas will normally be given serious consideration.

The functions of ministries conform to a fourfold classification:

1. policy planning
2. liaison with the Riksdag
3. instructions to agencies;
4. administrative matters.

These matters will be dealt with in due course.

THE BUREAUCRATS

There is very little surprising about the Swedish civil service as far as personnel is concerned, a fact which perhaps explains the paucity of recent research on the subject. The main feature which is common to many northern European bureaucracies, but not to Britain, is the extent to which a degree in law serves as an appropriate entry qualification. Despite the growth in the number of specialists - for example, economists and accountants - and the increased importance of scientific and technological expertise, the proportion of civil service entrants with legal training is still more than a half.

One of the consequences of this is that Swedish universities now incorporate such 'administrative' subjects as economics and sociology into their courses, and hence the entry qualification is not so narrow as may be supposed. Another consequence of the almost universal graduate requirement for entry to the levels of the civil service where real administrative responsibility lies is that inevitably people from economically better backgrounds predominate, indeed Elder (1970) writes of those with aristocratic backgrounds occupying many influential posts. It must be remembered, however, that access to higher education in Sweden is very much more open than in most European countries and also that the range of economic backgrounds for Swedish families is much narrower - certainly than, say, for the UK. There are, of course, very poor Swedes and very rich Swedes but the picture, even in the present time of some economic depression, is of a very unified society, lacking the stratification of Britain and the racial inequalities of North America. Thus the social effects of restricting entry to graduates and biasing entry towards law graduates has much less significance than in, say, Britain, where the bias towards Oxbridge is far more significant, or the US, where the better-off WASP has much more chance of success.

Reforms in the late sixties saw a considerable simplification in the number of classes and pay scales within the service and there is now no barrier to promotion from any grade to any grade within the bureaucracy. The trade unions, however, do indicate more clearly than the official position what the reality is. Three unions, SR, TCO and SSA, represent the interests of senior civil servants, white-collar workers and blue-collar workers respectively, while SACO acts as a general association for public sector interests. In 1969 the bureaucracy gained the right to strike, but this has been used sparingly in the last 15 years.

In principle, any Swede may become a civil servant at any stage in his or her career. It is worth noting, in this context, that the concept of civil servant in northern Europe is much wider than in the UK. There is much more movement between local government and central government and between the private and the public sector, so that whereas in Britain we think quite narrowly of a civil servant as employed specifically by central government, the northern European concept is much broader and embraces the whole of the public sector.

If, therefore, we restrict our analysis to those who work in positions of administrative responsibility within either ministries or agencies, we note that most career civil servants have entered the public service soon after graduation, applying for a specific post within a department or agency and receiving their training 'in house'. There is no civil service commission as such, although there is a training college and a training committee. Having entered the service, promotion is again by successful application for advertised vacancies. All vacancies are advertised, but, since many of them are advertised internally, the major competition is with one's colleagues already in the state's employ.

A significant feature of the Swedish system in this respect is a consequence of the Freedom of Information Act. The interview and application records are available to candidates and hence, if there is a feeling that a miscarriage of justice has taken place, the appeal system can be invoked and appointments can be set aside. In practice there are not too many overturnings on appeal: the effect has been to make interview and appointment panels very careful to demonstrate that justice is being done.

Another feature worth pointing out is that civil servants are able to follow political careers in central or local government with no effect on their careers. At lower levels the principle of 'the best person for the job' is applied and a person's political convictions are unlikely to have much relevance. At senior levels, particularly at under-secretary level, the political convictions do matter, but even there the corporatist tendency implicit in Sweden's political/administrative thinking may exclude only those with more 'extreme' political views.

Once appointed the Swedish civil servant enjoys considerable security of tenure; even 'political' appointments

will not be removed from office without consultation between
the relevant parties and the appeals system ensures again
that such dismissals as do occur are usually thoroughly
justified.

T. J. Anton reported (1973) on a survey of 300 top civil
servants. He found that they considered themselves satisfied
with their achievements, independent of thought and politically sophisticated. They are probably right. In 1979 there
was an anti-bureaucracy act designed to cut down the amount
of red tape. It failed miserably to achieve its aims!
Its ineffectiveness is evidence perhaps of the strength of
the Swedish bureaucrats.

POLITICAL ACCOUNTABILITY

It has already been remarked that the Swedes pursue the distinction between government and administration to its logical
conclusions. A policy once made (by politicians on the
advice of bureaucrats) is administered by agencies responsible via the bureaucrats to politicians. The people of
Sweden, perhaps more than in any other state in the world,
have access to and control over both bureaucrats and politicians. This section describes some of the main mechanisms by
which both arms of government are accountable to the people.

Clearly the government itself needs the support of the
Riksdag and this, in turn, needs the support of the people.
The Swedes are very conscientious and very informed voters
who, having a wide range of parties to chose from and a
rational electoral system, are able to produce the sort of
party mix in the Riksdag which probably satisfies the
majority of them. There seems little doubt that within the
liberal-democratic context the Swedish Riksdag is as legitimated by its accountability to the electorate as any other
state.

There is, however, evidence that the Swedish population,
despite the near ideal conditions of Sweden, do not trust
their politicians! A 1982 survey known as 'Opinion 82'
showed that over two-thirds of the population (71 per cent)
believed that little reliance can be placed on the intention
of political parties to turn their promises into realities,
while over half the population (55 per cent) believed that
parliamentarians paid little or no attention to the feelings
or thoughts of ordinary people. To those who see Sweden as a
good exemplar of democracy these figures are disquieting;
perhaps more disquieting is the fact that both percentages
had increased substantially over the years since 1968, the
first from 61 per cent, the second from 46 per cent. In
general terms it is the young, the rural and the blue-collar
workers who display least trust. Most highly educated people
show a much more positive attitude. Interestingly, the

disaffection cannot be ascribed to the instability of the
1976-82 period. The big increase in distrust occurred in the
early seventies while the Socialist bloc was still in power.

Between elections the Riksdag scrutinises the government
through a series of committees. In general terms there are
committees to correspond to each of the ministers of the
government and these committees are empowered to consider any
matter within their broad specialisation. The major activity
will be the consideration of bills as part of the process by
which they become acts, but other aspects of the work include
the examination of issues with the right to question agencies
and to invite ministers to the committee's hearings.

The degree to which Sweden is a corporate state has been
mentioned. An important manifestation of this is the involvement of presure groups in the political process. Pressure
groups are among the private groups which will be involved in
the preparation of policy and will be consulted by parliamentary committees on both the political and the administrative
aspects of legislation. This is dealt with more fully below,
but it is clear that the widespread tendency for ordinary
members of the public to involve themselves in pressure group
activity will result in an increase in public accountability.

An important role in the accountability process is
played by the media. There is extensive coverage of the
business of the Riksdag and the state provides information
services on a generous scale. More important, however, is
the check on the administration which is found in the Freedom
of the Press Act. This Act, one of the pillars of the constitution, embodies the principle of publicity which gives the
Swedish people a unique right of access to all government
documents, whether issued by or sent to the state. There are
exceptions to this in the cases of national security and personal privacy, but the general effect is far reaching. It
means that individuals can have access to all papers affecting them personally and the media can have access to every-
thing and can thus, through their specialist staff, interpret
and criticise all that is going on in government. Clearly
the latter feature will prove an important constraint on the
Swedish authorities.

Another well-developed Swedish safeguard lies in the
individual's right of appeal against the decisions of government which affect him or her. In the nature of things most
such decisions will have been taken by a bureaucrat, perhaps
in local government, perhaps in an agency. Whatever the
decision an appeal can be made to the next higher tier of
authority. Ultimately the government itself may be appealed
to and, of course, if an appeal gets so high it will probably
have been picked up as interesting by the media and/or a
relevant pressure group or even a political party. It will
therefore be in the interests of government to redress
genuine grievances and correct wrong decisions as fairly as

possible. The right of individuals to papers concerning
them, mentioned previously, is of great value in this process.
If the appeal involves a legal question then the Supreme
Adminstrative Court is the final arbiter.

The public also has the right of complaint to either the
Ombudsman or the Chancellor of Justice. The Ombudsman is, of
course, one of Scandinavia's 'exports' to the world – many
states now having officials who serve essentially the same
purposes. In fact there are four ombudspeople who have the
constitutional role of overseeing 'the application of laws
and ordinances in public activities'. Ultimately the Ombudsmen, who really represent the Riksdag's check on the bureaucracy, have the power to prosecute, but usually warning or
even just drawing attention to maladministration proves
effective. The Chancellor of Justice is the government's
check on its own administration.

Finally the Parliamentary Standing Committee on the Constitution maintains an annual check on all the activities of
government to ensure harmony with the constitution and the
will of the Riksdag as expressed in its statutes. The range
of devices developed to protect the Swede against maladministration at whatever level is impressive, but there are yet
more controls internal to government.

INTERNAL CONTROL AND MANAGEMENT

The internal control of the executive may be considered under
four headings. Some of the material has already been
discussed in outline earlier in the chapter.

Political Control

Apart from the system of debates and committees, members of
the Riksdag are permitted to direct questions and interpellations to ministers in order to obtain information and to
monitor a minister's performance. Questions are directed in
writing and are answered normally a week after submission. A
short debate usually follows in which only the questioner and
the minister may participate, according to strict rules
regarding time limits. The first speech for either side
lasts three minutes, the second two minutes and subsequent
speeches no more than one minute. Thus the maximum length of
debate is likely to be about 12 minutes and most debates substantially less. Debating points will, of course, be scored,
but the level of debate, because the parties to the debate
are informed, is likely to be high.

Interpellations are submitted less often. They too are
directed to a minister but are intended to provide major
debates on important issues. The submission must include

statements of content and motive. Ministers take great care
with their replies to interpellations, and so there is
sometimes delay in starting the debate. Any member of the
Riksdag may take part in an interpellation debate and there
are no severe time limits. Questions to ministers average
around 500 per annum, interpellations around 200 per annum.
    Parliamentary oversight of the bureaucracy is excercised
via the committee system and via the ombudsman, as already
discussed.

Financial Control

This has two aspects. The first is a detailed control over
the spending of each department and agency to ensure that it
corresponds reasonably closely to the budgeted forecast.
This control is undertaken by the Treasury. The second, less
detailed control, more concerned with principles, and the
audit which looks for efficiency, economy and effectiveness
are undertaken through the budgetary process and through the
parliamentary auditors.
    The budgetary process itself lasts about three years and
falls into three stages:

1. forming and approving the budget (1 year 8 months)
2. operating the budget (1 year)
3. closing the accounts, audit and publication (4 months)

    The Swedish fiscal year runs from 1 July to 30 June.
The budget is normally presented in early January and will
have been approved, possibly in amended form, by early June.
The actual budget will have been preceded by draft budgets
starting in the January of the previous year and this, of
course, will have been prepared in outline over the preceding
month or so.
    The timetable will thus look like this (Budget 1987/88):

December 1985: Preliminary work on draft budget.
January 1986: Draft budget presented to Riksdag.
The whole of 1986 will be taken up with negotiations within
    and between ministries as to detailed allocations and
    appropriations.
January 1987: The budget formally presented to the Riksdag.
The first half of 1987 will be taken up in voting on specific
    measures, department by department.
June 1987: Final approval of budget package.
1 July 1987 to 30 June 1988: Budget in operation.
July to October 1988: Audit and publication.

    Clearly all manner of occurrences may intervene between
the initial planning and the operating stages and so there

are three oppportunities for the government to ask for supp-
lementary budgets (in October, January and March). The
Riksdag thus has several opportunities to debate the principles on which the budget is constructed and the reason for
departure from the original estimates. It was the Riksdag
who decided in the late 1960s to abolish the distinction
between revenue and capital spending.

The Parliamentary Auditors, 12 in number, usually
selected from the Riksdag, have the right to 'inspect the
activites of central government'. They report annually on
anything which they find from the ministries and agencies.

Judicial Control

This has already been dealt with. The system of appeals is
extensive. The Parliamentary Commissioner and the Chancellor
of Justice investigate the administration on the initiative
of either the Riksdag or the Cabinet respectively.

The Hierarchical Pattern of Administration

This has also been discussed. The important role of the
Riksdag in providing board members for the agencies and the
political appointment of the under-secretary of state for a
ministry are among the devices that ensure control.

POLICY-MAKING

It is a feature of the Swedish administrative culture that
virtually all proposals for change, no matter where they
originate, will be thoroughly discussed at a variety of different levels and by a variety of interested parties. Only
after this preliminary work of preparation has been completed
and agreement ranging from assent to wholehearted commitment
gained from the majority of interested parties will the
policy be embodied in a bill, presented to the Riksdag and,
once passed, be the source of authority for decisions and
actions of the agencies of state. It is both the thoroughness of discussion and the feeling that general agreement is
important which are so characteristic of Swedish culture.

The first requirement for any policy formation is, of
course, information, and the major source of such information
will be the report of some authorised committee or body. The
majority of such committees are special, ad hoc committees
usually consisting of a full-time administrator and about ten
other personnel engaged on a part-time basis. At any time
about 300 such committees are at work, each under the aegis
of a ministry of state, working within terms of reference

stipulated by that ministry and with appropriate personnel
nominated by the minister.

The background of the committee's personnel will vary
according to the subject under discussion. For matters which
are mainly administrative or technical a handful of experts
drawn from the ranks of the ministry may suffice. For
matters which are more political then members of the Riksdag
will be included, with particular care being taken to ensure
that there is no 'loading' of the committee with one dominant
political view. For matters which are highly politically
sensitive, such as defence or constitutional reform, then the
whole committee may be made up of parliamentarians. Where it
is appropriate people from outside the ministries and the
Riksdag, for example from industry, commerce, the academic
world or the labour force, may be included.

The prime purpose of the committee is to produce a
report, and these reports, which may have taken several years
to compile, will be published as a Government Official
Report. Alternatively, for matters where the report is less
significant or very straightforward, the report may be replaced by a Ministerial Memorandum produced entirely from
within the ministry or by an Agency Study produced from
within an appropriate agency, but these modes are far less
common than the major consultative report.

Once the report has been published it will be circulated
to interested parties both within the public and the private
spheres. Everyone has a right to comment on the proposals,
the procedure for circulation having been enshrined in the
constitution. It will only be after such consultation that
moves will be taken to turn the ideas in the report into positive law. If the committee has done its work properly there
will not be too much adverse comment, but clearly it is
impossible to satisfy every party completely and the government will be looking for a policy which commands both widespread political support and acceptance from the groups, both
administrative and private, which will have to operate the
measure.

Ultimately the measure will be incorporated into the law
of Sweden by means of an Act of the Riksdag. This will be on
the basis of a bill presented by the appropriate government
minister. Such bills may vary in scope and complexity from a
simple bill concerned with the granting of an annuity to an
individual to a highly detailed and very long bill such as
the annual budget bill. The majority of bills will be intermediate in length and complexity, and where political principle is involved may be presented to the Riksdag in two
stages; the first intended to gain support for the principle,
the second to provide a detailed working out of that principle. The important points to grasp are that the policy
embodied in the bill has been the outcome of an extensive
process of consultation and research and that the subsequent

operation of that policy will be very largely delegated to
the ministry concerned, and, within that ministry, mostly
delegated to an agency.

ISSUES AND CONCLUSION

The picture of Swedish bureaucracy that has been painted so
far has been one of rationality and common sense. The problems of government have been eased by the mood of the people,
which is one of pragmatism coupled with a desire for consensus solutions to problems.

This portrait is essentially correct. The recent tragic
murder of the Swedish Prime Minister (March 1986) must be
seen as deeply ironic: Sweden is one of the few countries in
the world where the divisions do not seem to run deep and
where the mechanisms for sensible and satisfactory solutions
to pressing problems both exist and are understood by the
majority of a well-educated, prosperous and stable
population.

Nevertheless, two main questions can be asked about
potential problems. The first is about the underlying
stability of the governmental apparatus. Could it be that
the achievements in the field of democratic and consultative
administration have been made possible only because of the
economic prosperity and consequent financial security of the
polity? If so, then will the recession of the 1980s cause
not just a cutback in affluence but also declining political
stability?

The second question is about the nature of the corporatism that has been described; the deliberate inclusion of a
plethora of interested parties into the policy-making process.
On the one hand it can be argued, for example, that the non-
emergence of a successful 'green' party is a measure of the
success of corporatism - the views are already integrated
into the system. On the other hand it can be argued that the
establishment has found a way of excluding radical views and
of rendering them impotent - that the corporatism is to this
extent superficial.

There is no easy way of settling questions such as
these. The first can only be settled as time elapses and the
effects of economic decline affect (or otherwise) the polity.
It may be, of course, that the government is able to deal
with the economic problems, in which case there is a vindic-
ation of the Swedish system.

The second cannot so easily be resolved. If there were
to be an obvious change in the nature and stability of the
Swedish polity then there would be empirical evidence that
the corporatism was superficial. But without such a change
the arguments take place on a different level; the level of
interpretation of much more subtle and less dramatic evidence,

and the problem is that the stance of the interpreter may
determine the conclusion reached.

It is well outside the scope of this chapter to attempt
to discuss such issues. The next few years should prove very
interesting to the student of Scandinavian politics as the
institutions described here are put to the test.

REFERENCES AND FURTHER READING

Much basic material about Swedish government and administration can be found in books and pamphlets obtainable from the
Swedish Institute, PO Box 7434, Stockholm, Sweden or from the
appropriate local Swedish Embassy. This material includes:

Books

Gustaffson, A. (1983) Local Government in Sweden.
Vinde, P. and Petri, G. (1978) Swedish Government Administra-
    tion (2nd ed.).
Lindstrom, E. (1983) The Swedish Parliamentary System.

Factsheets These are regularly updated and include, for
example:

Constitutional Protection of Rights and Freedoms in Sweden
Swedish Political Parties
Local Government in Sweden
Swedish Government in Action
The Swedish Ombudsmen

The government of Sweden is also the subject of academic
publication.

Board, J. B. (1970) Government and Politics of Sweden,
    Boston, Houghton Mifflin; and
Elder, N. C. M. (1970) Government in Sweden: the Executive at
    Work, Oxford, Pergamon

are specific, but both rather dated. More recent publications giving a good insight into Swedish government include:

Elder, N., Thomas, A. H. and Arter, D. (1983) The Consensual
    Democracies? Oxford, Martin Robertson.
Gustaffson, G. and Richardson, J. J. (1984) 'Sweden' in
    Ridley, F. F. (ed.) Policies and Politics in Western Europe,
    London, Croom Helm, is very helpful.

Sweden

Journals

Scandinavian Political Studies, now in its second series,
contains much that is directly relevant and a good deal which
is applicable. Other directly relevant articles are occas-
ionally to be found in such journals as Public Adminstration
or Government and Opposition. A survey of 300 top civil
servants is reported in

Anton, T. J., Linde, C. and Mellbourn, A. (1973) 'Bureaucrats
    in politics: a profile of the Swedish administrator',
    Canadian Public Administration, 16(4), 627-651.

Chapter 8

THE UNITED STATES

J. A. Chandler

In comparison with Western European bureaucracies the
administrative system of the United States seems far removed
from the Weberian ideal type. It appears to be a highly
politicised structure in which its senior officers are
personal appointees of the President who will resign as soon
as the chief executive leaves office. The system therefore
appears to have stagnated in the early nineteenth century and
resembles, apart from its size, the pre-Northcote-Trevelyan
bureaucracy of Britain. It is, however, often presumed that
an advantage of this structure is that it ensures the
obedience of the bureaucracy to the elected chief executive.
These perceptions are misleading. The bureaucracy of the
United States may be very different from those of Europe but
it is also far removed from early-nineteenth-century patterns
of patronage. The country has developed a bureaucratic
system that is highly modern and efficient in the context of
a system of government based on very different principles
from European parliamentary systems that are founded on
cohesive party structures.

THE POLITICAL SETTING

The formal political system of the United States is governed
by the constitution, which outlines the federal structure of
the nation, the rights of individuals within the states and
the basic character of the federal government. The democratic
structure of the regime is based on a principle of checks and
balances which ensures that no single organisation or
individual can dominate the policy process.
     The most powerful individual within the United States is
the President who, with his deputy the Vice-President, occupy
the only offices elected by the nation as a whole. As chief
executive and head of state the President is responsible for
implementing the policy of the federal government. In
practice this extends not only to ensuring that laws are

enacted but in taking the initiative in proposing legislation
and steering the nation's foreign policy. Although head of
state and government the President's power can be kept in
check by the legislature. Congress is divided into a lower
chamber, the House of Representatives, whose members are
elected from approximately equally sized constituencies, and
the Senate, whose 100 members are elected two from each of
the 50 States. The Congress is the only body capable of
passing federal legislation or appropriating taxes, and hence
many of the major initiatives of the President must be
acceptable to the legislature. The Senate also has the power
to endorse or reject appointments made by the President to
the bureaucracy. Congress is, however, in turn subject to
checks by the President who can veto legislation. This power
can be overridden by a two-thirds majority vote of both the
Senate and the House of Representatives, which is rarely
achieved. Both Congress and the President must act within
the confines of the constitution, whose dictates are interpreted by the Supreme Court. This body consists of nine
judges who are appointed for life by the President.

The framework of checks and balances is only meaningful
in practice because of the underlying structure of the party
system. The United States is often depicted as a two-party
system, given the domination of the Republican and Democratic
parties in presidential and congressional elections. These
parties, however, differ greatly in structure and behaviour
from the ideologically based parties of Western Europe. The
Democratic and Republican parties are highly fissiparious
organisations that at national level consist of loose feder-
ations of State party organisations. Party members from one
State may have different political views from members f the
same party from another State. There is a much weaker attachment to a party line within Congress. Democrats may, for
example, vote for policies advocated by a Republican President
or oppose the initiatives of a Democratic administration.

Since the President cannot rely on the support of his
party colleagues in Congress he must gain approval for his
ideas through cultivating good relations with legislators.
The President will seek the support of congressmen not only
by persuading them of the political advantages of his programme but by arranging mutually beneficial deals with
congressmen. The President may, for example, persuade a
recalcitrant congressman to favour his initiatives by agreeing
to support one of the politician's favoured legislative
proposals or by implementing a package that would result in
greater federal expenditure in the congressman's constituency.
The ability of a President to implement his policies into
practice relies greatly on his skills in manipulating
Congress. Success is not very high. Presidents may expect
to get the majority of their Bills through Congress during
their first months in office but thereafter they are more

likely than not to see their proposed legislation defeated in Congress or subject to a protracted process of amendment.

THE EXECUTIVE

The bureaucracy of the eighteenth and early-nineteenth-century United States was organised on much the same principles of patronage as the larger states of Europe. Presidents, with the agreement of Congress, appointed to salaried government posts, ranging from secretaries of state to clerks and messengers, individuals who demonstrated that they would loyally support their political views. Many of the senior administrators were politicians who had actively helped in the campaign to ensure the President's election in the expectation that their loyalty would be rewarded with office.

The first Presidents chose as their chief secretaries and advisers individuals associated with the wealthy educated elite that had spearheaded the revolt against Britain. This elitist phase of American history came to an end in 1828 with the election of Andrew Jackson as President, representing a more populist and egalitarian ideology. He consequently opened up the patronage system to a much wider social strata. By the second half of the nineteenth century serious criticism was being voiced about the incompetence of many government officials and in particular that corruption was undermining the efficiency and fairness of the political system. Pressure for reform became steadily more strident and eventually received congressional support when President Garfield was assassinated by a disappointed office seeker in 1881.

The assassination was the catalyst for a major reform of the bureaucracy that was considerably influenced by the Northcote-Trevelyan reforms in Britain. In 1883 Congress approved the Pendleton Act, which established a Civil Service Commission to oversee the process of recruitment to the lower ranks of the administration. Although responsible to the President the Commission had to include members of both major parties. It created a system of entry to permanent posts within the civil service through competitive examinations. Initially only 10 per cent of administrative posts were subject to this merit system but the proportion increased rapidly until 45 per cent of officials were merit appointees by 1900. Today over 90 per cent of federal government employees are career officials. The remaining posts are, however, still allocated on the basis of political patronage, which involves some 200,000 individuals and many of the most senior positions in the bureaucracy. Many of these posts are, however, within the numerous agencies of government and their incumbents are not obliged to resign when the President ends

his term of office. Within the White House and departments
of government there are approximately 2,000 positions subject
to the continuation in office of the President (Heclo 1977:
36-7).

The division of the bureaucracy into merit and patronage
positions should be placed in the wider context of the
modernisation of the United States into a highly industrialised and populated nation. The development of a complex
governmental bureaucracy to regulate the expanding economy
and develop social services did not, however, take place
until the 1930s under the New Deal policies of President
Roosevelt, which aimed to get the United States out of its
economic depression. In 1816 the Federal Service encompassed
6,000 bureaucrats which by the presidency of Lincoln had
risen to 50,000 (Van Riper 1958: 24). Today there are over
two and a half million individuals in civilian federal
employment.

The bureaucracy has not only increased in size, it has
also become much more complex in respect to the range of
duties and the technical skills that it requires. For most
of the nineteenth century the government consisted of the
presidency and the departments of state. This pattern began
to be complicated by the creation of ad hoc governmental
agencies in the late nineteenth century. The first of these
bodies was the Inter-State Commerce Commission created by
Congress in 1887 to regulate competition between rail
companies in order to prevent monopolies controlling inter-
state transport. This agency, like many later creations, was
subject to control by a board whose members were selected by
the President for a fixed term and could not thereafter be
removed. Once appointed the Boards were empowered to operate
without, and on occasion in spite of, presidential or
congressional interests. Since 1887 there has been a steady
growth of governmental agencies which effectively cover a
further strand in the separation of powers. They encompass
organisations as important as the Federal Reserve Board, The
Environmental Protection Agency and the Food and Drug
Administration. The structure and functions of these numerous
regulatory agencies varies in accord with the ad hoc nature
of their creation and there are no clear rules determining
which subjects should be handled by a semi-independent agency
and which should be subject to departmental control. In
general, however, the staff serving these bodies are not
regarded as part of the civil service and most agencies will
determine their own methods of recruiting and grading staff.

A third sector of the bureaucracy, the Executive Office,
did not emerge until the 1930s. President Roosevelt began to
develop a small team of close personal advisers who would not
be subject to senatorial scrutiny. From small beginnings
post-war Presidents have created a considerable bureaucracy
under their personal direction. It encompasses the direction

of the budget, advice on defence and economic issues and the President's team of expert political and technical aides. The Executive Office of the President is still, however, a very small organisation in terms of personnel when compared with the departments and agencies although, on occasion, it can be argued to be the most important centre of power within the United States.

Although the bureaucracy is often informally divided into three major sections, the Executive Office of the President, the departments and the agencies, there are, in addition, organisations such as the General Accounting Office that are responsible to Congress. These elements of the administration are divided arbitrarily from one another largely in relation to their accountability. The Executive Office reports directly to the President. Departmental officials are in the first instance subject to the secretary of their department rather than directly to the President. The numerous agencies are much further removed from presidential control and in most cases their career officials are not subject to the regulations laid down for the civil servants who inhabit the departments.

It is almost impossible to classify the elements of the bureaucracy in terms of functions. The assignation of certain functions to agencies and others to departments or the Executive Office followed no predetermined rules but evolved as a consequence of numerous and often transitory factors.

There are also no clear functional divisions between political and career officials. As in all developed liberal democracies government officials can be involved not only in implementing decisions but in all stages of the policy process. The White House staff and many department officers are as much concerned with making policy as its implementation. Legislation in the United States, as in Western Europe, delegates considerable responsibility to the executive to determine the details of government regulations. The bureaucracy is also engaged in monitoring and evaluating the effects of government policies. The tasks of policy-making, implementation and evaluation cannot, moreover, be clearly assigned to either the political or career appointees. Whilst the most senior patronage appointments are more concerned with devising and evaluating policy rather than its implementation, civil servants in the United States may still have a considerable influence on the nature of the government's agenda.

STRUCTURE

The Executive Office of the President

The Executive Office of the President is a conglomerate of

individuals and committees that have coalesced as a result of numerous ad hoc decisions. It is difficult to define a single purpose or function for this organisation. It is in part established to provide the President with advice from close confidants; it also arranges his daily programme, manages his relations with the media, and monitors the extent to which his directives are carried out and have effect. In these respects the office is an organisation concerned with ensuring that the President can effectively undertake his duties, although its principle task is to aid the policy-making process. The Office of Management and the Budget and the National Security Council may, for example, take on roles that overlap with departmental interests and transcend the basic task of serving the office needs of the President.

The Executive Office can be divided into three sections, the White House Staff, who are generally the closest confidants of the President, a number of policy advisory committees, and the Office of Management and the Budget (OMB).

The White House Staff. At the heart of the Executive Office are the White House Staff. The number of staff steadily increased following the Roosevelt Presidency to reach a high point of 500 individuals serving Nixon, but following the Watergate affair subsequent Presidents have pruned the number of aides. The staff includes both advisers on policy and managers of the President's time and relations with the outside world. In the former category Presidents appoint as their aides associates who will be able to advise them on particular policy issues. In recent years individuals occupying these positions have been delegated considerable discretion in steering United States policy, especially on foreign affairs. Henry Kissinger as Nixon's Assistant for National Security Affairs was seen to have far greater authority over the direction of foreign policy than William Rodgers, the Secretary of State (Griffith 1983: 72), and was himself aided by a substantial staff.

In addition to policy advisers the White House Staff includes aides who act as personal assistants to the President. His entourage includes a number of press officers who brief the media on their master's thoughts and actions and also seek to ensure good relations with the press. Speech writers are employed to give some oratorical substance to his thoughts. Secretaries keep the President's diaries and ensure he arrives in the right city at the right time or is informed of matters of correct protocol. At the apex of this team is the White House Chief of Staff and his deputy, who are often among the closest confidants of the President and in most frequent contact with the chief executive. The role of the Chief of Staff can vary greatly depending upon the needs of the President. They may be a sounding board and discussant with the President concerning policy. They may like John

Erlichman, Chief of Staff to Nixon, be manipulators of patronage and electoral strategy to ensure that the President
retains his popularity. In most cases they have a vital role
as gatekeepers determining who should see the President and
in what circumstances.

Councils and Committees. The Executive Office of the
President also includes a number of advisory committees and
their staffs. The most prominent are the Council of Economic
Advisers and the National Security Council. They were
created respectively in 1946 and 1947 by Congress in order to
ensure better co-ordination of government services. The
Council for Economic Advisers comprises three prominent
economists selected by the President who advise him on the
financial state of the nation and prepare on his behalf an
annual economic report for Congress. The body is assisted by
a staff of some 30 to 40 individuals. The National Security
Council consists of the President, Vice-President, and the
Secretary of State for Defence, although a number of other
senior members of the executive, including the National
Security Adviser, the Chiefs of Staff and the Director of the
Central Intelligence Agency (CIA) usually attend its meetings.
It is serviced by between 50 and 100 officials, the number
varying in accord with the importance the President assigns
to the Council. Both the Economic and National Security
Councils have had considerable importance in policy-making but
their use is always subject to the views of the President.
Under Nixon the National Security Council, for example, had
greater influence than the Defence Department, whilst
President Johnson gave much less prominence to the
organisation.
      There are in addition a number of lesser consultative
committees advising the President. Nixon established a
Domestic Council to deal with non-military affairs. The body
was renamed the Domestic Policy Staff by President Carter and
has yet to establish itself as a permanent denizen of the
White House. The President has also acquired or been given
control of many more minor technical regulatory organisations
such as the Council on Environmental Quality or the Office of
Science and Technology. As Griffith succinctly points out
'their number and nature are constantly changing' (Griffith
1983: 74).

The Office of Management and Budget. The third major element
of the President's office was created in 1921 as the Bureau
of the Budget and was located within the Treasury Department.
In 1939 it was transferred to the President's direct control
and given further status by Nixon, who reorganised the Bureau
into the OMB which assumed not only the role of creating the
budget but of ensuring more efficient managerial techniques
in the bureaucracy and the power to advise on the level of

spending by other departments in the administration. The OMB
is, in effect, an important instrument through which the
President can attempt to control departments and agencies by
cutting or increasing funds and investigating their
managerial efficiency.

The Office has a further important function as an agency
for co-ordinating the work of the bureaucracy in accord with
presidential directives. Departments and some agencies
report to the OMB on their legislative proposals which can
then be supported or rejected in the light of the administration's programme. The Office will also advise the White
House on bills put before Congress by non-government sources
so that the President can, if necessary, organise opposition
to hostile proposals. In its capacity as a clearing house
for legislative initiatives the OMB acts as a co-ordinating
mechanism which can identify and resolve conflicts between
departments. Since the Nixon presidency the legislative
influence of the OMB has, however, diminished, whilst
advisory councils have become important bodies co-ordinating
major policy developments. The Office, nevertheless, still
retains a major role in ensuring that the mass of legislation
put before Congress bears some relationship to executive
policies.

The OMB currently has a staff of over 600 which includes
a considerable number of career-grade administrators. The
senior members are presidential appointees and its director
is regarded as an important adviser to the President. Reagan,
for example, appointed David Stockman to the office as the
man who promised that he could both increase defence
expenditure, cut taxation and still balance the books by
decimating expenditure on almost all domestic services. The
ability of the OMB to achieve its aims is, however, always
subject to Congress approving its budget proposals, whilst
its role in co-ordinating legislation is dependent on the
President's willingness to listen to its senior officials.

The Departments

The current departments are shown in Table 8.1. Some of the
newer departments are a result of the break-up of larger
departments, whilst one of the earliest creations, the Post
Office, has recently been hived off as an agency. The number
of departments is, nevertheless, smaller than those of most
Western European democracies reflecting, in part, the more
laissez-faire attitudes of American government and also the
greater prominence given to ad hoc agencies.

Each department has different internal structures
although there is, within those dealing with domestic policy,
a generally accepted hierarchy of personnel. At the highest
level are the executive grades which consist largely of

TABLE 8.1   The departments of state

Department	Year Created
Treasury	1789
State (foreign policy)	1789
Interior	1849
Justice	1870
Agriculture	1889
Commerce	1913
Labour	1913
Defence (formerly depts of War and Navy)	1947
Health and Human Services (formerly Health Education and Welfare	1953
Housing and Urban Development	1965
Transportation	1966
Energy	1977
Education	1979

political appointees. At the top of the hierarchy is the
Secretary who is usually deputised by a single Under-
Secretary. Below these posts are deputy under-secretaries
and assistant secretaries. Below this level are the highest
three grades of the civil service which may be tenanted by
both career officials or politicians occupying posts that
have been reserved for patronage appointments. The number of
these political appointees varies among departments. In a
smaller department such as Housing and Urban Development
there were in 1974 39 political appointees compared with 74
career civil servants in the senior echelons of the
organisation (Heclo 1977: 43). The political appointees are
usually allocated overall responsibility for a particular
administrative function or programme area but are also
expected to consult with the Secretary and play a direct role
in forging the overall policy of the department.

Below the largely patronaged-staffed executive level
departments are divided into further groupings which are in
general referred to as bureaux, but may individually be
called offices or divisions. The size, number and importance
of bureaux within each department varies in accord with the
eclectic pattern of growth of the bureaucracy. They include
huge organisations, such as the Inland Revenue Service (IRS)
which has a staff of over 80,000 within the Treasury
Department devoted to collecting federal taxes. Perhaps more
typical are bureaux such as the Animal and Plant Health
Inspectorate of the Department of Agriculture which employs a
work-force of just less than 5,000 to regulate diseases and

pests that could damage agricultural productivity. In most
departments the bureau marks the level at which the chief of
the section may be a career civil servant rather than a
political appointment. Generally the larger and less
specialised bureaux such as the IRS will be headed by a
patronage appointment. The smaller, more technical bureaux
may be controlled by individuals who have worked their way up
the career grades of the civil service. In most cases the
administrators immediately below the bureau chief will be
career officials. Each bureau will extend into further
groups and sections whose organisation reflects the needs of
the department rather than any pre-ordained bureaucratic
structure. Many of these sections will include regional
offices and in some cases such as the IRS or the Social
Security Administration a network of local offices.

RECRUITMENT AND PROMOTION

Political Appointments

The President will normally have personal direction over the
appointment of his senior aides in the White House and the
most senior positions within the departments and important
agencies. The holders of these posts are general policy-
makers who rely on their subordinates to facilitate the
implementation of their departmental strategies. The
President is, however, also formally responsible for the
appointment to many of the posts at the level of the bureau
chiefs or their equivalent although, in practice, these
appointments are generally made by the departmental secretaries or senior White House staff rather than by the
President himself. Many of these appointments are unknown to
not only the President but to his closest advisers. From his
selection to his inauguration the President has less than
three months to make numerous appointments and ensure that
his team is ready to take power.
     Nominations to these lower-level political positions come
from a wide range of sources. On occasions they are recruited
as individuals personally known to senior departmental
politicians but many names are put forward by congressmen or
interest groups. State party officials will also recommend
hardworking colleagues as possible political appointees.
Although most secretaries will endeavour to check the
credentials of nominees often through the help of trusted
head-hunting personnel officers, it is not unknown for the
administration to appoint bureaucrats with little sympathy to
its interests.
     The Reagan administration, however, made strenuous
efforts to appoint officials who were personally loyal to the
President's political philosophy. The White House staff, and

in particular Reagan's counsellor, Edward Meese, along with
his director of personnel, devised a rigorous process of
interviewing likely candidates for almost all posts under the
President's gift in order to ensure that appointees would be
sensitive to the administration's philosophy (Nathan 1983:
74). As a consequence it was not too difficult for Reagan to
find suitable incumbents to fill posts regulating industry
and commerce, but only with considerable difficulty were
individuals found to help wind down social security
programmes. The whole process of appointments under Reagan
became much slower, but in exchange much more careful, in
ensuring that its political appointees would act in tune with
presidential requirements.

Whatever the method of selection of political appointees
they are invariably culled from elite backgrounds. Most will
be white, male, and Anglo-Saxon, with a college degree.
Their working experience will vary depending upon the post to
which they are assigned and in certain areas such as
agriculture or transport preference will be given to specialists in these fields. There is, however, a tendency to
recruit in more generalist areas individuals who are senior
practising lawyers or high-ranking, if not the highest-
ranking, executives in large multinationals. A problem, however, that besets any administration in recruiting from these
fields is the difficulty of keeping individuals in government
service who can attract much higher salaries and equally, if
not more, secure jobs in the private sector. Experience in
government for a few years will, moreover, improve the
prospects for a young executive. After two or three years in
the administration he may greatly enhance his ability to gain
lucrative government contracts. Many patronage appointees do
not, therefore, stay for long in their posts and frequently
leave the administration before the President's term of
office comes to an end. At any time there are invariably a
considerable number of vacancies among positions reserved for
political appointments as a consequence of the transience of
incumbents in these positions. These vacancies are temporarily filled by career civil servants who, in consequence, can
gain a not inconsequential foothold in the higher ranks of
the administration.

The Career Civil Servants

The structure and conditions for recruitment into the civil
service is governed by the Office of Personnel and Management
which was created in 1978 by the division of the Civil
Service Commission. A further creation of this reform is the
Merit Protection Board which oversees complaints concerning
dismissal and discrimination. Entry to most levels within
the career grades of the civil service is by competitive

examinations which, like those of the British Civil Service
Commission, are largely geared to ascertaining the technical
competence rather than academic brilliance of recruits, and
will concentrate on issues such as literacy, numerical skills
and ability to comprehend written material. Entry can be
obtained by this system to several levels in the grading
structure and most college graduates who will hope to reach
the highest ranks will join at the seventh grade. Certain
entrants are, however, exempt from these arrangements.
Lawyers, for example, regard themselves as sufficiently well
trained not to be subject to entry by examination.

The civil service is organised on a single grading
structure ranging from General Service (GS) 1 to GS 18. The
three top grades form an elite echelon to which all ambitious
entrants to the service will aspire. The unified scale
encompasses both managers of services and programmes along
with technicians and specialists. There is, therefore, no
ethos within the service of separate status being accorded to
generalist managers and specialists. Individuals are, nevertheless, recruited to the managerial grades within the
service with little reference to their academic background.
Certain qualifications are, however, more prominent than
others and the most frequent degrees held by senior administrators are in law, economics and accounting. Science graduates may, nevertheless, be found in the managerial as well
as the technical posts. In order to attract highly skilled
scientists and economists to the service there are also
procedures to enable such specialists to enter the civil
service at the highest supergrade levels. Approximately
seven per cent of the senior administrators have been
recruited through this process (Corson and Shale-Paul 1966).

The structure was modified in 1978 by the Carter
administration which steered through Congress a Civil Service
Reform Act aiming to provide more attractive conditions of
service to the highest career officials and at the same time
secure greater commitment from these officials. The Act
created a senior executive service (SES) which comprised some
7,000 of the highest-ranking career civil servants who would
be prepared to act as generalist administrators and be capable of being moved from one department to another. They
could also be dismissed provided they did not have lengthy
experience within government service. In return these high-
level officials were able to obtain greater financial rewards
which included, as in private industry, bonuses for
efficiency and productivity. The reform was, in effect, an
attempt to provide the civil service with a senior executive
career structure similar to that of the major private
businesses which had been continually poaching more able
government employees with the lure of improved working
conditions.

Although the changes to the highest grades were intended

to make the civil service a more attractive career they
enabled the Reagan administration to manipulate the staffing
within these senior positions to the administration's
advantage. As part of his policy of cutting the cost of
domestic programmes the size of the domestic civil service
was considerably reduced. He was able to dismiss untenured
senior civil servants who did not enthusiastically advance
the government's policies and moved those with tenure to
unattractive positions in the remoter States.

ACCOUNTABILITY AND CONTROL

The system of checks and balances that characterises the
political system of the United States ensures that each
branch of the federal government has resources it may use to
check the activities of the bureaucracy.

The President

As chief executive the President appoints his own White House
staff and the senior officials of the departments. In line
with the adage used by Truman that 'the buck stops here', the
President, in the final analysis, can determine how the
bureaucracy should manage policy and can expect each section
of the administration to account to him for its actions.
    In as much as the President appoints the most senior
administrators he is also able to dismiss staff if he feels
that they are incompetent or not fit to carry out his
objectives. The power to dismiss is, however, seriously
limited. Most agency heads are appointed for fixed terms and
cannot subsequently be removed by the President. Career
civil servants with more than 15 years' service cannot be
removed from the service even though their job designations
and locations may be altered by the administration. In
practice many political appointees are chosen by the
secretaries and under-secretaries of departments rather than
the President himself, and are unlikely to be removed by the
President without the consent of the departmental chiefs.
The President himself will, therefore, remove relatively few
individuals from office although those people may themselves
be in the most powerful positions with responsibility for
shaping important elements of the administration's policies.
    In addition to his powers of patronage the President can
also control his bureaucracy by use of fiscal policies.
Through the OMB he will attempt to channel funds to those
officials who are developing or administering policies that
meet with presidential approval, whilst schemes that are not
favoured may be starved of resources. In extremis the
President may also have recourse to legislative initiative in

order to restructure a department or to create or curtail
policy programmes.

Congress

In as much as the President can attempt to control the
bureaucracy through appointments, dismissals, budgeting and
legislation, Congress may also insert itself into these
processes.

The Senate has formal powers to approve all presidential
appointees. This power is rarely invoked to the extent that
senior appointments by Presidents are rejected. It is, moreover, not conventionally expected that it should be used to
over-rule appointments on the grounds that the candidate is
politically unsuited to the views of congressmen, as opposed
to being morally unfit to serve in public office. Hence,
when John Tower, President Bush's nominee as Defense
Secretary, was rejected by Congress in March 1989, it was on
the grounds of his reputation for womanizing and because of
his over-cosy relationship with defence contractors. A
President will usually take care to select senior appointees
who will be above public reproach. Senators can also
influence appointments to more junior positions in the
bureaucracy through the tradition of senatorial courtesy,
that the selection must be made with the approval of the
senators supporting the President from the State concerned.
The device, in effect, gives some senators a share of presidential patronage.

A more powerful means through which Congress can check
bureaucratic power is through the investigatory powers vested
in congressional committees. Each of the subject area committees of Congress are allocated resources to enable them to
investigate the actions of the administration within their
area of competence. They may, therefore, choose to investigate the executive's handling of particular policy issues by
demanding the presence of administration members before a
committee to answer questions from its members. On occasion
a matter may be deemed sufficiently serious to necessitate
the formation of a special investigatory committee. The
committee of the House of Representatives formed to
investigate the sale of arms to Iran has been the most
sensational special investigation in recent years. Congressional committees have considerable powers to call before
them any member of the administration, with the exception of
the President himself, to answer on oath questions put before
them by the committee members. Congress also has powers to
see most government papers and require them to be submitted
to its committees.

Whilst subject committees of Congress can investigate
the role of the bureaucracy in terms of implementation of

policy there are a number of important standing committees
involved in detailed financial control over the bureaucracy.
The constitution provides Congress with the power to raise
taxes and resources for the executive. The President,
through the OMB, draws up a budget which must be submitted to
Congress before it can be enacted. Both the Senate and House
of Representatives have appropriations committees which
undertake the scrutiny of government estimates. These committees break down into a number of small subject area sub-
committees which carry out much of the detailed review of
estimates. They will, as a matter of course, call senior
political and career administrators before them to question
them on the need for their proposed appropriations. It is
possible at this point to ferret out overspending by departments, or through denying funds curtail some presidential
programmes.

The financial conduct of the bureaucracy is also subject
to audit through the General Accounting Office (GAO) which
is, in theory, a body subject to Congress with the power to
investigate whether departments have spent funds as directed
by Congress and also to recommend correct accountancy procedures for the executive. Since its creation in 1921 the GAO
has achieved a considerable degree of independence from
Congress as a consequence of its constitution which places
the organisation under a single Director who is appointed by
the President with senatorial approval for a 15-year term of
office. The GAO has until recently tended to frown on any
deviation from the terms of the appropriations laid down by
Congress and hence, on occasion, has not only restrained
abuse of spending but restricted sensible, flexible management of funds. The organisation, if it finds accountancy
failures, reports its conclusions to Congress, the President
and the press who can then take appropriate action.

Judicial controls

The United States bureaucracy has considerable discretion
delegated to it by Congress to both make regulations and
adjudicate on the extent to which the law has been upheld.
Rule-making and adjudicatory powers are particularly important characteristics of many of the regulatory agencies but
these powers are also central to the operation of many
departmental bureaux. The IRS, for example, is granted
considerable discretion in determining detailed rules on
taxation and whether any individual or corporation is in
default of their tax obligations.

The correct and proper use of these powers is subject to
control by the federal courts and in the final analysis by
the Supreme Court. These courts are considerably burdened
with administrative issues and it has been estimated that

between a fifth and a third of the cases brought before the
Supreme Court are concerned with the activities of the bureaucracy (Mainzer 1973: 50). The departments of state will
at any time have a considerable volume of cases undergoing
some form of judicial review. The federal courts are not,
however, specialised administrative courts in the style of
the French judicial system and deal with almost all forms of
legal adjudication. There are, however, a few highly
specialised administrative courts, such as the United States
Customs Court, which are not typical of the American judicial
system.

Whilst the courts are receptive to complaints against
the bureaucracy certain groups and individuals have, in
practice, a much greater capacity to use the system to their
advantage than others. The pursuit of a complex legal
issue against the government requires resources that can match
those of the government. Only the most wealthy individual
can, unaided, afford to pay for the legal expertise needed to
pursue his claims. Individuals will, moreover, have much more
to fear in terms of penal sanctions, should they lose a case,
than corporate organisations. Successful legal redress is,
therefore, largely the preserve of wealthy interests and in
particular corporate business (Woll 1977: 90-1).

THE CIVIL SERVICE AND POLICY-MAKING

From a European perspective it may initially be thought that
the ability of the President to select political fellow-
travellers to senior positions within the bureaucracy would
be a powerful weapon to curb the power of the civil service
to undermine the policy initiatives of the elected executive.
There are, nevertheless, a large number of studies which be-
moan the inability of the President to ensure that his
objectives are enacted by the bureaucracy (Woll 1977, Nathan
1983). Truman is said to have observed that 'I thought I was
the President, but when it comes to these bureaucrats, I
can't do a damned thing', whilst Kennedy told a petitioner
that 'I agree with you but I don't know whether the government will' (Nathan 1983: 1-2).

Established career bureaucrats can use all of the arts
of permanent officials to ensure the support of their immediate superiors. They can claim expertise and experience of
the traditions and professional working practices of their
departments. They can also be persuasive and will attempt to
forge a common interest with their political superiors in
order to defend the established interests of their bureaux.

The strength of the career civil servants is, however,
largely founded on their considerable experience both of the
structure of government and the problems that beset their
area of specialism. In contrast to the politicians who

command European ministries, the political appointees who head
United States departments may have little familiarity with
public administration and may have little acquaintance with
the interests of legislators most concerned with their area of
responsibility. Hugh Heclo points out that 'because most
political appointees require considerable help in government,
higher civil servants normally need do little by way of harm-
ful actions in order to prevail' (Heclo 1977: 172). They may
simply not bother to point out to their superior some of the
problems and difficulties that confront his department or lie
in the path of his proposals.

If the civil servant fails to gain much support from his
political superiors he can further thwart presidential
objectives by lobbying Congress. Although, in theory, civil
servants should not be lobbyists, in practice they can be
highly effective mobilisers of congressional support. Established bureau chiefs and congressional committee chairmen
both tend to enjoy longer tenures in office than political
appointees of the President. A committee chairman may often
greatly value the help and expertise of career civil servants
in his deliberations on policy and both can, on occasions,
forge strong alliances to protect and develop the interests
of a particular section of the bureaucracy.

The bureaucracy may also gain influence through links
with powerful interest groups. Regulatory agencies have, in
particular, been accused of establishing such close links
with the private interests that they are supposed to regulate
that they have reversed their principle function and, in
practice, protect private concerns from the public interest.
Established career civil servants will also forge close ties
with interests that are affected by their activities. These
ties will, in part, be a result of the need for close working
relationships between business interests and the bureaucracy.

The ability of the bureaucracy to check the power of the
President must, however, be seen as at most one of a number
of sources of control. The consequences of bureaucratic
intransigence must be placed alongside the checks upon his
powers from Congress, regulatory agencies, the judiciary, and
perhaps most significantly, the structure of the office
itself. The President is, apart from the subordinate and
often overlooked Vice-President, the single elected head of
government who must govern through his appointed departmental
heads and White House aides. He cannot hope to be in full
command of all elements of the governmental process and must
delegate considerable policy discretion to his appointed
staff. President Johnson, for example, was so concerned with
Vietnam that he gave almost total command of his domestic
policy to his Chief of Staff, William Calafino. The senior
members of the presidential team will, in turn, give their
appointed subordinates considerable discretion and, as the
chain of command lengthens, many political appointees of the

administration are placed at a considerable distance from the
White House. The politically appointed bureau chief or
assistant secretary will, however, be very close to their
subordinate senior career civil servants, who may well have a
greater facility to gain the heart and mind of their immediate political superior than the remote inhabitant of the
White House.

It would, however, be unwise to conclude that the United
States bureaucracy is a conservative organisation in which
established higher civil servants continually outwit temporary political appointments. The senior grades awarded on
merit contain individuals of considerable ability who are not
averse to pushing forward innovations and will greatly value
working alongside political appointees who have power within
the administration sufficient to achieve the collective goals
of the administration and the bureaucracy. Both elements of
the political system can operate in close and productive
harmony (Heclo 1977: 185).

Links between the civil service, interest groups and
Congress, moreover, do not necessarily corrode presidential
power since they are founded on the favourable ethos towards
private interest that pervades the elite ideology of the
United States and consequently the government and bureaucracy.
The interpenetration of powerful interests with the bureaucracy is, therefore, a political creation. Presidents
appoint to posts in the regulatory agencies and departments
businessmen and lawyers who will be expected to favour the
interests that they represented before assuming their
positions in government. This relationship is perhaps most
strongly and sinisterly developed between the Defence Department and military contractors. Among the overlapping circles
of elites classically identified by C. Wright Mills (1956)
service chiefs and senior civil servants in the Pentagon have
a common interest with major defence contractors to expand
the American arsenal.

The greatest divisions will, however, occur when a new
President wishes to impose policies that are radically
different from those being pursued by the established
bureaucracy. Kennedy's New Frontier created the need for
more radically minded bureaucracts. Reagan's reversal of
these policies of public intervention resulted in a concerted
strategy by his senior aides to remove the Kennedy-style
administrator who was unlikely to favour the cutback in the
scope and role of government occasioned by the new
conservatism. The civil service was being returned to the
years of Coolidge and Hoover.

REFERENCES AND FURTHER READING

Brown, R. E. (1970) The GAO, Knoxville, University of
Tennessee Press.

Corson, J. J. and Shale-Paul, R. (1966) Men Near the Top,
Baltimore, John Hopkins Press.

Grant, A. (1982) The American Political Process, 2nd ed.,
London, Heinemann.

Griffith, E. S. (1983) The American System of Government,
6th ed., London, Methuen.

Heclo, H. (1977) A Government of Strangers, Washington,
Brookings Institution.

Lees, J. D. (1983) The Political System of the United
States, 3rd ed., London, Faber and Faber.

Mainzer, L. C. (1973) Political Bureaucracy, Glenview,
Illinois, Scott, Foresman and Company.

Mills, C. W. (1956) The Power Elite, New York, Oxford
University Press.

Nathan, R. P. (1983) The Administrative Presidency, New York,
John Wiley.

Van Riper, P. R. (1958) A History of the United States Civil
Service, Evanston, Row Peterson.

Woll, P. (1977) American Bureaucracy, 2nd ed., New York,
W. W. Norton.

Chapter 9

WEST GERMANY

A. R. Peters

THE POLITICAL SETTING: INSTITUTIONS

The modern West German state dates from 1949 with the election
of the first post-war government led by Konrad Adenauer. The
technical distribution of power within the political system
is delineated by the Basic Law drawn up by a Constituent
Assembly in 1948. In effect, the format adopted has widely
been seen as reflecting the determination of the western
occupying powers to establish a system of government firmly
grounded in the principles of liberal democracy, with a
clear-cut separation of powers. To this end a federal system
was adopted, which built on the bedrock of local and state-
level administration progressively licensed by the Allies in
the period 1946-9, with power dispersed within the system
between ten states and a federal government established in
Bonn. Although the power of initiative, in terms of
legislative competence, lies in most fields with Bonn, the
states are guaranteed a voice in federal affairs through the
creation of a bicameral legislature incorporating an elected
chamber, the Bundestag, from which the Chancellor is drawn as
leader of the ruling political party or coalition, and a
second chamber, the Bundesrat, composed of delegates from the
states (Länder). The power of scrutiny and veto held by the
Bundesrat over vast areas of federal legislation, coupled
with the reliance of Bonn on the administrative apparatus of
the Länder to implement legislation and provide services, has
ensured that effective power in West Germany has not
gravitated to the federal government.
     The network of checks and balances within the West
German political system is reinforced by the explicit commitment within the Basic Law to the defence of individual rights
and in particular freedom of speech, religion, assembly,
association and security. While the political parties are
charged with expressing the will of the German people the
determination to prevent the suppression of basic rights is
indicated by the decision to make the Federal Constitutional

Court, composed of 16 judges elected by the legislature, the ultimate guardian of the Basic Law and all constitutional questions.

In a desire to eliminate the problems that contributed to the downfall of Weimar, the respective roles of the Chancellor and the President have been revised, with power clearly gravitating towards the Chancellor who is drawn from the dominant coalition within the Bundestag. In comparision to his pre-war prestige the President is no longer popularly elected and now holds a largely ceremonial position. In addition the propensity for party factionalism in the legislature has been reduced by a ruling that parties must secure five per cent of the vote at an election in order to gain seats within the Bundestag. It would appear, therefore, that the adoption of a federal system with a central legislature anchored in the tradition of responsible party competition and scrutiny, ultimately backed by the power of the Federal Constitutional Court, represents an attempt to instil in West Germany a political system firmly fixed in the mould of a liberal democracy.

To view the format, however, as purely a system implanted by foreign powers would be misleading. While except for the period of the Weimar regime Germany had only flirted with liberal democracy, parallels with the past can be drawn with the selection of a federal format which was used by Bismarck in the nineteenth century to weld together the first German state. Furthermore, it has been suggested that the establishment of a formal constitution backed by a constitutional court is indicative of the German preference for a legalistic framework in the conduct of government (Rechtsstaat). To an extent these parallels are justified, but the similarities with previous systems of government should not be pressed. Although Adenauer's interpretation of the power of the Chancellor was seen as echoing an innate desire for strong executive leadership, the focus of the post-war system lies firmly with the political parties which, through their need to command an electoral majority, must remain representative of popular opinion.

While, therefore, far from perfect and open to charges of perpetuating a legalistic approach to problem-solving, the Basic Law has provided within the new German state the framework for the implantation of the central tenets of liberal democracy.

POLITICAL SETTING: POLITICAL CULTURE

In dealing with comparative political culture there is always the temptation to draw upon national caricatures or stereotypes. In this sense the German approach to the conduct of politics is often analysed within a Hegelian perspective,

seeking to draw a distinction between state and society.
Within this approach the faith placed in political leadership
that is seen as objective and representative of a higher
national interest paves the way for the assertion that the
German people prefer and expect strong leadership that
positions itself above the competitive sectional interests of
civil society.

To an extent elements of such an analysis can be seen in
the study of post-war political culture conducted by Almond
and Verba in 1959. Their conclusions point firmly to the
suggestion that, while West Germans were well acquainted with
the mechanics of the political system, in general there was
little evidence of positive identification with the system
and a broad alienation toward political activism at all
levels. Support for the system was, therefore, based partly
on its ability to satisfy economic aspirations and also a
marked faith in the efficiency and impartiality of the state
bureaucracy. On this basis the authors concluded that while
there existed grounds for optimism, the values of liberal
democracy had by no means been widely accepted by the West
German people. More recent studies, however, have indicated
that to a remarkable extent Almond and Verba's optimism was
justified in that the West German people have displayed an
increasing willingness to participate in the democratic
process and have in general indicated their faith in the
ability of the political system to respond to their demands.

In attempting to account for this rapid change reference
has to be made to several factors that distinguish West
Germany from pre-war Germany. In particular, the changing
nature of partisanship has been significant. Widespread
system support was traditionally inhibited by deep-rooted
sectionalism in German society based on religious rivalry,
distinctive local traditions and the imprint of a heavily
class-divided society. To a great extent the FRG, which now
contains a numerical balance between Catholics and Protestants, has eliminated religious subcultures. In additon, re-
drawing of state boundaries and the influence of a modern
industrial society have largely reduced the significance of
regional groupings. The major change, however, lies in class
distinction, with the decline of traditional blue and white-
collar differentiation alongside wider access to education,
housing and welfare services. West Germany has, therefore,
witnessed an increase in social mobility and a blurring of
class distinctions. Furthermore, the assimilation of refugees
from eastern Europe and workers from southern Europe has seen
the establishment of a more cosmopolitan society.

Ironically, it could be suggested that the FRG has continued, and to an extent completed, a revolution in German
society initiated by the National Socialists. It was the Nazi
era that saw the first major challenge to the power of the
traditional elites - the landed aristocracy, the bureaucracy

184

and the armed forces - and the second world war that witnessed the discrediting of those who sought to succeed them as a
new ruling caste. In the flux and turmoil of post-war
Germany political power has gravitated increasingly into the
hands of the political parties, to the extent that West
Germany is now commonly referred to as a Parteienstaat. It
has to be remembered, however, that a system that encourages
participation must also display an ability to accommodate
political demands. To this extent the need to fulfil economic
expectations, the demands of those who see themselves as
disadvantaged, and the groundswell of interest in sensitive
policy areas such as the environment and defence have tested
and will continue to test the German political system severely
for some time to come.

THE POLITICAL PARTIES

There are three major political parties in West Germany: the
conservative Christian Democratic Union (CDU), with its autonomous Bavarian wing, the Christian Social Union (CSU); the
Social Democratic Party (SPD); and the liberal Free Democratic
Party (FPD). Their emergence as the driving force in the political system has had particular implications for the format
and role of the bureaucracy, which was traditionally seen as
representing national goals and cohesion above the turmoil
and rifts of civil society. It was widely respected for its
thoroughness and impartiality, given its position of authority
derived from the implementation of supposedly rationally
derived national guidelines. This role not only afforded the
bureaucracy an enhanced status in German society, but also
effectively insulated it from subservience to the party
political battle. In the post-war era, however, the position
of the bureaucracy has been significantly undermined by the
state's emphasis on their loyalty to the government and
therefore to the ruling political parties. The reorientation
of this relationship is symbolised by the effective politicisation of senior civil service posts, which are now controlled
by the ruling coalition and are generally given to civil servants who are members of, or sympathetic to, that coalition.
    In many senses, therefore, Parteienstaat is now a reality
in West Germany as the political parties attempt to provide
an adequate vehicle to fuse the interest of the state and
civil society. This role is particularly ambitious, given the
need in the immediate post-war era not just to aggregate
interests but also to educate the electorate to the values of
liberal democracy. As suggested earlier, high electoral turnout, party membership figures and the profusion of interest
group activity indicate that this role has been performed
more than adequately, although problems exist in certain
areas. In particular, increasing doubts as to the efficiency

of the parties in their role as agents of political communication led, in the 1970s, to an increase in locally based
pressure group politics. The Burger-initiativen have to an
extent rejuvenated local politics through the provision of an
alternative to the established patterns of party politics and
have forced the major parties to pay increased attention to
issues such as welfare and the environment and to re-assess
the nature of their links with the electorate at grass roots
level.

The relationship established between the bureaucracy and
the political parties has also been identified as an area for
concern. In that party support is a precondition for career
advancement, civil servants now play a central role in the
membership and running of the major political parties. Not
only has this generated charges of corruption but it has also
led to the assertion that the fusion of the bureaucracy and
the political parties has been conducted on terms that give
undue influence to the bureaucracy. Certainly it is
undeniable that the civil service is now one of the premier
pressure groups in the political process, in that
approximately 40 per cent of Bundestag deputies have civil
service backgrounds. Although the post-war reforms have
revolutionised the relationship between parties and the
bureaucracy, it is possible to suggest that the links have
been remoulded in a manner not unfavourable to the civil
service. Given the absence of severe ideological divisions
between the major political parties and the ability of the
bureaucracy to operate within the parties as an extremely
influential pressure group, some critics have suggested
that the bureaucracy is now the 'fourth' party in West
Germany.

WEST GERMAN FEDERALISM

The format of West German federalism has particular implications for the structuring and role of the bureaucracy. Constitutionally, the bedrock of the system is provided by the
11 states (Länder), each with its own constitution, legislature, civil service and the right to enact legislation on any
topic not specifically reserved for the federal government or
deemed by the Federal Constitutional Court to be inconsistent
with the Basic Law. In reality, however, the legislative
initiative has been appropriated by the federal government,
which holds exclusive control over areas such as foreign
affairs and defence in addition to retaining the authority to
intervene in a vast number of fields such as transport, trade
and commerce and the organisation of civil and criminal law.
These powers are reinforced by the use of framework legislation allowing the federal government to establish guidelines for the provision of a vast array of public services.

186

Quite clearly, the federal government has legislated on most
areas of importance and the Länder are left in effective
control only of those areas specifically exempt from central
direction - the local police force, cultural affairs, local
government and broadcasting.

While legislative competence lies primarily with Bonn,
the Länder do play an influential role in both service
provision and policy-making. Through the medium of the
Bundesrat the states have direct representation in the
deliberations of the federal government. In addition, their
autonomy is bolstered by the Basic Law that guarantees the
Länder and local government sources of independent finance.
At present the Länder are automatically allocated 45 per cent
of all revenue derived from taxation, alongside extensive
grants and fees received from Bonn for the execution of
services on behalf of the federal government. Furthermore,
although the Länder only hold exclusive control of a limited
number of services, in their capacity as agents for the
federal government they actually provide the vast majority of
services undertaken by the public sector in West Germany.
This role gives the Länder extensive discretion in the
determination of the level and format of service provision
and an influential voice in policy formulation and planning.
While it has been suggested that West German federalism is
little more than administrative decentralisation, it is more
accurately described as 'co-operative federalism'. Without
doubt, in the past decade Bonn has used its financial
leverage to increase its influence over the Länder, but the
latter still retain a significant element of autonomy. The
relationship is perhaps exemplified by the establishment, in
1967, of a framework for central-local collaboration in what
are termed 'Joint Tasks'. In the fields of higher education
and regional economic development projects are now jointly
funded by federal and state agencies, with Bonn holding the
right to establish national planning guidelines, but the
actual implementation still the preserve of state agencies.

Although there has been a drift towards centralisation
the Länder have utilised their constitutional independence to
retain an element of autonomy and have also been successful
in influencing decision-making in Bonn. Constitutionally the
Bund has to consult the Länder before implementing measures
that might affect their interests under what are generally
known as the 'Consent Laws'. To this end the Länder maintain
delegations in Bonn that play an active role in the lobbying
and negotiations that surrounds the policy-making process.
In addition the reliance of the federal ministries on the
Länder for administrative feedback and advice has necessitated
close links between the various arms of the West German civil
service. These connections have also been constantly cross
fertilised by the interaction of officials within a network of
permanent conferences covering areas such as finance,

education and interior affairs, and designed to co-ordinate information and policy guidelines between the various states and the federal ministries. It is within these committees that a vast array of administrative agreements are concluded that symbolise the interdependence of the federal and state governments.

German federalism is therefore a delicate inter-weaving of political and administrative responsibilities that hinges heavily upon the nature of the relationship between the federal and the state civil services. It has been contended that the system surrenders too much power to officials to interpret and implement political guidelines. In response, however, it has to be noted that the central links within the chain are the political parties that operate at both the state and federal levels. Through the ability to appoint and replace senior figures within the bureaucracy, channels of accountability alongside the normal legislative role are provided that suggest that the West German bureaucracy does not escape detailed scutiny.

THE EXECUTIVE

Although parallels can be drawn between the modern West German state and pre-war Germany in most instances the link- ages are tenuous. For example, as has been noted previously the relationship between the Chancellor and the President has been completely redrawn in that the President is now nomin- ated by a joint assembly of the Bundestag and the Länder (Bundesversammlung) rather than directly elected, as in the pre-war period. In addition, while the President has to approve the Bundestag's nomination of the candidate for the position of Chancellor, and retains the power to appoint several key personnel within the bureaucracy, the role has essentially been interpreted by its post-war incumbents as largely ceremonial and passive. Indeed, successive Presidents have rarely chosen to challenge the Bundestag or to oppose the Chancellor in the selection of his Cabinet.

The effective head of state is therefore the Chancellor, who is drawn from the Bundestag and commands the loyalty of a majority of its members. The Chancellor is the central figure within the policy-making process in that upon assuming office he holds the formal power to dispense all ministerial posts, dictate the number and format of ministries and estab- lish policy guidelines. Furthermore, unlike the British Prime Minister, the Chancellor cannot be ousted by a simple vote of no confidence registered by the Bundestag. In order to remove the Chancellor the Bundestag must accept the nomi- nation of an alternative candidate in what is generally termed a 'constructive vote of no confidence'. The replace- ment of Helmut Schmidt by Helmut Kohl in 1982 is the only example of a Chancellor being ousted in this manner in mid-term.

The Chancellor is supported by a large and influential secretariat known as the Chancellor's Office staffed by some 600 people. This unit is at the heart of the policy-making process, servicing the Cabinet and maintaining extensive links with the various ministries. Although attempts by Brandt in his first term to expand the Chancellor's Office to take on the role of a policy 'think-tank' were largely resisted by the bureaucracy and individual ministers, the Office still holds an influential position by virtue of its role as a channel of communication between the Chancellor and individual ministries, supervising the implementation of the Chancellor's policy guidelines and monitoring policy feedback.

During the 13 years that Konrad Adenauer held the post of Chancellor it was suggested that the office had excessive power, and indeed that Adenauer manipulated the position to adopt an almost presidential posture. Closer analysis and subsequent events, however, indicate that the Chancellor is, in fact, closely surrounded by a network of checks and balances. Perhaps the most visible counterweight is the Basic Law, which can only be amended with the consent of two-thirds of the Bundestag and the Bundesrat. Furthermore, interpretation of the Basic Law is vested in the Federal Constitutional Court, whose 16 jurors are elected by two-third majorities from the Bundestag and the Bundesrat. Even leeway on the selection of ministers is often restricted by the bargaining necessary to forge a governing coalition and the demands of senior figures from within the Chancellor's own party. Helmut Kohl, for example, in 1982 had to accommodate not only the expectations of CDU members but also to satisfy the FDP and CSU in order to forge a governing coalition. While to an extent the Chancellor is able to bind his Cabinet, once formed, by the extension of collective respons-ibility, he differs from his British counterpart in that he does not have the right to dictate policy to his ministers or interfere in the selection of senior civil servants. In addition, given the tradition in West Germany of Bundestag deputies being drawn from commerce, interest groups, or seconded from the civil service, the Chancellor is often confronted by ministers with a vast amount of experience in their assigned area and a fair amount of formal freedom to develop policy initiatives.

The power of the Chancellor is, therefore, most often seen in the negative sense. While he is able to outline policy guidelines, his main strength lies in the ability to veto ministerial decisions that conflict with his guidelines. As with most of his counterparts in Western Europe, the West German Chancellor is a key figure in setting the tone and goals of government and holds certain powers of patronage and policy initiation. In order to achieve these goals, however,

he relies heavily on the co-operation and support of his
Cabinet colleagues, particularly the inner circle holding the
key ministries of Finance, Interior and Foreign Affairs, who
dominate both the proceedings of Cabinet and the limited
number of functional sub-committees. The delicate tightrope
walked by the Chancellor is exemplified by his relationship
with the Bundestag. Given the discipline of party voting
patterns, the Chancellor is not generally expected to give
the fighting performance in debate that is associated with
the British Prime Minister, but he is often confronted by
powerful figures within his own party in the form of party
chairmen and Fraktion chairmen, who will ensure that the
executive does not lose touch with the main body of the
party. While, therefore, the Chancellor undoubtedly holds a
central position in the policy-making process, his effective
power is largely conditioned by his ability to mobilise support, and particularly by his ability to build bridges with a
number of influential forces within the governing coalition.

STRUCTURES

One of the salient features of the West German political
system is the relative autonomy enjoyed by ministers.
Certainly the role played by the Cabinet in policy evolution
is limited due to the problems created by coalition government that often result in policy guidelines being formulated
within the party caucus rather than within the Cabinet arena.
In this sense the Cabinet is generally preoccupied with the
scrutiny of draft legislation and recommendations emanating
from the ministries rather than being actively engaged in
policy formulation. This restricted role is reflected in the
absence of an extensive network of Cabinet subcommittees and,
in the face of a general acceptance of an element of departmental autonomy, the convention of collective responsibility
is relatively weak. Within this context the minister is seen
primarily as a departmental leader and spokesman rather than
as a member of a policy-making team. Certainly, when in
office, although ministers are bound to observe the broad
guidelines established by the Chancellor and are ultimately
accountable to the Bundestag, they are offered a wide degree
of freedom to run their departments. The success of this
approach is largely based on the fact that while generalists
are not unknown within ministerial ranks, appointments are
usually made from area specialists within the parties who
often remain in post for long periods, given the stability of
governing coalitions in the post-war era. Although the
facility exists to appoint ministers who are not Bundestag
deputies, it has rarely been utilised.
        Given the general reluctance to appoint ministers without
portfolio, the size of the Cabinet has generally oscillated

between 16 and 22. The number attending meetings, however,
varies markedly, given the acceptance of the convention that
deputies can represent absent ministers and the willingness
to include additional experts, such as the party chairmen and
Fraktion leaders at key discussions. In general, although
the number and format of departments has changed considerably,
the Cabinet draws upon ministers from the following areas:

Interior	Labour and Social
Finance	Affairs
Foreign Affairs	Postal Communications
Economic Affairs	Planning, Building and
Defence	Urban Development
Justice	Inner German Affairs
Education and	Youth, Family Affairs and
Science	Health
Agriculture	Economic Co-operation
Transport	Research and Technology

The division of responsibility reflects a combination of
traditional structures, such as Foreign Affairs and Justice,
alongside bodies targeted at programme areas, such as Research
and Technology, and specific client groups, such as Labour
and Social Affairs. Quite clearly, within this structure
certain ministries are identified as senior partners, generally due to the fact that their responsibilities cut across
the roles of junior departments. For example, all departments
must operate within a budget approved by the Ministry of
Finance, the Ministry of Justice scrutinises the legality of
departmental activity, while the Ministry of the Interior has
overall responsibility for the domestic civil service.
    It would be a mistake, however, to overemphasise the
role of the federal ministries. In 1980 it was estimated
that approximately 90 per cent of public employees were
employed at either state or local level. Furthermore, of
those classified as federal employees, the majority were
employed within the limited number of ministries that have an
extensive structure beyond the confines of Bonn, such as the
Ministry of Foreign Affairs and the Ministry of Defence. Many
more are involved in the running of the few district and
local services actually provided by the federal ministries,
such as rail transport, postal services and the collection of
certain taxes. Finally, a large number are employed in
agencies such as the Meteorological Office and the Federal
Statistical Office which, while under the overall jurisdiction of the federal government in effect enjoy a semi-
autonomous status. Of those classified as federal employees,
therefore, only approximately 20,000 actually work in the
various ministries based in Bonn. This reflects in essence
the role of the federal ministries which is, in most
instances, to establish policy guidelines and then supervise

and co-ordinate the provision of services by other agencies.
In terms of internal organisation each ministry is
structured on a hierarchical basis. At the apex of power sits
the minister, assisted by a parliamentary state secretary
drawn from the Bundestag, who is permitted to deputise for
the minister both in Cabinet and in the Bundestag. Depending
on the size of the department, the minister is assisted by one
or two state secretaries. The duties of the department will
be allocated to a number of divisions, with specific responsibilities given to subdivisions and ultimately to sections.
In general, the state secretaries and divisional heads are
seen as political appointments, although several departments
have a tradition of appointing career civil servants to
divisional and state secretary posts that are not considered
to be politically sensitive.

The heart of the department is the section, which consists of a small team of approximately five. It has been
suggested that the subdivision of responsibility within a
ministry into as many as 100 sections reduces efficiency and
co-ordination, given that the only cross-functional agencies
are those providing services such as personnel, finance and
legal advice. In addition, just as the minister is ultimately
responsible for the work of his department, section and
divisional heads are held accountable for decisions taken
within their specific areas. While this creates clear lines
of responsibility and allows the most successful to be ear-
marked for rapid promotion, it has been contended that it
encourages a cautious approach to policy-making and the avoid-
ance of risk taking and innovation.

In most cases, therefore, federal ministries are relatively small in terms of personnel and finance. Where they
pursue a more expansive role it is generally through the
medium of a range of semi-autonomous agencies such as the
Federal Insurance Office, which, under the direction of the
Ministry of Labour and Social Affairs, supervises the national
network of compulsory insurance schemes covering accidents,
sickness and unemployment. Most of the major ministries have
responsibility for a range of agencies, one of the most not-
able being the Ministry of the Interior, which has jurisdiction over the Federal Office for the Protection of the Constitution and the Federal Archives. In addition, ministries
often sponsor a range of research institutes. In most cases
the agencies are established by virtue of legislation or
decree and effectively operate autonomously within an overall
budget and policy guidelines established by the parent body.
Although the agencies stand one step removed from the rigid
hierarchy of departmental accountability, control is exerted
by virtue of tight legal and financial limitations on their
activity and the ability of individuals and groups to seek
redress of grievances through the network of administrative
courts.

THE BUREAUCRATS

In comparison with Britain the term 'public servant' is used
in a different context in West Germany in that it refers to
all those who are in the employment of the state.. With the
inclusion of groups such as postal workers, teachers and
railway workers, approximately 12 per cent of the working
population of West Germany can be classified as public
servants, the vast majority being employed by the Länder or
local government. Despite the variety of institutions
employing public servants, their conditions of service,
however, are effectively governed by federal legislation in
the form of the Federal Civil Service Laws of 1977 and 1983.
By virtue of its power to control legislation affecting
public servants the 'federal government has established a
national pattern for conditions of service and promotion. In
general, public servants are recruited into one of four categories, each with an internal ladder of posts:

Higher service	A13-B11
Executive	A9-A12
Clerical	A5-A8
Basic	A1-A4

These ladders are staffed by three broad categories of
employees:

Beamten   (officials)
Angestellten   (white-collar employees)
Arbiter   (workers)

A place amongst the ranks of the Beamten has traditionally been prized in German society, for although obliged to
swear loyalty to the constitution and accept a no-strike
agreement, the West German civil servant is afforded high
status in society, derived not only from his/her position of
responsibility but also from the financial rewards attached
to the post in the form of a lifetime job guarantee and a
generous non-contributory pension scheme. Although, in
recent years, the distinctions between Beamten and
Angestellten have been reduced and career patterns in the
private sector have become increasingly lucrative, a position
in the higher civil service is still held in high regard.
    The higher grades of the West German civil service are
dominated by the Beamten by virtue not only of their superior
educational background but also due to the fact that public
law vests formal authority solely in the Beamten, with the
Angestellten seen simply as ancillary white-collar workers.
Recruitment to the higher grades and subsequent training are
still largely conditioned by the standards established over a
century ago by the Prussian administrative apparatus. The

Prussian influence is manifest in the retention of rigid
grading levels with entry determined by educational qualifications and little scope for movement between levels.

While there is no equivalent to the British Civil
Service Commission, with federal ministries operating
independent recruitment schemes, there is broad uniformity in
the level of academic achievement required for entry into the
higher civil service. Candidates are expected to have passed
the Arbitur - an examination of general competence only undertaken at the Gymnasium (the highest of the three categories
of secondary school) - and to have completed three years at
university. Traditionally, the study of law alongside social
sciences was seen as the natural precondition for undertaking
the two formal entrance examinations and two-year probation-
ary period. This reflects yet again the legalistic image of
the civil service as the impartial adjudicator and implementor
of established guidelines and legislation. To an extent this
tradition has been reduced, with increasing emphasis placed
on the social sciences, but the preference for a legal background is still marked within the higher civil service,
particularly within the federal bureaucracy. In comparison
with other nations, this position has been allowed to continue
due to the tendency to hive off specialist technical functions
to semi-autonomous agencies, thus avoiding the clash between
specialists and generalists. While, therefore, senior civil
servants are encouraged to take further academic qualifications and may pass through a network of in-service training
in administration provided by individual departments or the
High School for Administrative Sciences based in Speyer, the
Prussian tradition is still much in evidence.

Although acceptance into the higher civil service is
technically on merit, the insistence on formal educational
qualifications and the preference for a legalistic background
has effectively restricted those eligible for application.
While not comparable to the British public school-Oxbridge
network, the West German civil service undoubtedly draws
largely on those from a middle-class background. The absence
of extensive promotion between broad classifications, and
indeed the rigid departmentalisation that often precludes a
rotation of senior civil servants between different ministries, have at times been heavily criticised. Certainly doubts
can be cast on the ability of the West German bureaucracy to
keep in touch with the changing demands of a sophisticated
industrialised society.

The danger of ministers being unduly influenced by their
officials is increased by the absence of an inner cabinet of
political advisers within West German ministries. To an
extent, however, the influence of the bureaucracy is mitigated by the open acknowledgement that within the higher civil
service all posts above the position of B7 are potentially
political appointments. Alongside, therefore, the Prussian

promotion-by-merit network, operates a network of patronage aimed at ensuring that civil servants observe the needs of their political overlords. While many posts are seen as non-political, socialist governments in particular have used this capacity to make sweeping changes at all levels of the public service. Although fears of corruption have been expressed, the system has allowed an infusion of different talents and backgrounds into the higher civil service and has encouraged increased flexibility in the appointment and movement of officials between departments.

Resistance within the federal higher service to political appointments has been muted. This can partly be explained by the fact that the influx of 'new blood' has often consisted of officials drawn from the higher service in the various Länder who are quickly assimilated within the federal bureaucracy. In addition, it has to be noted that the changes have been cushioned by a guarantee that displaced officials will receive an alternative post or equivalent pension. Finally, West German civil servants are now free to join political parties and stand for elected office. New horizons have been opened for the civil service and the promise of subsequent re-employment has encouraged many civil servants to stand for election to the state and federal assemblies. Indeed public servants are now the largest occupational grouping within the Bundestag deputies.

The West German civil service therefore retains much of the Prussian tradition in the form of career structure moulded around a rigid hierarchy of posts with entrance determined by academic qualifications. Undoubtedly, however, the admission in the post-war period of the artificiality of the distinction between political and administrative policy has changed the ethos of the civil service. The intermeshing of the bureaucracy and the parties has proceeded relatively smoothly and encouraged the bureaucracy to acknowledge that policy-making must be conditioned by the acknowledgement of the realities of party politics.

ACCOUNTABILITY

As in most liberal democracies, the relationship established between the executive and the legislature is of great significance in ensuring that governments are accountable for their actions. In this sphere West Germany outwardly reflects the British tradition, with accountability being based on the acceptance by the Cabinet of collective responsibility for the overall policy guidelines established by the government, supported by individual ministerial responsibility for the running of particular departments. Within this format, the Bundestag is expected to scrutinise the activities of government, by seeking information from ministers in the course of debates and Question Time. In addition, the Bundestag has a range of specialist committees shadowing most of the major ministries.

The committee network is probably the primary vehicle used by the Bundestag to monitor executive activity, and at the centre of the process stands the Appropriations Committee, which holds overall responsibility for scrutinising and approving all government expenditure as part of a process that is initiated by the submission of ministerial accounts to the Federal Court of Accounts. The court, which holds independent legal status, is presided over by a President, who generally also holds the office of Commissioner for the Efficiency of the Administration. The report compiled by the court is passed for approval to the Appropriations Committee, thus presenting the Bundestag with the opportunity to comment on government expenditure. One final weapon in the armoury of the Bundestag is the ability to establish, upon request of a quarter of the deputies, a Committee of Investigation to examine misdemeanors allegedly perpetrated by the executive. Although such committees have often been stifled by an inbuilt government majority, they have been used increasingly to extract information from the executive, most notably in the scrutiny of the suggestion that political parties have illegally received significant contributions to their funds from the business organisations.

In most respects, however, parallels should not be drawn between the British House of Commons and the Bundestag. While accountability within the British system is founded on a tradition of active and constant scrutiny by the Opposition, it is not unusual for government legislation in the Bundestag to be widely and openly supported by the Opposition and, in comparison with the House of Commons, Question Time and parliamentary debates are often rather tepid affairs. Quite clearly, the Bundestag does not see itself as primarily concerned with checking initiatives emanating from the executive but prefers to play an active role in policy formation. The focus of activity in the Bundestag, therefore, is the network of specialist committees that examine proposed legislation. The rejection of the British pattern of confrontation between Government and Opposition is indicated by the organisation and proceedings of the committees. Committee members tend to be specialists in their field, often acting as representatives of outside interest groups with the expertise and support to challenge complex pieces of legislation. As a result the executive is often forced to negotiate and strike bargains during the passage of legislation. The committee system is, therefore, an important focus for policy formulation and meetings are almost always attended by ministers and senior civil servants.

The linkages thus established between ministries and the Bundestag provides the legislature with access to the

decision-making process and assist in the breaking down of
barriers between politicians and the bureaucracy. Informally
these ties are further reinforced by the attendance of
selected civil servants at the working groups on policy
formation established by individual parties.

The rather tepid nature of the party battle within the
Bundestag is largely conditioned by the appreciation that
while Parliament in Britain carries extensive responsibility
as a counterweight to executive power, in West Germany the
defence and interpretation of the constitution is clearly
vested in the Federal Constitutional Court. Ultimately,
therefore, behind the Bundestag the Basic Law provides a
reference point for the examination of government action. In
this light it is not surprising to find that there is little
pressure for the expansion of the powers of the Bundestag to
review government activity. Although an ombudsman now exists
to deal with complaints relating to the military and at Land
level Rhineland-Pfalz has experimented with an ombudsman for
administration, the institution is unlikely to be duplicated
at the federal level.

Scrutiny of the administration is, therefore, largely
left to the judicial system. The right of citizens to legal
redress against the actions of the state is encompassed in
the establishment of a network of Administrative Courts at
the district, state and federal levels. The courts are
empowered to investigate the use of the legal and discretion-
ary power vested in the bureaucracy and to take action against
their improper use. The network of courts is supplemented by
specialist courts covering matters such as taxation, labour
law and social security, which provide relatively accessible
channels through which citizens can challenge administrative
acts.

The system is, however, not without its problems, for
cases can often be lengthy and expensive, with applicants
bearing the full cost if a case is lost. In addition, the
courts are largely confined to making comments on the legality
of administrative decisions, with little power to deal with
inefficiency and maladministration. In this context, there
is pressure for the reform of the Administrative Courts,
particularly as a result of doubts surrounding the ability of
the system to control the mounting data banks held by federal
ministries on individuals and organisations. The creation in
1978 of a Federal Commissioner for Data Protection, empowered
to receive complaints from citizens and report to the
Bundestag, has partially resolved the problem, although the
central issue of whether administrative review should be
conducted by the judiciary is still undecided.

CONTROL

Control of the bureaucracy is generally regarded as an essential element of the political system. Attention in this area focuses not only on channels of legal redress open to the public but also on the means by which elected representatives exert direct and indirect influence over the bureaucracy. In comparision with Britain it is tempting to treat the question of internal political control as rather academic in West Germany, with the acceptance that all senior and influential posts within the bureaucracy are political appointments. In this light, given the ability of federal ministers to 'hire and fire' their senior civil servants and influence appointments at all levels within the system, it could be contended that the West German civil servant is unable to escape the reality of having to work within a system that is constitutionally and effectively dominated by the politicians. Whilst, therefore, civil servants still have a degree of discretion in the exercise of their administrative role, it would appear that the conflict of interests that might occur between politicians and permanent officials is less likely in the West German context.

It would be a mistake, however, to underestimate the influence of the West German civil service in that, unlike many of their counterparts in other countries, the civil service plays an active part in the political arena. Given the numerical size of the West German public service and its control of many essential services in society, the bargaining power of the public sector unions representing officials, employees and workers is extensive, both in internal negotiation of terms of service, conducted through a network of Personnel Councils (on the pattern of the British Whitley Council network), and as a general pressure group on wider issues. In addition, the civil service is one of the most successful interest groups within the political parties. It is hardly surprising, therefore, that the Bundestag has generally been reluctant to challenge the role and privileges of the bureaucracy, given the influence of the civil service lobby, which is generally over-represented as a percentage of both party and Bundestag membership, in comparison with other occupational groups in West Germany.

Financial Control

As noted previously, the bureaucracy is subject to formal financial scrutiny, given the necessity for departmental accounts to be audited by the Federal Court of Accounts and approved by the Bundestag. While this procedure applies only to expenditure already undertaken by the executive, the Bundestag does retain the ability to influence future expend-

iture patterns through its examination of the annual budget
proposals. Although the expertise of the Appropriations
Committee enforces a certain discipline on departmental
spending projections, much of the value of this exercise is
negated by party discipline. The central role within the
allocation of expenditure is therefore played not by the
Bundestag but by the Ministry of Finance. Through negotiations with individual departments the Finance Ministry wields
extensive power in the allocation of department and project
budgets. The process of assembling the budget proceeded
fairly amicably in a climate of spiraling economic growth,
but since the mid-1960s West Germany has witnessed an expansion of public expenditure to a level that threatens to out-
strip incoming revenue. The adoption, therefore, in 1967 of
a rolling medium-term (five-year) expenditure plan was indicative of the need to establish priorities in the allocation
of resources. As the agency charged with implementing the
programme the Finance Ministry has increased in power and
influence, for although its projections are not binding, its
role is central in determining spending priorities and
resolving clashes between departments.

Control of expenditure, however, is by no means as rigid
as in other countries. A large slice of annual expenditure
is in practice delegated to local and state-level government,
while the medium-term strategy only takes the form of a guide-
line. In addition, federal ministries have yet to evolve a
network of programme review and monitoring to assess in depth
whether expenditure is allied to clearly established goals,
and to what extent the goals are achieved. The Ministry of
Finance has therefore been accused of an overall preoccupation with the levels of total government expenditure and
individual departmental expenditure patterns, rather than
with a value-for-money analysis of individual projects.

BERUFSVERBOT

The loyalty of public employees to the ideals of the Basic Law
has been a particularly sensitive matter in West Germany for
the past two decades. Although all public employees are bound
to actively defend the constitution, it was suspected in the
latter half of the 1960s that radicals from both ends of the
political spectrum were infiltrating the public service, particularly the education sector, in an attempt to destabilise
and eventually topple the democratic order. In response to
what was identified as an attempt by radicals to mount a
'long march through the institutions', in 1972 the federal
government, in concert with the Lander, issued an executive
decree (subsequently known as the Radicals Decree) that re-
emphasised the need to ensure that all public employees supported the democratic order. As a result it was recommended

that all public employees and future applicants be disquali-
fied from public service if it could be shown that they were
members of groups with anti-constitutional goals or were
engaged in activity directed against the democratic order.
    While few would disagree with the need for loyalty, the
ambiguity contained within the Radicals Decree and the subsequent ruling by the Federal Constitutional Court in 1975 have
been the subject of concern. In particular, fears have been
expressed at the sweeping powers granted to the Länder and the
Office for the Protection of the Constitution to amass information on current employees and applicants to all sections of
the public sector. It has also become evident that the
interpretation of what constitutes anti-constitutional
activity varies widely. While the SPD city-states of Hamburg
and Bremen largely restrict extensive investigations to
security-sensitive posts, more right-wing authorities, such
as the CSU government in Bavaria, have built up extensive
information systems on most of their employees, and it has
been suggested that mere participation in demonstrations has
been recorded and used as evidence of disloyalty.
    In this context the Radicals Decree has been seen as a
threat to the freedom from political persecution explicitly
guaranteed under the Basic Law. Certainly it appears absurd
to carry out rigorous checks on manual workers within the
public sector and civil servants holding non-sensitive posts.
Consequently, since the latter half of the 1970s SPD-control-
led authorities have increasingly relaxed the network of
investigations and there are indications that the CDU will
follow this pattern in the future.

MANAGEMENT

The federal ministries located in Bonn are relatively small,
rarely numbering over 2,000 employees in even the largest
ministries, and often staffed by as few as 300. Their size
is conditioned by the role of the Länder and local government
in both implementing and supervising the provision of the vast
majority of services to the extent that the federal ministries
are largely restricted to the creation of broad policy guidelines. In order to fulfil this goal ministries are outwardly
organised as rigid hierarchies headed by a minister and probably two state secretaries, with functions allocated between
a number of divisions which further break down tasks to subdivisions and ultimately sections. It would appear that the
power flow within the system is downwards, with objectives
being established by the minister and implemented by the bureaucracy, all of whom, from divisional head upwards, will be
political appointments. In reality, however, the leadership
function within the West German ministry is relatively weak.
Although the minister will be assisted by a parliamentary

secretary (a junior deputy drawn from the ruling coalition within the Bundestag), his personal staff will generally be limited to a small press section and secretariat. Ministers' do not employ teams of political advisers, nor is there provision for an inner cabinet or a 'think tank' to direct the workings of the department. To some extent this function is provided by consultation with senior officials, but to most intents and purposes ministers only have time to take a direct interest in politically sensitive issues and to direct the allocation of functions to divisions and sections.

The focus of activity within the ministry is therefore effectively the section, which is led by a section head and probably consists of no more than six people. Working within clearly established lines of authority, it is the role of the section to deal with its allocated tasks and funnel proposals upwards to divisional heads, who attempt to match policy guidelines with the work performed by sections. In terms of management style the West German ministries are open to criticism in that it is contended that rigorous task allocation, with section and divisional heads accountable for each area of work, discourages innovation. In addition, the entire process appears highly fragmented with divisional heads attempting to play a co-ordinating role but without extensive support staff to examine policy developments in detail. Within the ministries the only cross-cutting agency is Division Z, which provides personnel and legal services and attempts to co-ordinate expenditure. Division Z also works actively with the Ministry of Finance in negotiating the annual departmental budget.

While experiments have been attempted with project or task-orientated groups bridging sections (and at times ministries), the traditional structure still predominates. Although it provides clear lines of responsibility, there appears to be little attempt to further increase co-ordination of the work undertaken by sections, and there is a heavy reliance on the role of division heads to monitor the entire process and provide feedback to the minister and the state secretaries. While these problems might, to an extent, be mitigated by the relatively small size of the ministries, the absence of a planning unit at a senior level free of day-to-day administrative duties must cast doubt on the ability of the system to plan effectively, and to co-ordinate and monitor existing initiatives. Certainly the system is plagued by intense departmentalism and internally relies heavily on the ability of the bureaucracy to tailor their proposals to keep in step with the policies outlined by the ruling coalition.

PLANNING

The rebuilding of the West German economy on free market
principles initially did not require the creation of an
extensive framework for economic planning. This philosophy
was only subject to significant revision in the 1960s, with
increasing demands for long-term economic projections and the
creation of public sector spending targets both as a means of
establishing project priorities and as a lever to manipulate
the overall level of economic activity in an attempt to
eradicate the worst effects of the trade cycle. As a result
of this pressure, the government established in 1967 the
medium-term financial strategy with joint federal-state
bodies to collaborate on the assembly of expenditure guidelines to be overseen by the Ministry of Finance.

Two years later, in 1969, the SPD-FDP coalition government sponsored a major project to develop an extensive
government-wide planning agency. Each ministry was instructed
to appoint a Planning Commissioner responsible for monitoring
project development and amassing a detailed breakdown of
departmental work to be made available to the Chancellor's
Office. The intention was quite clearly to expand the role of
the Chancellor's Office from simply policy co-ordination to
acceptance of the responsibility for the evaluation and prior-
itisation of all new major project developments alongside the
monitoring of existing projects. This necessitated the rapid
expansion of personnel within the Chancellor's Office and the
establishment of highly specialised programme teams capable
of interpreting the data supplied by the departments in order
to determine long-term policy goals. This highly ambitious
experiment had essentially floundered by 1972, when it became
apparent that, in an attempt to guard their independence,
departments were unwilling to co-operate actively with the
Chancellor's Office. Given the unwillingness of Brandt to
force the issue, since 1972 the Chancellor's Office has
reverted to its traditional role of simply monitoring and
prompting departmental activity.

Long-term planning, therefore, remains something of a
moot subject within the bureaucracy. In essence, it runs
against the German bureaucratic tradition in that it threatens
both to infringe the latitude afforded to the administration
and to challenge the concept of the bureaucracy as simply an
administrative machine interpreting and implementing a given
legal framework. Yet the need to look to the future and co-
ordinate the allocation of resources is self-evident in a
complex industrial society, particularly where political power
is effectively fragmented between three tiers of government.
The response to this problem, however, has been piecemeal.
The creation of federal-state joint tasks in 1969 in the
fields of education and regional economic development has
necessitated the establishment within the respective federal

and Land ministries of internal planning units and joint
liaison bodies. In addition, the need for collaboration has
encouraged most departments to establish a planning unit,
although few have gone as far as the Ministry of Labour and
Social Affairs in delegating to the unit extensive power to
evaluate all new developments within the department. In some
areas, such as environmental protection, interdepartmental
co-ordination has been vastly improved. Yet while many
departments have now created planning units, the resources
and powers allocated to them are often restricted. Given the
absence of a central government-wide co-ordinating body,
interdepartmental collaboration is still not extensive and
one is left with the suspicion that its role is primarily one
of policy co-ordination rather than programme initiation and
evaluation.
    Perhaps to hope for much more is overoptimistic, given
the difficulty of assembling adequate information for long-
term planning, the shifting nature of party priorities, and
most of all the conflicts and jealousies of a fragmented and
decentralised political system.

POLICY-MAKING

Few would doubt that the West German bureaucracy, and in
particular the higher civil service, is at the centre of the
country's policy-making process. The influence of the
bureaucracy is manifest in almost all elements of the political system in that unlike in Britain, where the role of the
civil service is shielded by anonymity and the principle of
ministerial responsibility, the West German bureaucracy is
overtly politicised and is expected to be actively involved
in policy formulation. Not unnaturally, this has led to
doubts as to the advisability of permitting the bureaucracy
to wield such extensive influence. It has been suggested
that in addition to playing a major role within the federal
ministries in determining policy options, the bureaucracy is
itself a formidable pressure group, with particular influence
within the Bundestag by virtue of the extent to which the
major parties have recruited members and Bundestag deputies
from those employed in the public sector. Furthermore,
through the accepted formula of civil servants deputising
for ministers, bureaucrats play a leading role in the formulation and scrutiny of policy at all levels, from Cabinet sub-
committees and Bundestag proceedings through to agencies
established to co-ordinate policy with state and local
government.
    Against these charges it has to be noted that the polit-
icisation of senior levels of the bureaucracy has to some
extent undermined the Prussian tradition of a civil service
recruited from a limited social background with a cohesive

outlook anchored in a belief in the status afforded to those empowered to interpret and implement the law. The post-war bureaucracy has had to come to terms with the reality of party politics and the need to tailor its initiatives to accommodate its political overlords. The use of political appointees has not only injected new blood and ideas into the senior levels of the bureaucracy but has also acted as a constant reminder of the upgrading of party status incorporated within the Basic Law. Furthermore, the changing demands of the West German populace can no longer be met by simple reference to the principles of Rechtsstaat. The ambiguity of the law and the determination of sections of the population to challenge government attitudes on a variety of issues such as environmental protection, defence policy and nuclear power has arguably swung power away from the bureaucracy to the political parties which are the only agencies able to filter, aggregate and ultimately respond to new demands.

In other fields the power of the bureaucracy in policy-making is constantly hedged and restricted. By virtue of the narrow academic background from which the bureaucracy is recruited and the tradition of hiving off technical functions, the West German bureaucracy is ill equipped at times to compete with other agencies. In particular, it has been suggested that it is heavily reliant on key pressure groups in the formulation and administration of policy. West Germany has an extensive network of occupational and professional associations that effectively regulate standards, supervise training and act as bargaining agents for their particular profession. Together with the major economic interests these groups have undoubtedly forged close ties with the bureaucracy, to the extent that it is often dependent upon them for expertise, statistics and collaboration in the implementation of policy. While it is tempting to applaud the integration of such groups into the decision-making process, concern has been expressed at the nature of the relationships established, in that certain groups appear to wield inordinate power, due to the leverage that they hold over the bureaucracy, while other groups with extensive support, particularly in the fields of environmental protection and defence policy, are effectively excluded.

While, therefore, criticism of the bureaucracy is voiced in West German society, it is tempered, to some extent, both by the traditional deference afforded to the Beamten and the appreciation that, within the post-war political system, while elites are arguably still identifiable, the elevation of the parties and the adoption of a federal format have ensured that the bureaucracy is only one of a number of groups seeking to influence the decision-making process.

CONCLUSION

The role of the bureaucracy in West Germany is outwardly
dictated by the demands and constraints established by the
Basic Law in the post-war era. It is apparent, however, that
while the bureaucracy has undergone several major structural
changes, in effect it is still heavily conditioned by the
ninteenth-century Prussian administrative tradition. Parallels
with the past are manifest in the adoption of a fairly rigid
hierarchical administrative structure, staffed largely by
career civil servants recruited on the basis of educational
qualifications into one of the administrative groups. In
addition, despite the supremacy afforded to the political
parties by the Basic Law, the continued image of the bureaucracy as the guardian of the legal framework suggests that
the concept of Rechtsstaat is still an influential factor in
popular perceptions of the role of the civil service. It is
hardly surprising, therefore, that critics of the West German
bureaucracy have questioned the ability of an administrative
structure based on a nineteenth-century code of ethics to
respond to the needs of a modern industrial society.

The charges levelled at the bureaucracy are not entirely
without substance, for the West German political system
certainly appears to be at its best in reacting to a crisis
rather than anticipating and taking steps to prevent its
occurrence. Despite efforts to establish indicative financial
planning and policy units within each department, the only
major co-ordinating agency within the political system is
still the Cabinet. The absence of an extensive network of
Cabinet subcommittees is indicative, however, of the limited
role that the Cabinet is able to play in this sphere. It
would seem, therefore, that the West German political system
is still heavily dominated by the defence of departmental
independence and there has been resistance to the creation of
units seeking to impose interministerial guidelines. While,
therefore, policy co-ordination and planning have not been
ignored, and the past decade has witnessed the rapid expansion
of an extensive data base, the planning function is still
relatively weak.

To attribute this, however, primarily to the inherent
conservatism of the bureaucracy would be an overstatement of
its influence in decision-making. It can be contended that
the preference for pragmatic and incremental policy-making is
largely conditioned by a continual search for compromise and
consensus that results naturally from a system founded on
coalition government, with a strong tradition of corporatism
and with power distributed between three levels of government.
In addition, it has been argued that the real danger in the
relationship between party and bureaucracy lies in the possibility of the latter being overwhelmed by the pressures generated by a Parteienstaat. While the politicisation of the

bureaucracy has marginally devalued the status and role of
the Beamten, there is little evidence to suggest, however,
that the bureaucracy has been reduced to a completely
subservient role. In general it is agreed that the post-war
era has witnessed a successful intermeshing of party and
bureaucracy, with continued respect for the values inherent
within a 'professional' civil service together with an acceptance of the need for pragmatism on the part of the bureaucracy in accepting policy and targets determined by political
priorities.

The nature of the political system, therefore, and the
ethos of the bureaucracy, still founded on the public law
tradition, naturally converge towards the acceptance of a
system that is conservative in outlook and likely to adopt a
pragmatic and incremental approach to policy-making. While
this model has served West Germany well in the post-war era,
the challenge of economic recession and the emergence of
pressure for wider popular participation in the political
process is likely to result in demands for a more energetic
style of leadership and a more management-orientated approach
to the role of the administrator. Although the West German
bureaucracy has taken tentative steps along this path,
exactly how far it can successfully accommodate the pressure
for change within its existing structures is a question that
will have to be confronted during the next decade.

FURTHER READING

This bibliography is confined to texts in English and is by
no means exhaustive, but indicates the range of material
available.

General introductions to government, institutions and political culture in West Germany

Almond, Gabriel and Verba, Sidney (1963) The Civic Culture,
Princeton, Princeton University Press.

Almond, Gabriel and Verba, Sidney (1980) The Civic Culture
Revisited, Boston, Little, Brown.

Childs, David and Johnson, Jeffrey (1981) West Germany:
Politics and Society, London, Croom Helm.

Conradt, David (1986) The German Polity, New York, Longman.

Schweitzer, C.C. et al. (1984) Politics and Government in the
Federal Republic: Basic Documents, Leamington Spa, Berg.

Smith, Gordon (1984) <u>Democracy in Western Germany</u>, London, Heinemann.

Books with more detailed reference to the role of the bureaucracy

Döring, H. and Smith, G. (1982) <u>Party Government and Political Culture in Western Germany</u>, London, Macmillan.

Dyson, K. (1977) <u>Party, State and Bureaucracy in Western Germany</u>, London, Sage.

Johnson, Nevil (1983) <u>State and Government in the Federal Republic of Germany</u>, Oxford, Pergamon.

Mayntz, R. and Scharpf, F. (1975) <u>Policy-making in the German Federal Bureaucracy</u>, New York, Elsevier.

Articles

Kaltefleiter, W. (1972) 'Modernisation of the bureaucracy', <u>International Journal of Politics</u>, 20, 5-9.

Krieger, K. (1979) 'Worrying about West German democracy', <u>Political Quarterly</u>, 50, 192-204.

Mayntz, R. (1980) 'Executive leadership in West Germany', in R. Rose and E. Suleiman (eds) <u>Presidents and Prime Ministers</u>, Washington, American Enterprise Institute, pp. 139-170.

Southern, D. (1979) 'West Germany', in F. F. Ridley (ed.) <u>Government and Administration in Western Europe</u>, Oxford, Martin Robertson, pp. 107-155.

A. P. Barham

accountability and control
   (see also financial
   control; judicial
   control; political
   control)
   Britain, 24-6
   Canada, 45-6, 53-7
   France, 82-7
   Ireland, 95, 103-12
   Italy, 135-9
   Sweden, 151, 154-8
   US, 167, 169-70, 175-8
   W. Germany, 192, 195-9
Adenauer, Konrad, 182, 183,
   189
administration
   public and private
   distinguished, 4, 29; not
   by Glassco Commission, 58
administration-politics
   dichotomy (see also
   policy-making), 3-4
administrative law and
   courts, 8
   absence of, 25, 110, 178
   France, 83-5
   Italy, 139
   Sweden, 156
   W. Germany, 197
administrative reform, see
   reform
advisers, government
   Britain, 17, 23, 31
   Canada, 62
   Ireland, 114
   Italy, 139

Sweden, 159
US, 168, 169, 179-80
agriculture, Irish dependence
   on, 90
Aireacht department
   structure, 94-5, 112-13,
   117
Andreotti, Giulio, 123, 124
anonymity, decline in, 24,
   53
Appropriations Committee,
   196, 199
Auditor General, 56
autonomous agencies, 130

Basic Law, 182-3, 187, 189,
   197, 204, 205
   civil servants' loyalty to,
   199-200
Beamten, 193
Berufsverbot, 199-200
bilingual policy, 51-2, 58
bi-partism, imperfect, 125
Bozzi Committee, 140
Britain, influence of
   on Canadian government and
   administration, 35, 36,
   55-6, 57, 62
   on French civil service
   recruitment and training,
   76-7
   on Irish government and
   administration, 90, 92,
   96, 100, 103, 114, 116
budgetary processes
   Britain, 28

Canada, 56-7
Ireland, 110
Italy, 136, 138
Sweden, 157-8
US, 169-70, 177
W. Germany, 199
Bundesrat, 182, 187, 189
Bundestag, 182, 183
  accountability to and
    control by, 195-7, 198-9
  Chancellor and, 188-9, 190
  members' civil service
    backgrounds, 186, 195,
    198, 203
Bunreacht na hAireann, 91-2,
  103, 106, 110-11
bureaucracy (see also civil
  servants; civil service)
  concept of, 2
  confidence in and acceptance
    of, 5, 40, 54

Cabinet (see also Council of
  Ministers)
  Britain, 15-17
  Canada, 35, 41-3, 53
  Italy, 123-4, 125-7
  Sweden, 145-6
  W. Germany, 190-1, 195, 205
cabinet, inner (consiglio di
  gabinetto), 126
cabinet, ministerial
  France, 71, 86-7
  Italy, 129, 137-8, 139
cabinet secretariat (see also
  Chancellor's Office), 17,
  43
career structure and develop-
  ment (see also recruit-
  ment and promotion)
  Britain, 32
  Canada, 59-60
  France, 72-3, 75
  Ireland, 100, 102-3
  Italy, 131-2, 134, 137
  Sweden, 152-3
  US, 171-2, 173-4
  W. Germany, 193
Catholic Church, influence of
  Canada, 37
  Ireland, 91

Italy, 121-2
Cavour reforms, 119
centralisation
  Canada, 46
  Ireland, 100
  W. Germany, 187
Chancellor, role and
  authority of, 182, 183,
  188-90
Chancellor of Justice, 156
Chancellor's Office, 189, 202
checks and balance (see also
  accountability)
  US, 163-5, 175
  W. Germany, 182-3, 189
Chirac, Jacques, 69, 70
Christian Brothers' schools,
  101
Christian Democratic Party
  (DC), 122, 123, 124, 125,
  126, 131
civil servants
  characteristics and
    behaviour (see also
    education; policy-
    making; recruitment;
    social class etc.), 7;
    Britain, 21-3; Canada,
    48-52; France, 73-80;
    Ireland, 100-7; Italy,
    131-3, 136-7; Sweden,
    152-4; US, 165-7, 172-5;
    W. Germany, 193-5
  numbers of: Britain, 21,
    33; Canada, 43-4, 48;
    France, 72; Ireland, 99;
    Italy, 120, 131-2;
    Sweden, 148, 149; US,
    166, 168, 170, 171-2,
    175; W. Germany, 191,
    193, 200
  politics and, see
    patronage; policy-
    making; political
    participation
civil service
  agencies outside formal
    structure of: Britain,
    19, 20, 21; Canada,
    45-6, 54, 57, 61;
    Ireland, 99; Italy,

130-1; Sweden, 149-50;
US, 166; W. Germany, 192
concept of, 2-3, 153, 193
evolution, see history
Civil Service Commission
Canada, 48, 58
Ireland, 93, 106
US, 165, 173
class, see social class
coalition government
France, 66
Italy, 123-4, 138
Sweden, 144
W. Germany, 189, 190
Commission of Inquiry into
the Civil Service, Report
of, 93
committees
accountability through:
Britain, 25; Ireland, 107;
Sweden, 155; US, 176-7;
W. Germany, 196
congressional, 176-7, 179
federal-Länder links
through, 187-8
policy-making role: Sweden,
156-7; US, 169
select, 25, 107
Communist Party, Italian
(PCI), 121, 122, 124-5
comparative study, 1
Comptroller General, 56
Congress, US, 164-5, 176-7,
179-80
accountability to and
control by, 167, 176-7
consensus
extent of in Sweden, 144,
158, 159, 160
conservatism, Irish, 90-1, 116
Conservative Party
Britain, 13, 15-16, 33
Canada, 39, 49, 62
Consiglio di Stato, 139
constitution
Britain, 11-12, 16, 36,
Canada, 35-6
France, 64, 65, 67-71
Ireland, 91-2, 103, 106,
110-11
Italy, 125, 126, 133, 135,

138, 139
Sweden, 143, 144, 145, 156
US, 163, 164
W. Germany, 182-3, 189,
199-200
constitutional court
Italy, 139
W. Germany, 182-3, 189,
197, 200
control, see accountability
and control
co-ordination, inter- and
intra-departmental
Ireland: attempt to
increase, 94, 95, 113
Italy: lack of, 126-7,
128, 129-30, 134
US: role of OMB, 170
W. Germany: need for, 201,
202-3, 205
corporatism
Britain, 17
Canada, 41
Sweden, 147, 155, 160
W. Germany, 205
corps, French officials
organised through (see
also grand corps),
72-3, 74-80
Corte dei Conti, 138-9
Council of Economic
Advisers, 169
Council of Ministers, 71
Council of State
France, 83-5
Italy, 139
county agencies, 149-50
Court of Accounts, 85
Court of the Exchequer,
138-9
courts
accountability and control
through: Britain, 25-6;
Ireland, 103, 110-11;
US, 177-8
administrative, 8; absence
of, 25, 110, 178;
France, 83-5; Italy,
139; Sweden, 156; W.
Germany, 197
constitutional: Italy,

139; W. Germany, 182-3,
189, 197, 200
Crispi, Francesco, 120
Crown Corporations, 45-6

Dail Aireann, 92, 96
accountability to, 95, 103-7
data banks, control of, 197
de Gaulle, General Charles,
66-7, 68, 70
de Valera, Eamon, 90, 91-2, 96
decentralisation
Britain, 19, 20-1
Canada, 44, 48-50
France, 72
Italy, 129-30
Sweden, 149-50
W. Germany, 187
decision-making, routine (see
also policy-making)
Britain, 27
Ireland, 94-5, 113
Sweden, 146, 151, 154
W. Germany, 177
deference, 12, 13, 38, 40
Democratic Party, 164
departments and ministries
allocation of funds between
(see also expenditure):
Britain, 28; Canada, 56-7;
US, 169-70, 177; W.
Germany, 199
Britain, 17, 18, 19-20
Canada, 44
co-ordination, see co-
ordination
Ireland, 97-8
Italy, 120, 127-8
number of: Canada, 44;
Ireland, 93, 97; Italy,
120, 128; US, 170
organisation, see manage-
ment; organisation
size: Britain, 20; Italy,
127; W. Germany, 192, 200
Sweden, 147-8
US, 166, 170-1
W. Germany, 191
deputies, Irish, administrative impact of, 105-7
deputy minister

managerial and policy-
making role, 59-62
as political appointment,
55, 60-1
Devlin Report, 93-6, 98, 99,
103, 112-13, 116
Deifenbaker, John, 49
director generals
Italy, 120, 129
Sweden, 151
dirigisme, 75, 80
divisions, German civil
servants organised into,
192, 200-1

Ecole Libre des Sciences
Politiques, 76
Ecole Nationale d'Administra-
tion (ENA), 74, 76-8, 80
Ecole Polytechnique (X), 78-9
education and training, 7
Britain, 14-15, 22-3
Canada, 51
France, 74, 76-80
Ireland, 92-3, 100-2, 114
Italy, 133-4, 135
Sweden, 152, 153
US, 174
W. Germany, 193-4
efficiency, quest for (see
also inefficiency)
Britain, 29-30
Canada, 57-60
France, 65
Ireland, 94-5, 112-13
US, 169-70
elections and electoral
systems
Britain, 15-16
France, 68
Ireland, 96-7
Italy, 123
Sweden, 143-4, 154
elite, administrative
France, see grands corps
Italy: cultural gap
between politicians and,
137
elitism, 7
Britain, 22-3, 32-3
Canada, 51

France, 75-6, 77, 78,
   79-80, 88
Sweden, 152
US, 165, 173, 180
English Canadians, values
   and attitudes of, 37,
   38
enti pubblici, 130-1
examinations
Britain, 14
France, 77
Italy, 133
US, 165, 174
W. Germany, 194
executive, political (see also
   Cabinet; Chancellor;
   ministers; President;
   Prime Minister), 6
Britain, 15-17
bureaucrats appointed by,
   see patronage
bureaucrats' relationship
   with (see also political
   control; politicians), 9;
   Britain, 27; Canada, 43;
   France, 80-1, 86-7;
   Ireland, 94-5, 109-10;
   Italy, 136-8, 139-40;
   Sweden, 146; US, 175-7,
   179-80; W. Germany, 185,
   188, 194-5, 196-7, 198
Canada, 41-3
France, 67-71
Ireland, 96-7
Italy, 123-7
Sweden, 145-6
US, 163-4, 165-7
W. Germany, 188-90
Executive Office of the
   President, 166-70
expenditure, regulation of, 8
Britain, 24-5, 28
Canada, 55-7, 58
France, 85-6
Ireland, 110
Italy, 136, 138-9
Sweden, 144, 157-8
US, 169-70, 175, 177
W. Germany, 196, 198-9

Federal Constitutional Court,

182-3, 189, 197, 200
Federal Court of Accounts,
   196, 198
federal-provincial relations
Canada, 46-8, 53, 62
W. Germany, 182, 186-8,
   191, 202-3
federalism
Canada, 35, 46-7
W. Germany, 182, 186-8
field agencies
Britain, 19, 20-1
Canada, 44
France, 72
Italy, 129-30
Sweden, 149-51
Finance, Ministry of (W.
   Germany), 199
Finance Inspectorate
   (France), 85-6
Financial Administration Act,
   46
financial control, 8
Britain, 24-5, 28
Cananda, 55-7, 58
France, 85-6
Ireland, 110
Italy, 138-9
Sweden, 157-8
US, 169-70, 175, 177
W. Germany, 196, 198-9
fragmentation
Italy, 128, 129, 140
W. Germany, 201
Freedom of Information Act,
   153, 155
French Canadians, 37, 38,
   47, 62
recruitment, 51-2, 58
Fulton Committee, 20, 21, 22,
   29, 33
functional organisation
Britain, 19-20
Canada, 44
Ireland, 97-8
Sweden, 149
functions, administrative, 1
Britain, 18-21
Canada, 44
increase in, 18-19, 166
Sweden, 147, 151-2

Index

US, 166, 167-70
W. Germany, 191-2

Garfield, President James A., 165
gatekeepers, civil servants as, 115, 169
General Accounting Office, 177
generalists (see also specialists), 7
  Britain, 22
  Ireland, 100, 102-3
  US, 173, 174
Glassco Commission, 56, 57, 59, 61
government, see Cabinet; executive; ministers, etc.
government documents, Swedish public access to, 155
government instability
  France, 64, 66-7, 81
  Italy, 119, 123-5
government stability
  Sweden, 144, 146, 160
Governor General of Canada, 35, 38, 41, 42, 60
grades, see career structure
grands corps, 7
  in control agencies, 83-7
  recruitment to, 75-80
  role and significance, 74-5, 88
  technical, 78-9

Haldane Committee, 19
hierarchical organisation
  Britain, 27
  Canada, 45, 55
  France, 71, 72-3, 82
  Ireland, 100
  Italy, 129
  Sweden, 148, 150-1, 158
  US, 170-2, 174
  W. Germany, 192, 200-1, 205
Higher School of Public Administration, 135
history, bureaucratic, 5
  Britain, 2, 13-15, 18-19
  Canada, 41
  France, 65-6

Ireland, 92-6
Italy, 119-20
US, 163, 165-7
W. Germany, 193, 195
House of Commons
  Britain, 15
  Cananda, 36
House of Representatives
  Ireland (Dail Aireann), 92, 96; accountability to, 95, 103-7
  US, 164, 177

immobilisme, 66, 82
immobalismo, 140
impartiality, political (see also patronage; political participation)
  Britain, 23, 32
  Canada, 48-50
independence, Irish, contribution of administrative continuity to, 93
Indian Civil Service, 2, 14
industrialisation, 13-14, 18
inertia
  Britain, 33
  Italy, 139-40
inefficiency, Italian
  due to fragmentation, 128, 129, 140
  in recruitment process, 134
Information Canada, 53
Intendants, 65
interest and pressure groups
  Britain, 26, 30-1
  Canada, 40-1, 61
  France, 81
  Ireland, 115
  Sweden, 155, 158-9, 160
  US, 179, 180
  W. Germany, 186, 204; civil servants as, 198, 203
interpellations, 156-7

Jackson, President Andrew, 165
Johnson, President Lyndon B., 179
judicial control, 8
  Britain, 25-6

213

Index

Canada, 36
France, 83–5
Ireland, 103, 110–11
Italy, 138–9
Sweden, 155–6, 158
US, 177–8
W. Germany, 197

Kennedy, President John F.,
  178, 180
King, Mackenzie, 38, 43
Kohl, Helmut, 188, 189

Labour Party, 13, 15
Lambert Commission, 59, 60
Länder, role and importance
  of, 182, 186–8, 200
law (see also administrative
  law; courts; judicial
  control)
  civil servants' background
    in: Sweden, 152; US, 174;
    W. Germany, 194
  Swedish respect for, 144
legal framework
  German liking for (Rechts-
    staat), 183, 204, 205
  Italian civil service
    rigidly bound by, 127,
    133, 135
legislation, delegated, 19
Lemass, Sean, 108
Liberal Party
  Britain, 15, 16
  Canada, 39, 40, 49, 61, 62
liberal subculture, Italian,
  121
local government, role and
  importance of (see also
  federal-provincial
  relations; Länder)
  Italy, 128
  Sweden, 143, 147; relation-
    ship to central govern-
    ment, 149–50
loyalty
  of German civil servants to
    Basic Law, 199–200
  importance in Irish
    political culture, 91

maladministration, redress
  of, see courts; ombuds-
  men
management (see also organ-
  isation), 8–9
  Britain, 28–30
  Canada, 57–60
  Ireland, 94–5, 112–14
  Italy, 131–2
  US, 169–70
  W. Germany, 200–1
managerial skills, lack of
  Britain, 29
  Canada, 57, 59
  Ireland, 112
media, accountability
  through
  Ireland, 107–8
  Sweden, 155
merit, recruitment and
  promotion based on (see
  also patronage)
  Britain, 23
  Canada, 48–50
  France, 77–80
  Ireland, 102
  Italy, 133, 135
  Sweden, 153
  US, 165–6, 173–4
  W. Germany, 194
ministers
  cabinets: France, 71, 86–7;
    Italy, 129, 137–8, 139
  roles and responsibilities:
    Britain, 16, 17, 24, 27,
    30; Canada, 45, 53, 54,
    60; France, 70–1, 86–7;
    Ireland, 93, 95, 103–5,
    109–10, 113, 114, 115,
    117; Italy, 119, 120,
    125–6, 135–6, 137–8, 139;
    Sweden, 145, 146, 151,
    156–7; W. Germany,
    189–90, 192, 200–1
ministeries, see departments
  and ministries
monarchy
  Britain, 11, 12
  Sweden, 143, 145
Mulroney, Brian, 38, 42, 49,
  50, 61

Napoleon, 64, 65, 88
National Assembly, 68-9
    accountability to, 82
National School of Administra-
    tion (ENA), 74, 76-8, 80
National Security Council, 169
neo-corporatism, 81
Nixon, President Richard,
    168, 169, 170
Northcote-Trevelyan report
    and reforms, 2, 14-15, 22,
    92, 165

Office of Management and
    Budget, 169-70, 177
Oireachtas, 92, 96-7
    accountability to and
    control by, 103-7
ombudsmen
    Britain, 26
    Canada, 54
    Ireland, 95, 108-9, 111
    Sweden, 145, 156
    W. Germany, 197
organisation and reorganisa-
    tion (see also management;
    reform; structure)
    Britain, 19-20, 27
    Canada, 45, 55, 59
    France, 71, 72-3, 82
    Ireland, 94-5, 97-8, 100,
    112-13, 116
    Italy, 120, 129-30
    Sweden, 148-51
    US, 170-2, 174-5
    W. Germany, 192, 200-1, 205

'parallel administration'
    system, 130-1
Parliament (see also
    Bundestag; Congress;
    National Assembly;
    Oireachtas; Riksdag)
    Britain, 11, 15
    Canada, 35-6
    civil service accountability
    to: Britain, 24-8; Canada,
    45-6, 53-7; Italy, 135-8
    Italy, 123-5
Parliamentary Commissioner for
    Administration, 26

Parteienstaat, 185, 205
participation, see political
    participation
parties, see political
    parties
patronage and political
    appointment
    Britain, 17, 23, 31
    Canada, 42, 43, 48-50, 55,
    60-1
    Italy, 131
    Sweden, 148
    US, 163, 165-6, 167, 170,
    171-3, 175-6, 178-9
    W. Germany, 192, 194-5,
    198, 203-4
Pearson, Lester, 60
permanent secretaries,
    British: appointment by
    Prime Minister, 23, 31
planning, economic
    French tradition of, 65-6,
    75, 80, 88
    German attempts at, 202-3,
    205
planning units
    in Canadian departments, 59
pluralism (see also corpora-
    tism)
    Britain, 17, 26, 30-1
    Canada, 40-1, 53, 61
    France, 81
    Italy, 124-5
policy advisers, see advisers
Policy Expenditure and Man-
    agement System (PEMS), 57
policy implementation, 1
    artificial distinction bet-
    ween politics and, 3, 9
    Ireland: politicians'
    involvement in, 105-6,
    116-17; recommendations
    for separation between
    policy-making and, 94-5,
    113
    Italy: bureaucratic delay,
    140
    Sweden: clearly distinct
    from policy-making, 146,
    151, 154
    W. Germany: Länder role,

182, 187
policy-making (see also
   planning) 3-4, 9
   Cabinet's limited role:
      Italy, 126-7; W. Germany,
      190, 205
   Chancellor's role, 188-90
   civil service involvement
      in: Britain, 27, 30, 31-2;
      Canada, 53, 60-2; France,
      79, 80-1; Ireland, 94-5,
      112-13, 114-16, 117;
      Italy, 139-40; US, 167,
      168-9, 178-80; W. Germany,
      196-7, 203-4, 205-6
   interest groups and:
      Britain, 30, 31; Canada,
      40-1; Sweden, 155, 158-60;
      US, 179, 180; W. Germany,
      204
   ministerial role: Italy,
      139; Sweden, 151; W.
      Germany, 190
   President's role: US, 164-5,
      178, 179-80
   provincial (Länder) govern-
      ment importance in, 186-8
   routine decision-making
      distinct from: Sweden,
      146, 151
political control and account-
   ability (see also finan-
   cial control; judicial
   control), 7-8
   Britain, 24, 26-7
   Canada, 45, 53-4, 55
   France, 82, 86-7
   Ireland, 95, 103-10
   Italy, 135-8
   Sweden, 151, 154-7
   US, 167, 175-7
   W. Germany, 192, 195-7, 198
political culture (see also
   deference; loyalty;
   secrecy), 4-5
   Britain, 12-13, 15-17
   Canada, 36-40
   dualism: Canada, 37, 51-2;
      Italy, 122-3
   France, 64-6, 81-2
   Ireland, 90-1, 116

   Italy, 120-3, 140
   Sweden, 144-5, 154-5, 158
   W. Germany, 183-6
political executive, see
   executive
political impartiality
   Britain, 23, 32
   Canada, 49-50
political institutions and
   systems (see also Cabi-
   net; political parties;
   President; Prime
   Minister)
   Britain, 11-12, 15-17
   Canada, 35-6, 41-3
   France, 64, 66-71
   Ireland, 91-2, 96-7
   Italy, 123-7
   Sweden, 143-4, 145-6
   US, 163-5
   W. Germany, 182-3
political participation (see
   also patronage)
   by civil servants: Sweden,
      149, 153; W. Germany,
      185, 186, 188, 195, 203,
      205-6
   extent of: Canada, 38-9;
      Sweden, 144, 154; W.
      Germany, 184-6
political parties (see also
   individual parties)
   Britain, 13, 15
   Canada, 39-40
   France, 66, 68
   Ireland, 96
   Italy, 121-2, 123, 124-5
   Sweden, 144
   US, 164
   W. Germany, 183, 185-6,
      189, 190, 197; civil
      servants' importance in,
      185, 186, 188, 195, 198,
      203, 205-6
politicians
   civil servants' relation-
      ship with: Britain, 23,
      27; Canada, 43, 53, 55;
      France, 80-2, 86-7; Ire-
      land, 94-5, 103-7, 109-
      10; Italy, 136-8, 139-40;

Sweden, 146, 151; US, 167,
175-7; W. Germany, 185,
186, 188, 194-5, 196-7,
198
  Irish: unconstitutional
  involvement in administration, 106
  Swedish distrust of, 154-5
politics-administration
  dichotomy (see also
  policy-making), 3-4
Pompidou, President, 69, 70
President, role and authority
  of
  France, 67, 68, 69-70
  Ireland, 96
  US, 163-5, 166-70, 172-3,
  175-6, 177, 178-80
  W. Germany, 183, 188
presidential government, style
  Britain, 16, 17
  Canada, 42
pressure groups, see interest
  and pressure groups
Prime Minister, role and
  authority of (see also
  Chancellor; President)
  Britain, 15, 16, 17, 23, 31
  Canada, 42, 43, 49-50, 55,
  60-1
  France, 69-70
  Ireland (Taoiseach) 96, 97,
  98
  Italy, 123, 125, 126-7
  Sweden, 145
private sector
  administration: public
  administration distinct
  from, 4, 29, 58
  attraction of higher-paid
  jobs in, 135, 173, 174
  managerial skills from, 29,
  31
Privy Council Office, 43
Progressive Conservative
  Party, 39, 49, 62
promotion, see career
  structure; recruitment
  and promotion
Prussian administrative
  system, 193-4, 195, 203-4,

  205
Public Accounts Committee, 25
public administration
  courses in, see education
  and training
  distinct from private
  sector administration,
  4, 29, 58
Public Expenditure Survey
  Committee (PESC) process,
  28
Public Service, Department
  of, 95, 110, 113, 116
Public Service Advisory
  Council, 95
Public Service Alliance, 50
Public Service Commission, 58
Public Services Organisation
  Review Group, see Devlin

Quebec, 37, 47, 48
questions, parliamentary,
  accountability through
  Britain, 24
  Ireland, 104-5
  Sweden, 156-7

Radicals' Decree, 199-200
Radio Telefis Eirann, 108
Reagan, President Ronald,
  170, 172-3, 175, 180
Rechtsstaat, 183, 204, 205
recruitment and promotion
  (see also education and
  training; patronage), 7
  Britain, 14-15, 22-3, 32
  Canada, 42, 48-50, 51-2,
  59, 60-1
  France, 72-80
  Ireland, 100, 101-3
  Italy, 132-5, 137
  Sweden, 152-4
  US, 165-6, 171-5
  W. Germany, 192, 193-5, 200
reform, administrative (and
  proposals for)
  Britain, 2, 14-15, 18, 92;
  little impact of, 20,
  22-3, 29
  Canada, 57-60
  France: little impact of,

76
Ireland, 92, 93–5, 103,
  112–13, 116, 117; little
  impact of, 95–6, 103,
  113–14
Italy, 119–20, 131–2; avoid-
  ance of, 131, 140; need
  for, 140; in recruitment,
  134, 135
US, 165
W. Germany: need for, 201,
  202–3, 205
regional disparities, Italian,
  123
influence on civil service,
  132–3, 137
regulation, government role
  in (see also state:
  interventionist role),
  18–19
regulatory agencies, US, 166,
  177, 179
Republican Party, 164
responsibility
  collective: Britain, 24;
    Canada, 53; Ireland, 103;
    absent from Italy, 135–6;
    W. Germany, 195
  ministerial: Britain, 24;
    Canada, 45, 53, 55;
    Ireland, 93, 95, 103–5;
    absent from Italy, 135–6;
    not for routine decisions
    in Sweden, 151; W.
    Germany, 192, 195
Revolution, French, 64, 65
Riksdag, 143–4, 145–6, 154,
  159
  accountability to and
    control by, 154–8
Roosevelt, President Franklin
  D., 166

salaries
  Britain, 32
  Italy, 135
  US, 173, 174
Schmidt, Helmut, 188
Scuola Superiore della
  Pubblica Amministrazione,
  135

Seanad Aireann, 92, 96–7
secrecy, official
  Britain, 12–13, 32
  Canada, 40, 53
  Ireland, 91, 111
secretary of state
  France, 70–1
  W. Germany, 192, 200
sections, German ministries
  organised into, 192,
  200–1
Senate
  Canada, 35–6, 41
  Ireland (Seanad Aireann),
    92, 96–7
  US, 164, 176
social class, 7
  Britain, 22–3
  Canada, 40, 51
  France, 75–6, 77
  Ireland, 100–1
  Sweden, 152
  W. Germany, 184, 194
Social Democratic Party
  Britain, 15, 16
  Sweden, 144
southern Italy, civil
  servants predominantly
  from, 123, 132–3, 137
special agencies, 119
specialists (see also
  generalists), 7
  Britain, 22
  Ireland, 100, 102–3
  US, 174
  W. Germany: ministers, 190
structure and function (see
  also organisation), 1, 6
  Britain, 18–21
  Canada, 43–8
  changes and reforms in (see
    also reform, administra-
    tive): Britain, 19, 20,
    21; Ireland, 93–6, 98–9,
    113, 116–17; Italy,
    119–20, 131–2
  France, 72–3
  Ireland, 97–100
  Italy, 127–31
  Sweden, 147–52
  US, 167–72

W. Germany, 190-2
state
  extension in role: Britain,
    18-19; Canada, 39, 41,
    46-7; US, 166
  interventionist role,
    French tradition of,
    65-6, 70, 75, 80, 88
  reality of concept in
    France, 64-5
state secretary
  France, 70-1
  W. Germany, 192, 200
state-sponsored bodies, 99
states, German, see Länder
stato di diritto, 127
Supreme Court, US, 164, 177-8

Taoiseach, 96, 97, 98
Thatcher, Margaret, 13, 16,
  17, 23, 29, 31
Tomlin Commission, 2
Tower, John, 176
training, see education and
  training
Treasury, control by, 28
Treasury Board, role of, 56,

57, 58
Trevelyan, Sir Charles, 14
tribunals, appeals to, 112
Trudeau, Pierre, 42
Truman, President Harry S.,
  175, 178

under-secretary
  Italy, 120, 129
  Sweden, 148
unions
  Canada, 50
  Sweden, 153
  W. Germany, 198
United States, Canada influ-
  enced by, 36, 37, 48, 62
university education
  Britain, 14-15, 22, 23
  France, 77
  Ireland, 101, 102
  Italy, 134, 135
  US, 174
  W. Germany, 194

welfare state, Swedish, 144
White House Staff, 168-9,
  172

For Product Safety Concerns and Information please contact our EU
representative GPSR@taylorandfrancis.com
Taylor & Francis Verlag GmbH, Kaufingerstraße 24, 80331 München, Germany